The History of Medicine in Context

Series Editors: Andrew Cunningham and Ole Peter Grell

Department of History and Philosophy of Science
University of Cambridge

Department of History
The Open University

The Rise of Causal Concepts of Disease:
Case Histories

The Rise of Causal Concepts of Disease

Case Histories

K. CODELL CARTER

ASHGATE

Published by
Ashgate Publishing Limited
Gower House
Croft Road
Aldershot
Hants GU11 3HR
England

Ashgate Publishing Company
Suite 420
101 Cherry Street
Burlington, VT 05401–4405 USA

Ashgate website: http://www.ashgate.com

British Library Cataloguing in Publication Data

Carter, K. Codell, 1939–
    The rise of causal concepts of disease: case histories. –
    (The history of medicine in context)
    1. Diseases – Causes and theories of causation 2. Medicine –
    History
    I. Title
    616'.071

Library of Congress Cataloging-in-Publication Data

Carter, K. Codell, 1939-
    The rise of causal concepts of disease: case histories / K. Codell Carter.
    p. cm. – (The history of medicine in context)
    Includes bibliographical references.
    ISBN 0-7546-0678-3
    1. Diseases – Causes and theories of causation – History. I. Title. II. Series.

RB151.C37 2003
616.07'1—dc21

2002019418

ISBN 0 7546 0678 3

Printed on acid-free paper

Typeset in Sabon by Manton Typesetters, Louth, Lincolnshire, UK.
Printed and bound in Great Britain by MPG Books Ltd, Bodmin, Cornwall.

Contents

Preface

Like many undergraduates, I did hard time in a one-year college physics course. Later I studied the history and philosophy of the physical sciences. By the time I graduated I had some grasp of what classical physics was all about. By contrast, the closest I ever came to studying medicine was a required ten-week course in personal health and hygiene. The local physician (not a regular professor) who had been recruited to teach the course told us to be careful with alcohol and sex, and that chiropractic didn't really work, but he never discussed medicine as a collection of theories in the same way that physicists taught physics. Otherwise, no course in medicine or even in the history or philosophy of medicine was ever available to me at any point in my entire college career. Of course I could have studied microbiology, physiology, anatomy, or genetics, but to study medicine – theories of what can go wrong in your body and how – one had to be admitted to medical school. The same holds true today at most universities. One can't even buy a decent book on internal medicine in ordinary college bookstores (I don't count self-help books written on a sixth-grade level). Medical bookstores, like dealers in pornography or illegal drugs, seem to have their own sources of supply and to keep a close check on their customers.

I emerged from college realizing that I knew a whole lot more about physics than about medicine which, even at that age, seemed a little odd. Through the years I've spent lots of time and money on doctors, but I've never once had professional dealings with a physicist, and I'm sure my experience is not unique. So now I find our educational priorities even stranger. I'm certain that nothing in medical school is anywhere near as hard to grasp as, say, Maxwell's equations or tensor algebra. So why aren't students forced (or even allowed) to study something that touches all their lives so profoundly and on which they will expend so much time and money?

Within a few years of completing my education, I began to suspect a conspiracy by the American Medical Association (after all, controlling knowledge is a source of power just like controlling drugs), and I became interested in penetrating the great mystery – I wanted to find out what doctors were trained to believe. Through the years, as I've slaked my curiosity by reading medical books, my suspicions about a conspiracy have faded (although never quite vanished). I've become convinced that members of the medical establishment really aren't trying to keep their views secret; in fact, most of them don't seem to know or care much about the theories that inform their own professional activities – they are too caught up treating patients. Imre Lakatos wrote that 'scientists tend to understand little more *about* science than fish about hydro-dynamics' (Lakatos, 1968, p. 148n.) which, if you think about it, is not really an insult – after all, why should fish care about hydrodynamics? Perhaps members of most professions know how to do what they do (and even succeed in doing it well) without thinking much about what they do or why. In any case, this seems true of most physicians (which may be all for the best – what would happen to a fish that became preoccupied with theories about how to swim?).

This book reflects my own modest efforts to figure out something about the theories of disease that ground current medical practice. History provides one kind of understanding; conceptual analysis (philosophy) provides another. Ideally they are complementary. Adapting a famous sentence from Immanuel Kant,[1] Lakatos observed that 'philosophy of science without history of science is empty; history of science without philosophy of science is blind' (Lakatos, 1971, p. 102) – a comment that is no less true of the history and philosophy of medicine. Having been trained as a philosopher, not as a historian, I'm mainly interested in conceptual analysis, but, without historical context, philosophical analysis can become sterile (if not quite empty). So, in trying to figure out current theories of disease, my approach is to embody analysis in an historical context. I like to think the result is the sort of thing Lakatos himself advocated: 'in writing a historical case study, one should, I think, adopt the following procedure: (1) one gives a rational reconstruction; (2) one tries to compare this rational reconstruction with actual history and to criticize both one's rational reconstruction for lack of historicity and the actual history for lack of rationality' (Lakatos, 1968, p. 138).

Honestly speaking, I suspect that any philosopher who happens to read this book will find the philosophy nearly empty, and I already know that many historians regard my attempts at history as blind. So, ironically, my work probably resembles (and in a way confirms what I've always thought about) opera: combining drama and music ends up serving neither interest well. Hopefully someday someone will come along who will do it better. In the meantime, I can only say that I've had great fun doing what I've done – I can't think of anything I'd rather have studied.

Parts of this book are based on earlier publications several of which appeared in *Medical History* (Carter, 1977, 1980, 1982b, 1985a, 1985b) and in *The Bulletin of the History of Medicine* ('The Koch–Pasteur Dispute on Establishing the Cause of Anthrax' (1988) and 'The Development of Pasteur's Concept of Disease Causation and the Emergence of Specific Causes in Nineteenth-Century Medicine' (1991)) and I am most grateful to the editors and publishers who permit me to use them. Through the years, however, I've become persuaded that some of what I thought I knew was incorrect, and, for this volume, I've completely reworked all my earlier papers. Unless otherwise noted, all translations are my own.

I'm genuinely pleased for the opportunity to thank, publicly but mostly without listing names, the several people (including some students and even a few historians and philosophers) who have encouraged me in this effort. I must mention particularly Jackie Duffin (who seems to get similar thanks from every author I read these days) and Ann Carmichel (who, without knowing it, happened to provide encouragement at one point just when I needed it most). I also very much appreciate Andrew Cunningham, editor of the series in which this volume is honored to find a place; it was his idea to resuscitate a moribund earlier project and cast it in its current form. Over the years I have enjoyed very generous research support from Brigham Young University, the stimulation of interested students, the rejuvenating *Aufhebung* of a disputation of congenial colleagues, and the help of innumerable librarians in many interesting places. Most of all a sincere thanks to my wife, Barbara, who somehow managed to keep herself occupied on Oxford Street and Mariahilferstrasse while I read dusty books in the basements of London's Royal Society of Medicine and Vienna's Allgemeines Krankenhaus.

Note

1. The sentence is 'Thoughts without content are empty, perceptions without concepts are blind'; it comes at B75 in the *Critique of Pure Reason*.

Introduction

Of the numerous changes that have occurred in medical thinking over the last two centuries, none have been more consequential than the adoption of what Robert Koch called the etiological standpoint (Koch, 1901, p. 905). The etiological standpoint can be characterized as the belief that diseases are best controlled and understood by means of causes and, in particular, by causes that are *natural* (that is, they depend on forces of nature as opposed to the wilful transgression of moral or social norms), *universal* (that is, the same cause is common to every instance of a given disease), and *necessary* (that is, a disease does not occur in the absence of its cause).[1] This way of conceiving disease has dominated medical thought for the last century. As new diseases like Legionnaires' disease or AIDS emerge, efforts to control and to understand them focus immediately on the quest for such causes.[2]

The fertility of the etiological standpoint is obvious from the history of diseases like anthrax, smallpox, or rickets. At the same time it is clear from historical and anthropological literature that an interest in universal necessary causes is unique to modern western medicine. There is no such interest in non-western medicine or in western medicine prior to the middle of the nineteenth century. This concept is a defining characteristic of modern western thinking about disease.

Adoption of the etiological standpoint and of the concept of necessary causes can be seen as part of the quest for understanding and control that characterizes science. And, as with other fundamental theoretical innovations in science, the ramifications of this way of thinking transcend any specific discipline: they inform our concept of the human situation and shape our beliefs about society and about our place in nature. In an 1872 novel, *Erewhon*, Samuel Butler portrayed a society in which illness was regarded as willfully chosen while criminality was a natural condition that people occasionally fell into in spite of their best efforts to resist. We respond to willful deviance by moral expostulation and by legal sanctions; we respond to unintentional deviance by treatment. With the beliefs portrayed in *Erewhon*, it was inevitable and entirely rational that the sick were punished while criminals received treatment and care. However, given the etiological standpoint, it became difficult to think of illness as resulting from the willful violation of religious, moral, or social norms. While the way of thinking that Butler portrayed may still have been feasible in 1872, it was fundamentally incompatible with the idea that each disease had a specific natural cause – an idea that was emerging just at the time Butler wrote his novel.

Thus the etiological standpoint encourages us to interpret an important part of human experience – disease – in terms of natural processes rather than in terms of free choice or of the violation of norms. Along with Freudian psychology and the theory of biological evolution, the etiological standpoint promotes a mundane and naturalistic concept of human nature.

Because of the success of the etiological standpoint, there have been persistent efforts to expand the range of human abnormalities that are approached by way of causes. In recent decades, criminality, substance abuse, hyperactivity, spouse abuse, obesity, and other forms of deviance have been interpreted as diseases (Conrad and Schneider, 1980). Such attempts are motivated by the belief that these abnormalities, much like tuberculosis or cholera, may be more tractable and more intelligible within a medical model than if approached through sanctions or admonitions. This approach presupposes that natural causes can be found for these forms of deviance and, therefore, that they stem from natural forces rather than from individual choice. Thus, accepting the etiological standpoint fosters an ongoing re-examination of the boundary between events deemed manageable by the exercise of individual will and those regarded as controllable only through the manipulation of natural forces.

In respect to its pervasiveness in contemporary thought and to its uniqueness to the modern age, the etiological standpoint resembles the great nineteenth-century biological innovation: the theory of evolution. And because medicine consumes a huge percentage of the world's economic resources and touches virtually every human life, it is *imminent* in a way that no other aspect of science can ever be. Yet, in contrast to evolution or to the theories of physics, the etiological standpoint receives remarkably little philosophical or historical scrutiny. This book is a collection of case studies concerning the rise of the etiological standpoint.

It is enlightening to regard the etiological standpoint as a scientific research programme. This requires some explanation. In response to what he saw as deficiencies in earlier attempts to characterize scientific progress, Imre Lakatos formulated the concept of scientific research programmes and proposed that the history of science be regarded as a history of research programmes rather than as a history of theories (Lakatos, 1968, p. 132). Lakatos explained his concept of research programmes in terms of what he called 'progressive and degenerating problemshifts', and he explained these concepts as follows:

> Let us take a series of theories, T_1, T_2, T_3, ... where each subsequent theory results from adding auxiliary clauses to ... the previous theory in order to accommodate some anomaly, each theory having at least as much [empirical] content as the unrefuted content of its

predecessor. Let us say that such a series of theories is *theoretically progressive* (or *'constitutes a theoretically progressive problemshift'*) if each new theory has some excess empirical content over its predecessor, that is, if it predicts some novel, hitherto unexpected fact. Let us say that a theoretically progressive series of theories is also *empirically progressive* (or *'constitutes an empirically progressive problem-shift'*) if some of this excess empirical content is also corroborated, that is, if each new theory leads us to the actual discovery of some *new fact*. Finally, let us call a problemshift *progressive* if it is both theoretically and empirically progressive, and *degenerating* if it is not. We *'accept'* problemshifts as 'scientific' only if they are at least theoretically progressive; if they are not, we *'reject'* them as 'pseudoscientific'.

(Lakatos, 1968, p. 118)

Later in the same essay, Lakatos used the preceding distinction as a basis for characterizing scientific research programmes:

I have discussed the problem of objective appraisal of scientific growth in terms of progressive and degenerating problemshifts in series of scientific theories. The most important such series in the growth of science are characterized by a certain *continuity* which connects their members. This continuity evolves from a genuine research programme adumbrated at the start. The programme consists of [mostly implicit] methodological rules: some tell us what paths of research to avoid (*negative heuristic*), and others what paths to pursue (*positive heuristic*).

(Lakatos, 1968, p. 132)

While not immune to criticism, Lakatos's account of scientific progress provides a convenient framework for describing the history of causal thinking in medicine over the last century and a half.

By providing research models for their contemporaries and successors, Louis Pasteur and Robert Koch directed research away from such questions as whether diseases arise spontaneously or from moral transgression and toward the quest for bacteria that stand in the relation of necessary and universal causes of diseases. Subsequent researchers 'added auxiliary clauses' to the initial framework to account for new bacterial diseases. Within the etiological standpoint, subordinate programmes arose to deal with psychological abnormalities, protozoal, viral and rickettsial infections, nutritional deficiencies, metabolic and genetic disorders, and other classes of anomalies.[3] Each of these additions was made within the context of the quest for specific causes and each addition expanded the original research programme in a way that was (using Lakatos's phrase) adumbrated from the start. Attempts to identify causes for new diseases like AIDS, or especially for deviant behavior like addiction or abuse, can be seen as further attempts to expand the programme or to generate subordinate programmes. Each successful

assimilation of a new anomaly reinforces the credibility of the programme as a whole. On the other hand, the credibility of the programme
is threatened by the accumulation of recalcitrant anomalies, like cancer,
that seem to defy comprehension in terms of necessary causes and by
the discovery that the etiologies of some diseases are more complex
than originally thought. These developments erode confidence in the
research programme and threaten to replace its fundamental concept by
such notions as multicausality, risk factors, or causal webs (Kunitz,
1987; Susser, 1973, pp. 22–4).

It is impossible to predict whether the quest for necessary causes will
yield further successes or be replaced by other ways of thinking. But,
whatever may ensue, there is no denying the centrality of the concept of
necessary causes in medical thought for the last one hundred years. And
even if this concept ceases to prove useful, there is no clear alternative
to approaching diseases etiologically. One can imagine a medical system
in which risk factors replace universal necessary causes – this requires
only a change *within* an etiological framework. However, it is virtually
impossible to imagine how any future medical system could be organized except around some causal concepts or other.

By definition, a research programme is a temporally continuous co-
operative endeavor to which different persons can contribute (Lakatos,
1968, p. 132). But what are its boundaries? In tracing a single research
programme, one would like to distinguish the programme itself from
such extraneous elements as, first, general background knowledge or
research methods shared and exploited both by contributors to the
programme and by other researchers who may be contributing to other
(even competing) programmes; and second, ideas and methods advanced
by precursors who did not contribute directly to the programme but
who merely anticipated some of its features. Lakatos defines research
programmes as collections of methodological rules, but this definition
yields no clear practical basis for individuation. However, at least in
modern scientific literature, boundaries can be approximated by taking
account of citations. There is no need for citations when drawing on
shared background knowledge. References are required only for claims
that are not universally acknowledged or that are recognized as part of
the proprietary domain of some individual or group. Moreover, a new
idea or method contributes to a continuous research programme only if
others adopt it, and one expects such borrowing to be acknowledged by
citations. Thus, a research programme can be regarded approximately
as a collection of works linked through citations, and one can individuate
programmes by constructing citation indexes. One begins with a work
central to a programme, say Koch's first paper on tuberculosis. One
then identifies all the works that cite or are cited in that work, all the

works that cite or are cited in those works, and so on. The collection of all these works approximates a research programme. In logical terms, over the domain of all published works, a research programme is approximately the equivalence class defined by any particular work under the relation 'cites or is cited by'. This criterion has obvious weaknesses; however it provides a practical standard for the selection of materials, and I have chosen the topics in this book with this criterion in mind. The works here discussed are directly and indirectly linked by citations.

One final concept requires clarification. Lakatos defined 'research programme' in terms of series of scientific theories, and most of this book concerns ideas that are analytically connected to the concept of theories. At the start, therefore, we must give some attention to how the word 'theory' is to be understood. In ordinary life, 'theory' often refers to any belief or opinion, but in science the term is used more narrowly. Wim J. Van der Steen and Harmke Kamminga gave the following succinct account (which is compatible with other recent discussions in the philosophy of science):

> A statement is a law if it satisfies the following criteria: (i) it is general in the sense that it contains a universal quantifier, (ii) it is general in the sense that it does not mention particular individuals, times or places, (iii) it has empirical content, (iv) it is well-confirmed, and (v) it is well-entrenched (i.e. it belongs to a theory). ... *Theories* will be viewed as sets of interconnected laws.
> (Van der Steen and Kammingen, 1991, pp. 445f.)

As this account makes clear, theories and laws are conceptually linked: neither is possible without the other. When formalized, some of the laws comprised by a theory typically function within the theory like axioms in geometry or in other deductive systems. For example, here is a set of assumptions (axioms) for the kinetic theory:

> (1) A pure gas consists of a large number of identical molecules separated by distances that are great compared with their size. (2) The gas molecules are constantly moving in random directions with a distribution of speeds. (3) The molecules exert no forces on one another between collisions, so between collisions they move in straight lines with constant velocities. (4) The collisions of molecules with the walls of the container are elastic; no energy is lost during a collision.
> (Oxtoby, 1990, p. 104).

These assumptions have the qualities identified by Van der Steen and Kamminga (so they are laws in their sense), and from them, other laws (for example, Boyle's Law, Charles' Law) can be derived mathematically much as one derives theorems in geometry. As a second example, in their classic book on the general theory of relativity, Charles W. Misner, Kip S. Thorne, and John Archibald Wheeler observed that 'of all theories ever conceived by physicists, general relativity has the simplest, most elegant geometric foundation (three axioms: (1) there is a metric; (2) the metric is governed by the Einstein field equation $G = 8\pi T$; (3) all special relativistic laws of physics are valid in local Lorentz frames of metric)' (Misner et al., 1973, p. 302).

And there is one other important fact about laws and theories. Just as a statement cannot be a law without being 'well-entrenched (i.e. part of a theory)', it is impossible to fully justify a law abstracted from the theory of which it is a part. As Norwood Russell Hanson explained, the point of a theory is 'to offer an intelligible, systematic, conceptual pattern for the observed data. The value of such a pattern lies in its capacity to unite phenomena which, without the theory, are either surprising, anomalous, or left wholly unnoticed' (Hanson, 1963, p. 44). In short, a theory is justified by tying together and explaining observations. Laws, which can exist only within theories, are justified by being part of justified theories.

Obviously, in medicine (or in the biological sciences generally), one does not find formalized theories stated as elegantly as relativity or the kinetic theory. But ultimately the nature of theories must be the same. Even in medicine, if one is to talk of scientific theories, say, the bacterial theory of disease or the deficiency theory, one must mean more than simply that people opine that bacteria are, somehow or other, involved in disease. While different people may have different beliefs (theories in the loose sense) about the pathologicality of bacteria, if there is such a thing as the (or a) bacterial theory of disease (where 'theory' is used as it is used elsewhere in science) it must comprise a system of law-like statements. Believing, as I do, that 'the bacterial theory of disease' is not just a misnomer, in other words, believing that there are genuine theories in medicine, one of my main goals in this book is to identify some of the laws that constitute these theories.

In this context, I must comment on the relation of my book to Michael Worboys' excellent recent study: *Spreading Germs: Disease Theories and Medical Practice in Britain, 1865–1900* (Worboys, 2000). Among contemporary historians of medicine, there is precious little interest in scientific theories,[4] and Worboys' volume is an auspicious sign that this omission may someday be corrected. But what does Worboys mean by 'theory'? He never explains the term, but it seems clear that, *for the most part*, he is using the word in the loose sense of any belief or opinion rather than in the narrow sense discussed in the three previous paragraphs. For example, he makes it a point to talk about *disease theories* (plural)[5] and here is how he introduces this concept: 'the first and most important theme to acknowledge is the range of *germ theories of disease* current between 1865 and 1900. In the 1860s and 1870s, there were many views on what disease-germs were, for example, chemical poisons, ferments, degraded cells, fungi, "bacteria" or a class of parasites' (Worboys, 2000, p. 2). So what Worboys is considering is different 'views' about germs and their possible relation to disease. I say *for the most part* Worboys seems to use the term 'theory' in the loose sense because in his first chapter, he does once refer to the narrow use of the word: 'Yet, by the 1870s, the term [germs of disease] was firmly linked to the modern concept of the "germ theory of disease" [singular] – the etiological construction of disease in which external agents entered the body to produce septic, infectious and other diseases' (p. 22). This reveals the first difference between my interests and Worboys': I use the term 'theory' *exclusively* in the narrow sense explained in previous paragraphs and tersely exemplified in this quotation from Worboys. Thus, it is no accident that, in my opinion, the first explicit formulation of a bacterial theory (Klebs') came in 1876 – the same decade in which Worboys sees 'germs of disease' finally linked to the modern concept of the germ theory. As I use the term 'theory', there was no germ theory (at least no explicit germ theory) prior to that time while obviously there were lots of opinions about germs. I am interested in the laws (in Van der Steen and Kamminga's sense) comprised by the bacterial theory of disease (in the narrow sense of 'theory') – something to which Worboys gives no attention.

A second difference between Worboys' book and my own is this: my main interest is not really even the bacterial theory of disease. Rather, it is a broad movement – the etiological standpoint or research programme – of which the bacterial theory is one part. For me, the bacterial theory is only one example (albeit an important one) of the quest for universal necessary causes that characterizes medicine since the middle of the nineteenth century. Thus, while I have enormously enjoyed Worboys' fine book and have learned a lot from reading it, there is – unfortunately for me – almost no intersection between his work and my own.

The etiological research programme arose in the nineteenth century, and, while boundaries are as much created as discovered, one can distinguish three stages in this process. First, between about 1830 and 1860 a few researchers independently, nearly simultaneously, and apparently for the first time in medical history, began to think of several different organic disorders as having causes that were *universal* and *necessary*. A new strategy arose – the adoption of etiological characterizations – that provided a way of classifying individual illnesses so that, in principle, every recognized disease could be ascribed to a universal necessary cause. Basic methodological principles emerged forming what Lakatos would call the heuristic of the programme, and researchers began focusing on a particular domain of organisms – bacteria – that were later seen as causes of disease. As with many conceptual innovations, these developments were accompanied by little philosophical reflection or analysis – none of those who first used them may have considered how these approaches differed from those of their predecessors or why the differences were important. Indeed, such matters can only become clear in retrospect.[6] For example, we are better able to appreciate the nature and significance of, say, Koch's Postulates than Koch himself could ever have been (in this regard, I freely confess a *presentist* and partly *Whiggish* bias).[7] The issues here are the structure and subsequent use of published arguments, not how the authors of those arguments would have characterized their own work or how they would have compared their positions to those of other writers. It is worth emphasizing that, during this period of its inception, the research programme was *not* exclusively about bacteria or bacterial diseases. While the bacterial theory may be the most striking single achievement of the programme, the programme did not begin or end with the study of germs. As explained in the previous paragraph, this book is *not* primarily about the germ theory of disease.

Second, between about 1860 and 1890 researchers focused, with enormous success, on bacterial diseases. A coherent and explicit bacterial theory of disease emerged. In this period, researchers gave attention to the concept of disease causation: they identified, discussed, and refined various criteria for proving causation, and they deliberately organized their experiments to satisfy such criteria. Among these criteria were those now known as Koch's Postulates. There was also an awareness of and a conscious interest in the basic heuristic principles of the emerging programme.

Third, from about 1890 on, as the power of the new causal model became apparent, researchers addressed whole new ranges of disorders that were not bacterial. This required adjustments in the basic principles and methods of the programme, for example, in causal criteria. But collectively the results of these efforts bear such strong *family resemblances* (in Wittgenstein's sense) to one another and to the core of the programme that they must all be seen as falling within the etiological standpoint.

The case studies in this volume are organized around these three stages in the rise of the research programme: Chapters 2 through 4 concern the first stage; Chapters 6 and 7 the second; and Chapters 9 through 11 the third. The first chapter provides background, and Chapters 5 and 8 are transitional.

Notes

1. The usual term is 'specific cause'. However, as this term is currently used, it is both vague and ambiguous. When possible I avoid the term altogether, but when it appears, it should be understood to mean a natural, universal, and necessary cause.

2. F. Kräupl Taylor uses the term 'monogenic' for diseases associated with universal and necessary causes. In a philosophically sensitive and insightful book that has received too little attention, he writes that while most diseases recognized in medicine today are not monogenic 'the final hope and aim of medical science is the establishment of monogenic disease entities' (Taylor, 1979, p. 21). Alfred S. Evans has traced efforts to assimilate numerous new diseases to a model much like the one elaborated in this book (Evans, 1993).

3. Lakatos writes that all of science can be seen as one huge research programme within which special programmes focus on particular problems (Lakatos, 1968, p. 132). In the same way the entire etiological standpoint can be regarded as a single research programme or one can think of it as a collection of separate programmes each dealing with a class of diseases with similar causes. This is a useful ambiguity and there is no reason to eliminate it arbitrarily.

4. I will have more to say about this in the chapter entitled 'Some Final Thoughts' at the end of the book.

5. What could it mean to talk about 'kinetic *theories* of gasses'? While different accounts of the kinetic theory may employ different basic assumptions or state equivalent assumptions differently, the consequences of every such set must be isomorphic with the consequences of every other. In this sense, there can be only one kinetic theory. No doubt, early on, there were innumerable opinions about diseases and even about the nature of germs and about their possible relations to diseases, but, in my mind, to use 'theory' in these contexts verges on false advertising. Worboys does cite one 1878 work in which the word 'theories' (plural) was used in this way.

6. This point is related to Lakatos's thesis that so-called crucial experiments can never be seen as crucial until decades after they have been performed (Lakatos, 1968, p. 158).

7. Back when they may have hoped there was still a chance of saving my immortal soul, Adrian Wilson and Andrew Cunningham kindly presented me with a copy of Butterfield's *The Whig Interpretation of History*. But I found Butterfield's strawman arguments only about 40 per cent persuasive so, while confessing, today, to be 60 per cent Whig is about like calling oneself a witch in 1692 Salem, there is little point in denying what will, soon enough, be apparent to the reader.

CHAPTER ONE

Causes of Disease in Early Nineteenth-century Practical Medicine

Early nineteenth-century medical texts are superficially similar to our own. Textbook discussions of most diseases include sections with such titles as pathology, etiology, therapy, and prognosis, and the contents may seem readily intelligible to a modern reader. One could surmise that our medical system is part of a continuous tradition extending back through these decades and beyond – that changes have come mostly through the accumulation of facts within a shared framework of fundamental beliefs and objectives (King, 1982, pp. 5–15). However, earlier medical texts contain statements that now seem strange, and these statements sometimes point to fundamental discontinuities separating earlier thinking from our own.

In 1845 James L. Bardsley, a prominent British physician, wrote that diabetes 'has been traced by some patients to sleeping out the whole of the night in a state of intoxication' (Bardsley, 1845, p. 609). This statement seems curious not simply because Bardsley identified a cause we no longer find plausible; more fundamental issues are involved. Bardsley assumed that patients' opinions were important or even decisive in identifying the causes of their illnesses, and this assumption suggests that different cases of the same disorder may have entirely different causes.

In the same year, Wilhelm Friedrich Scanzoni, director of the Prague maternity clinic, proposed to study the etiology of childbed fever, an often fatal disease that struck women a day or two after delivery. As part of his study, Scanzoni urged the authorities to require local physicians to report each case of childbed fever that occurred in their practices. In their reports they were to give 'particular attention to the causal factors of the disease' (Scanzoni, 1850, p. 32). Scanzoni intended to study the etiology of childbed fever by determining the frequency of the different causes to which local physicians ascribed individual cases. Like Bardsley, Scanzoni assumed that different cases of a given disease could have completely different causes.

Medical texts contain the results of surveys like the one Scanzoni proposed to conduct. Seven years earlier, in 1842, A. F. Chomel, a leading French internist, explained that one could investigate the causes of pneumonia 'by interrogating carefully a certain number of individuals struck by this affliction, and by directing one's questions to the causes that produced it' (Chomel, 1842, pp. 165f). In his own study, 'made with great care on seventy-nine pneumonia patients', he found the following: fourteen patients reported experiencing some form of cooling, five had consumed too much wine, two had worked excessively, one had experienced a lively emotion, and another had inhaled carbon vapor. The 56 remaining patients were unable to explain how they had become ill. Chomel also reported an earlier study of 125 patients in which the following causes had been established: contusions of the throat, 2; cooling, 38; violent effort and fatigue, 12; depression, 4; excess of drink or upset regimen, 3; and in 66 cases no cause could be identified.

Proceeding in this case-by-case way, physicians accumulated extensive lists of possible causes for each disease. For example, in his account of diabetes, Bardsley identified the following causes: frequent exposure to sudden alterations of heat and cold, indulgence in copious draughts of cold fluid when the system has been over-heated by labor or exercise, intemperate use of spirituous liquors, poor living, sleeping out the whole of the night in the open air in a state of intoxication, checking perspiration suddenly, and mental anxiety and distress (Bardsley, 1845, p. 609). Similar lists can be found for virtually any disease in most German, English, or French medical texts from the period.

In order to characterize more precisely the causes included in these lists, one must first be clear about the meaning of the terms 'necessary' and 'sufficient'. A set of conditions C is sufficient for events of type E if the presence of C always precedes or accompanies an event of that type (or, equivalently, if the absence of such an event always accompanies or follows the absence of those conditions); a set of conditions C is necessary for events of type E if the absence of C always precedes or accompanies the absence of E (or, equivalently, if such an event always accompanies or follows those conditions). In connection with these definitions, several points require emphasis:

1. Necessity and sufficiency apply only to *classes* of events. To say certain conditions are necessary or sufficient for a single event can only be understood to mean that the event belongs to a class of events that stand in the specified relation to the conditions.
2. Necessity and sufficiency are strictly empirical relations. This implies that conditions C may be necessary or sufficient for event E

without either being the cause of the other: my having swallowed a vitamin pill may always and only precede my saying grace over breakfast – having taken the pill may be necessary and sufficient for saying grace, but neither is the cause of the other. Thus, proving causation requires more than simply demonstrating necessity or sufficiency (or both). (Some of what more is required in a proof of causation will emerge in subsequent chapters.)

3. While we often talk of *events* as being necessary or sufficient for other events, as Kant taught us, causation is fundamentally a relation between *sets of conditions* and events.

Since we will generally be interested in necessity and sufficiency in the context of causation, Kant's insight is reflected in the above definitions.

Causal concepts are rooted in everyday interests in controlling and understanding the world. Our interests vary, and so does our language about causes. We talk about causes of individual events (what caused the accident) and of classes of events (what causes lightening); we use causes to explain what has happened or is happening now (what caused the power failure) and to predict what will happen in the future (adding iron will cause the leaves to turn dark green); causes insure that events will happen (what will cause the tree to bear fruit) and prevent events from happening (what causes wilt). In discussing causes, the terms 'necessary' and 'sufficient' (as defined above) mark two broad kinds of causes both of which interest us in daily life. In general when we want to explain why some event or class of events happens or to insure or predict that such events will happen, we look for a cause whose occurrence will be accompanied by the event – that is we look for a sufficient cause. However when we want to explain why some event or class of events doesn't happen or to insure or predict that such events won't happen, we look for a cause whose absence will be accompanied by the absence of the event – that is we look for a necessary cause. So, depending on our interests, we sometimes seek sufficient and sometimes necessary causes. Because our interests in the two kinds of causes are different, most causes are not both necessary and sufficient.

What was the nature of the causes identified in early nineteenth-century practical medicine? Physicians actually distinguished different kinds of causes. There were proximate and remote causes and remote causes were further classified as predisposing or exciting (or occasioning). The proximate cause of a disease was the anatomical abnormality, if any, with which the disease was associated. One writer defined 'proximate cause' as 'the essence of disease, its intimate nature, the special alteration of the solids or fluids. ... [the effect of which is] to fix the new relations that occur in the economy of the ill body' (Lagasquie, 1849, p. 313). This made good sense until, under the influence of pathological anatomy, some diseases were identified with specific lesions. Given such characterizations, the proximate cause and the disease became one and the same: 'The proximate cause is nothing else than the actual disease itself – the actual condition of that part of the body, from which the whole train of morbid phenomena essentially flows' (Watson, 1858, p. 76). Writers acknowledged that this use of the term 'cause' was confusing. 'It is ... a puzzling term, and tends to give to the study of disease a scholastic and repulsive aspect' (Watson, 1858, p. 76). Some physicians dismissed all talk of proximate causes as redundant and urged that the term be abandoned. 'If we retain the term proximate cause, it signifies ... the pathological condition of the throat, the pleura, or the joints; but we think the term may be advantageously banished from medicine' (Conolly, 1845, p. 677; Watson, 1858, p. 76).

In contrast to proximate causes, remote causes were factors normally external to the patient that explained the onset of disease. This was the most common sense in which the word was used, and all the causes identified in the first section of this chapter were remote causes.

What was the relation between some particular remote cause, say anxiety, and the disease it occasioned? Clearly, no one cause was necessary for the onset of any specific disease since, as we have seen, different cases of each disease were ascribed to different remote causes. Physicians explicitly denied that the same cause was present in every case of any disease: 'No inference can fairly be drawn from the identity of the effect, for certain diseased states are produced by a variety of remote causes, this expression being used in the sense usually annexed to it by medical men' (Brown, 1845, p. 505). It is also clear that the remote cause identified in a particular disease episode was not necessary even for that episode because, if a given patient did not contract her disease from one cause, she might contract the same disease from other causes. Or, conceivably, several causes (no one of which was necessary) might contribute equally to the onset of a particular episode. Thus no single cause was regarded as *necessary* for any one of the diseases it could cause.

However, particular remote causes seem not to have been thought of as *sufficient* either. A typical factor, say anxiety, could be listed as a possible cause for many diseases. For example, one widely used British medical encyclopedia identified anxiety as a possible cause of dozens of diseases including acne (1:48),[1] catalepsy (1:379), diabetes (1:609), ecthyma (1:739), fever (2:177), herpes (2:449), hydrocephalus (2:490), impetigo (2:594), senile dementia (3:74), psoriasis (3:733), scrofula (4:139), and tetanus (4:168). Thus anxiety was not expected always to result in the same disease – one anxious person might become diabetic but others might contract impetigo or tetanus. So remote causes were not sufficient either. Christopher Hamlin, who has discussed accounts of disease causation in this period, recognizes that 'the presumption of a single exciting cause as sufficient could not be sustained' and seems to infer that 'all remote causes could plausibly be thought of as necessary causes' (Hamlin, 1992, p. 51). But clearly this doesn't follow and (as we have seen) it is inconsistent with what contemporary physicians themselves reported about how they used the words. Hamlin gives no further evidence for this surprising claim.

However, while individual causes were not thought of as sufficient, they could be part of a combination of factors that was sufficient. To understand this, we must take account of another distinction important in nineteenth-century etiology. Remote causes were classified as predisposing or exciting (or occasioning). Predisposing causes 'render the body liable to become the prey of something, which has a tendency to excite the disease. The exciting cause of the disease might have no effect, unless the body had been predisposed; and the predisposition might not have had the effect, unless the exciting cause had occurred' (Elliotson, 1844, p. 43). Typically, in an account of any disease, both predisposing and exciting causes were listed. One discussion of tetanus mentioned these predisposing causes: warm climate, humid situations, bad or insufficient nutriment, close and ill-ventilated habitations, inattention to cleanliness, and neglect of the bowels. The same discussion listed these exciting causes: mechanical wounds, application of cold and damp, the irritation of worms, terror, sympathy, mental anguish, the suppression of perspiration, the accumulation of cherry-stones in the intestines, suppression of lochia, and gastric inflammation (Symonds, 1845, p. 368). Contemporary writers observed that, over time, predisposing causes could become exciting, and what were usually exciting causes could become predisposing (Elliotson, 1844, p. 45). Moreover under suitable circumstances, either kind of cause alone could seem to bring on a disease (Conolly, 1845, p. 678). One writer observed that 'the same occasional cause can provoke the development of all the diseases, and the same disease can be created by every kind of occasional cause' (Chomel, 1835, p. 425). If, as this suggests, a typical remote cause is neither necessary nor sufficient, how can distinguishing between predisposing and exciting causes help provide a complete sufficient causal explanation?

Several discussions of disease causation included some version of this hypothetical case:

> Of several individuals exposed to the same exciting cause, scarcely two will be affected alike. From exposure to cold, for instance, one

will be attacked with catarrh, another with rheumatism, a third
with inflammation of the bowels, a fourth with sore throat; while
by far the greater number will escape altogether. Were the exciting
cause solely chargeable with these several effects, they would unquestionably be marked with greater uniformity. The truth is, that
the exciting cause produces its effect because the body exposed to
it is prone to be morbidly affected in consequence of its own
previous derangement; and the specific form of the disease is determined, partly by the operation of the exciting cause, but chiefly by
the predisposition of the parts affected to undergo those morbid
actions to which the general indisposition of the system and their
own partial weakness render them liable.

(Barlow, 1845b, p. 555)

Thus it was believed that any single remote cause could, in principle, be
filled out into a fully sufficient explanation of the onset of a case of
illness with the help of other predisposing and exciting factors. In 1835,
while explaining why different persons react differently when exposed
to a cold damp wind, a French writer observed that

This experiment proves only that which observation confirms every
day, namely, that the same cause can give rise to different effects,
according to the particular state of the individual on which it acts.
Thus the same frozen drink given to several perspiring persons
produces in one a simple loss of voice, in another a cold, in a third
a very serious laryngitis, etc.

(Trousseau, 1835, p. 338)

Fourteen years later, another French physician wrote that no one could
predict what would happen when persons were exposed to an exciting
cause, say, sudden chilling – some become rheumatic, some develop
pulmonary catarrh or diarrhea, and others remain healthy. He then
observed that 'a previous examination of each [victim] would no doubt
solve the problem' (Lagasquie, 1849, p. 313). Of course, in practice, no
examination could be thorough enough to identify all the relevant
'indispositions and partial weaknesses' to enable one to predict the
exact outcome of some trauma. However, in principle, the collection of
all the remote causes – both predisposing and exciting – would be
sufficient for the particular effect. Moreover, presumably, any two persons
affected by the same set of predisposing and exciting causes would
suffer the same effect.

All of this suggests that a remote cause, such as those identified at the
beginning of this chapter, could be any trauma that seemed especially
striking to the patient or physician and that helped explain the onset of
one case of a disease. Such a cause was thought of as one of a combination of conditions that, together, constituted a sufficient cause for the
particular instance of disease. There is nothing unreasonable about such
causal explanations: they are exactly what one would look for, today, if

one were interested in explaining why some individual became ill. It was also reasonable to think patients could be aware of salient traumata that might be part of such an explanation. From our point of view, no less than from that of nineteenth-century physicians, patient-reported experiences such as overexertion, sleep deprivation, or poor diet could be part of a sufficient explanation of the onset of a particular case of illness. This is how one must understand Bardsley's comment that some patients had traced illness to 'sleeping out the whole of the night in a state of intoxication'.

In the early nineteenth century, there was an elegant symmetry between causes of disease and causes of death. In 1839 the Registrar General of Great Britain began publishing annual reports of births, deaths, and marriages. The first report was mostly compiled by William Farr who explained that 'the registration of births and deaths proves the connection of families, facilitates the legal distribution of property, and answers several other public purposes, which sufficiently establish its utility' (Farr, 1839, p. 86).

Farr illustrated what was to be understood by a cause of death: 'A man falls from a height, and breaks his neck; a woman takes arsenic, which corrodes the coats of the stomach, and in both cases death is the result. The arsenic and the fall, or the fracture of the neck and the corrosion of the stomach, may be viewed as the causes of death' (Farr, 1839, p. 89). While Farr recommended that causes of both kinds (the external factor and the internal morbid process) be registered and considered as causes of death, he acknowledged that in many cases only one or the other could be found, and, in practice, usually only one was reported. In a letter accompanying his second annual report, he observed that some identified causes of death were 'diseases, which terminate in the extinction of existence', but at other times 'the attention of the observer was less attracted to this class of facts, and overlooking the proximate, passed directly on to the more impressive external causes' (Farr, 1840, p. 75). He then observed that a 'vast number of the deaths ... are referable to cold, and to effluvial poisons ... and it is scarcely necessary to state that many of the diseases had their origin in intemperance, and in the want of proper food', and he then discussed each of these as a cause of death. These quotations illustrate not only that, like causes of disease, causes of death were thought of and classified as proximate and remote, but also that one could pass back and forth between causes of death and causes of disease, often mentioning the same factors – cold, intemperance, starvation, effluvial poison – sometimes as one and sometimes as the other.

Farr's idea was this: suppose a woman is exposed to some trauma, say cold, and that an ensuing morbid process (that is, a disease) causes her death. Then there was no distinction between the remote cause of the disease and the remote cause of death.

Not only were particular causes of disease and of death similar and sometimes the same, but causal explanations were also similar in kind or form: for both disease and death, the object was to explain what happened to one individual at one time. This called for identification of a sufficient cause for a particular event. As we have seen, having found causes of many individual disease episodes, physicians like Scanzoni and Chomel tried to discern patterns. In the same way, Farr sought patterns among the causes of individual deaths; for example, he thought that the record of causes of death could help one decide which parts of the country would be safe retreats from serious diseases like consumption or whooping cough (Farr, 1839, p. 87).

The causes of death we identify, today, are still sufficient causes for particular events. 'The certificate wants to find out not why every patient died but why *this* patient died' (King, 1982, p. 213). And so, although more precise and detailed, they are of the same general form as the causes of death identified 150 years ago. Moreover, we still accumulate information about causes of death by surveys like those that Scanzoni and Chomel proposed for investigating the causes of childbed fever and pneumonia. However, as will become clear in the course of our investigation, the symmetry between causes of disease and causes of death has been destroyed by a change in the kind of causes we now identify for diseases (Carter, 1997).

We can now appreciate one important discontinuity between etiological discussions in the 1840s and causes of death, on the one hand, and the causes of disease that most interest us, today, on the other. Today, in both ordinary everyday conversation and in technical medical discourse, one speaks of '*the* cause of X' where X is the name of some disease; for example, 'the cause of diabetes' or 'the cause of tuberculosis'. And the causes that are typically identified in such contexts are among those that nineteenth-century physicians would have called remote. However, in literature from the early decades of that century, one looks in vain for any talk of '*the* cause of disease X'. Among remote causes, one finds only exciting and predisposing causes of individual cases such as those we have listed and characterized. One reason for the apparent strangeness of James L. Bardsley's discussion of the etiology of diabetes, considered in the first section of this chapter (pp. 10–11), is that, in a general discussion of the etiology of diabetes, such as he was purporting to give, we now expect an account of *the cause* of diabetes (so far as it is understood) not just a list of factors contributory to individuals becoming diabetic. But in the early 1800s, there were no such accounts; there simply was no concept of 'the cause of disease X'. Why might this have been?

One reason is this: given how diseases were then defined, it was reasonable and virtually inevitable that different episodes of any disease would be attributed to a variety of unrelated causes. In the early nineteenth century, individual diseases were almost always characterized in terms of prominent signs and symptoms (or, under the influence of pathological anatomy, of particular morbid alterations in the body). For example, in a lecture delivered at the University of Paris in 1832 and reprinted in the British journal, *Lancet*, Gabriel Andral defined 'hydrophobia' as 'complete horror of fluids, reaching to such a degree, that their deglutition becomes almost impossible' (Andral, 1832–33, p. 806). Thus, hydrophobia was defined in terms of one prominent symptom: an extreme inability to swallow. However, if hydrophobia is a horror of swallowing, then, as Andral cheerfully acknowledged, fully authentic cases could be caused by blows to the throat or by psychological problems as well as by the bites of rabid dogs.[2] Given a symptomatic definition like Andral's (or even a definition in terms of a specific lesion), it was logical and inevitable that hydrophobia, or any other disease so defined, would have a range of different remote causes that varied from case to case. So it is not simply that earlier physicians failed to notice a commonality among individual cases that we have since managed to discern. There was no commonality: within their system of ideas, the phrase 'the cause of disease X' could have no meaning.

There are ways of characterizing diseases other than in terms of symptoms. Early nineteenth-century anatomical studies revealed that phthisis, a prominent disease at the time, was often associated with distinctive caseating tumors or tubers in the lungs. By contrast, the presence of non-caseating tubers was called tuberculosis. At the beginning of the century, phthisis and tuberculosis were often regarded as separate conditions because each was known to occur without the other. However, when phthisis symptoms and tubers occurred together the tubers seemed to explain the symptoms, and phthisis could be regarded as a particular manifestation or development of tuberculosis. In 1832, Johann Lucas Schönlein, a prominent German pathologist, wrote: 'In recent times phthisis has been regarded, not as a unique disease, but as a direct sequel and higher development of tuberculosis. This opinion arose first in [Marie François Xavier] Bichat's school and has spread through France, England, and even part of Germany' (Schönlein, 1832, p. 134). Schönlein did not agree with this way of thinking; he objected on the grounds that some genuine cases of phthisis did not involve tubers. However, he wrote, 'one cannot deny credit to the pathologists who have provided this material basis for phthisis'. By providing a 'material basis', the pathologists explained symptoms and made diagnosis more objective and precise. For these reasons, and because it seemed so enlightening, phthisis was ultimately recharacterized in terms of tubers; non-tuberous cases, which had formerly been genuine instances of phthisis, were reclassified in other categories.

Because the new characterization of phthisis seemed superior and because, at the time, phthisis was such a prominent disease, this approach was followed in characterizing other diseases. Physicians dissected corpses, sought morbid remains, and, when possible, redefined diseases in terms of what they found. The new characterizations were greeted as important advances. 'The great improvements which have taken place of late years in pathology, by enabling practitioners to connect symptoms with their organic causes more accurately, have necessarily diverted attention from the artificial [symptomatic] combinations of the old nosology' (Forbes, 1845, p. 106). However, the influence of pathological anatomy went further than just providing new ways of defining diseases. Thomas Watson began a lecture on morbid anatomy by noting that the topic

> is not one of merely curious interest, but has a direct bearing upon the proper treatment of diseases. It will teach us what we have to guard against, what we must strive to avert, in different cases. In speaking of particular diseases, I shall constantly refer to the facts and reasonings which I am now about to lay before you.
>
> (Watson, 1858, p. 68)

Thus, the examination of corpses became a major source of knowledge about the proper and improper functioning of the body – about health and disease. Physicians were inevitably influenced not only by the content – the specific observations and explanations – but also by the *form* of the explanations that pathologists provided.

Of what form were the causes that interested pathologists? The causes pathologists identified (and that physicians took as a basis for their 'facts and reasonings' about diseases) were causes of death and causes of the successive stages of morbid processes. As we have seen, it was natural to associate causes of disease with causes of death. Indeed, it could not have been otherwise: whenever possible, diseases were defined as morbid processes, and unchecked morbid processes end in death. Thus, in contemporary medical texts, the discussion of individual diseases was often immediately preceded by a discussion of causes of death (Watson, 1858, pp. 67–76). But, as we have seen, a cause of death or the cause of a certain morbid alteration, like the cause of an accident or of the malfunction of a watch, is a sufficient cause for a particular event; one is asking: 'Why did this person die now?' From their symptomatically oriented predecessors, anatomically oriented physicians inherited a preoccupation with sufficient causes for particular events; the fascination with pathology only reinforced this preoccupation. Thus, etiology was almost unaffected by the change from symptomatic to anatomical characterizations of diseases. The lists of remote causes of diseases quoted above spanned, essentially unchanged, the shift from symptomatic to anatomical characterizations.

Insofar as one is interested in explaining why an individual becomes sick or dies, it is (from our point of view no less than from that of an 1840s physician) logical and correct to look for a sufficient cause for that single event and such a cause would inevitably include a variety of both predisposing and exciting factors. The result will be an historical explanation of a sort familiar in the biological sciences (Kamminga, 1993).[3] However, in the early nineteenth century, given symptomatic or anatomical characterizations of diseases, there simply was no other way of thinking about causes. In respect to remote causes, the nearest a nineteenth-century physician could come to our concept of 'the cause of disease X' was a collection of different causes found in individual cases – just the sort of collection Scanzoni and Chomel sought to accumulate in studying childbed fever and pneumonia. Thus, in the 1840s physicians focused on a kind of cause that receives relatively little medical attention today, while causes of the sort that dominate our etiological thinking were almost entirely absent. To help understand this striking contrast, we will now consider one final aspect of early nineteenth-century etiology.

Even a casual reader of the medical literature from the early nineteenth century must be struck with the extent to which medical theory and practice were bound up with traditional morality.[4] Etiological discussions of most diseases included references to such factors as drunkenness (1:79),[5] intemperance (2:595), gluttony (1:89), luxury (1:219), indulgence (4:331), debauchery (2:209), dissipation (4:137), vicious habits (2:559), solitary vice (4:139), excessive venereal indulgences (1:72), lustful excesses (2:621), indolence (1:48), sloth (1:739), envy (2:631), jealousy (2:631), and anger (1:116). Physicians observed that excess was the foundation of most disease (Barlow, 1845a, p. 751). Indeed, in the etiological discussions of one multi-volumed and multi-authored medical encyclopedia, such terms as 'excessive diet', 'gross and luxurious diet', 'gluttony', 'high feeding', and 'full and stimulating diet' appear four times as frequently as terms like 'insufficient food' or 'want of stimulating diet' (Dunglison, 1845). Through more than 3000 pages of text, 'excessive venereal indulgence' is repeatedly mentioned as a cause of disease, but celibacy is mentioned only once – as a possible cause of insanity (Prichard, 1845b, p. 48). The specific choice of terms in these etiological discussions is crucial – by identifying such factors as indolence (as opposed to inactivity), drunkenness (as opposed to alcohol intoxication), and solitary vice (as opposed to masturbation), *moral* concepts are invoked that necessarily permeate all subsequent theory and practice. If immorality causes disease, virtue becomes an important prophylaxis: 'Moderation in the pursuits of pleasure, of study, and of business; strict temperance and virtuous habits; may be said to comprise all that is most likely in our mode of living to give protection throughout life against the occurrence of scrofulous disease' (Cumin, 1845, p. 140). 'Few things are better preservatives against infection than fortitude and equanimity. Nothing, we are informed by those who voluntarily exposed themselves to the contagion … was found so great a preservative against its effects, as a steady adherence to what they believed their duty, banishing from their minds … all thoughts of danger, and avoiding every kind of passion' (Tweedy, 1845, p. 177).

Adherence to traditional standards was not only a protection against disease, it was central to treatment. One frequently reads that the 'moral management of the patient' constitutes an important or even the 'most efficacious' part of therapy (Prichard, 1845a, p. 560). Thus, in both prophylaxis and therapy, the nineteenth-century physician inculcated and defended traditional moral and social norms; 'his main endeavor was to see that individuals were capable of playing their social roles successfully in a traditional structure of social position. Illness was for him a mark of undue deviation from the norm' (Turner, 1967, p. 392). In this quotation, Victor Turner is discussing the social role of one *chimbuki* (which Turner translates as 'doctor' although he points out that '"ritual specialist" or "cult-adept" would be equally appropriate') among the Ndembu, a tribe in Zambia (Turner, 1967, p. 359), but, without much of a stretch, the quotation also applies in the present context.

Understanding this aspect of the physician's role, may shed light on the dominance of medical interest in sufficient causes of particular events. Suppose one is interested in discouraging some practice (for example, solitary vice). A natural response is to portray that practice as liable to bring on undesirable consequences like disease (for example, blindness). However, many immoral people do not become sick (so moral infraction by itself cannot be sufficient) and some people become sick without being immoral (so the infraction cannot be necessary or universal) – it can only be part of a complex cause that is sufficient for some particular events. Mary Douglas drew attention to the frequency with which conformity is encouraged (both in primitive societies and in our own) by portraying deviancy as a threat to such assets as time, money, nature, or divine favor (Douglas, 1975). Douglas does not mention health as one such asset but, clearly, endangerment of health is used at least as frequently for the same purpose. Representing infractions of moral and social norms as liable to bring on disease is a natural, almost universally espoused, and (possibly) even mildly effective strategy for influencing behavior. One must expect any culture whose physicians are concerned with reinforcing norms to focus on sufficient causes for particular disease episodes (Carter, 1991).

Nineteenth-century physicians were more interested in questions like 'Why does this person now have mumps?' than in questions like 'How does mumps come about?' Exactly the same priority of interests has been repeatedly noted in explanations of misfortune in primitive societies (Foster, 1976; Frankfort et al., 1949, p. 25; Evans-Pritchard, 1976, pp. 19–23). The reason is always the same: the primary objective is not controlling or explaining misfortune but reinforcing norms. Of course, this should not be construed as minimizing the significance or social utility of *chimbuki*-medicine:[6] Whether in twentieth-century Zambia or in nineteenth-century Europe, the wilful violation of norms is far more destructive than illness.

Years ago Erwin Ackerknecht warned that 'a fundamentally rational therapeutic method may be misunderstood because of its magic, semantic cloak' (Ackerknecht, 1946, p. 474). A sort of reverse confusion is also possible: What appears to be an essentially scientific vocabulary may cloak beliefs, concepts and objectives totally alien from our own. In the early nineteenth century, physicians spoke so much as we now speak that we see continuity where there was fracture and we overlook strands of their language that bind them inextricably to other systems of thought. Castiglioni describes early nineteenth-century physicians as scientists (Castiglioni, 1947, p. 760) and Foucault celebrates the rise of pathological anatomy as the origin of a science of the individual (Foucault, 1973, p. 197). In fact, scientific medicine is a more recent development that began with the rise of a research programme focusing on causes of disease.[7] One superficial clue marking the origin of this programme is a change in talk about causes of diseases. This change is connected to more fundamental changes in the concept of disease, in the organization of medical knowledge, in the selection of therapies,[8] and in professional expectations of physicians (Carter, 1993; Schlich, 1996).

Earlier causal talk was not wrong or irrational. It was part of a reasonable, coherent, and remarkably tenacious system of thought and action that had enormous social utility (Rosenberg, 1979, pp. 1–5). However, it was profoundly different from our own and was driven by interests quite different from those that have dominated the practice of medicine since about the middle of the nineteenth century.

Notes

1. Through this sentence, such numbers as the preceding are volume and page references to Dunglison (1845).
2. As this case illustrates, while early nineteenth-century physicians used many of the same disease names we use today, such names applied to dramatically different sets of cases, and they had altogether different meanings than they now bear. Michel Foucault (Foucault, 1973) and others (Schlich, 1994; Wilson, 2000) have made this point, but the lesson is difficult to learn.
3. For an independent analysis of causes of disease in individual patients that reaches similar conclusions see Wulff (1984). Michael Worboys has, appropriately, emphasized that 'germ theories of disease, explicitly or implicitly, always included ideas about the interactions between germs and bodies ... the seed and soil analogy, or some variant, was routinely used to explain both disease and its absence from the first uses of modern germ theories of all types' (Worboys, 2000, p. 281). John Harley Warner has discussed an exactly parallel focus on individual cases in the therapy of the period (Warner, 1986, pp. 58–80).
4. Charles E. Rosenberg has given attention to this issue but from a different perspective (Rosenberg, 1989).
5. Through this sentence, numbers such as the preceding are volume and page references to Dunglison (1845).
6. I occasionally use the phrase '*chimbuki*-medicine' as a convenient label for any medical system in which immorality, per se, is regarded as a cause of disease in the sense that it is taken as part of a sufficient cause for particular episodes of illness. No disrespect is intended either to nineteenth-century practitioners or to the *chimbuki*.
7. Lakatos pointed out that, in the absence of a research programme, there is 'a mere patched up pattern of trial and error' (Lakatos, 1968, p. 175) – so something less than mature science. Arguably the first research programme in *medicine* (that is, the first attempt to understand and control diseases by the formulation of scientific theories) is the one we are investigating.
8. 'Between the 1820s and the 1880s medical therapeutics in America was fundamentally altered. Traditional medical practices, founded on assumptions about disease shared by doctor and patient and oriented toward visibly altering the symptoms of sick individuals, began to be supplanted by strategies grounded in experimental science that objectified disease while minimizing differences among patients' (Warner, 1986, p. 1; see also Carter, 1982a).

CHAPTER TWO

Universal Necessary Causes

In 1844, Jacob Henle and Carl Pfeufer founded the *Zeitschrift für rationelle Medizin*. The first issue contained a long essay in which Henle distinguished three approaches to medicine: a speculative or theoretical approach, strict empiricism, and rational medicine (a combination of theory and observation). In his essay, Henle was sharply critical of existing causal thinking in medicine. He wrote that typical etiological discussions were so fallacious that medicine appeared ridiculous in comparison to the exact sciences, and he continued:

> Only in medicine are there causes that have hundreds of consequences or that can, on arbitrary occasions, remain entirely without effect. Only in medicine can the same effect flow from the most varied possible sources. One need only glance at the chapters on etiology in handbooks or monographs. For almost every disease, after a specific cause or the admission that such a cause is not yet known, one finds the same horde of harmful influences – poor housing and clothing, liquor and sex, hunger and anxiety. This is just as scientific as if a physicist were to teach that bodies fall because boards or beams are removed, because ropes or cables break, or because of openings, and so forth.
>
> (Henle, 1844a, p. 25)

This paragraph contains three different criticisms of existing causal thought in medicine and, by implication, three ideals that physicians should strive for in identifying causes. (1) In the first sentence Henle objected to accepting, as causes, factors that can have different effects or even no effect at all. Thus to be acceptable to Henle, a cause must always have the same effect; in other words it must be *sufficient* for its effect. (2) In the second sentence Henle objected to accepting, as causes, factors that need not be present for a given effect to occur (because the same effect could flow from other possible causes); in other words, he objects to factors whose absence does not insure the absence of the effect. Thus, to be acceptable to Henle, the absence of a cause must always accompany the absence of the effect; in other words, the cause must be *necessary* for its effect. In Henle's view, only factors that are both sufficient and necessary should be accepted as causes in rational medicine.

(3) The last two sentences contain a third criticism. Henle objected that for most diseases a 'horde of harmful influences – poor housing and clothing, liquor and sex, hunger and anxiety' – were recognized as

possible causes of each disease. This is exactly what we saw in our account of remote causes in the last chapter. Henle continued: 'This is just as scientific as if a physicist were to teach that bodies fall because boards or beams are removed, because ropes or cables break, or because of openings, and so forth.' Henle believed physicists seek a single common cause (perhaps gravitational attraction) to explain each instance of a class of similar events (instances of falling) instead of explaining those events in terms of the unique circumstances of each event itself (for example, the removal of a beam). His idea was that rational medicine should follow this example. In medicine, the counterparts to the different instances of falling are episodes of illness. So Henle is calling for the identification of universal causes – causes that are also necessary and sufficient – to explain every episode of each different disease. Later in the same essay, Henle observed: 'explanation is always the unification of the special under universal law' (Henle, 1844a, p. 31). Henle was interested in causes that were universal, necessary, and sufficient.

In fact, by 1844, when Henle published his essay on rational medicine, a few researchers had already identified causes that achieved his ideal. In 1835, Simon-François Renucci and Philippe Ricord in France and Agostino Bassi in Italy associated scabies, syphilis, and muscardine with a parasitic insect, a 'special ferment', and a minute fungus respectively.[1] Each of these causes was universal, necessary, and sufficient. In the same year, James Paget discovered encapsulated worms in human muscle tissue that, by 1860, were recognized as the universal, necessary and sufficient cause of trichinosis. In 1837 Alfred Donné described a parasitic protozoan, *Trichomonas vaginalis*, associated with inflammation of the vagina, and one year later Angelo Dubini discovered the hookworm parasite (Kunitz, 1988). In 1839 a German pathologist, Johann Lucas Schönlein, discovered that favus was always due to a minute fungus, and in the early 1840s David Gruby, an Hungarian microscopist working in Paris, described this fungus more adequately and traced several other human skin disorders to other fungi. These nearly simultaneous discoveries, most of which were known to Henle,[2] were nearly all independent of one another. How did each of these persons conclude – in stark opposition to the usual ways of thinking – that a particular cause was universal, necessary and sufficient for a certain disease? As a sample we will consider Renucci, Bassi, Gruby, and early research that culminated in the recognition of trichinosis.

The background to Renucci's claim to have discovered the cause of scabies is long and complex.[3] For more than 200 years, various persons had associated mites with the disease. However, the connection remained unclear and controversial.

In 1828, Jean Lugol, a French medical professor, having taught for many years that scabies was due to acari, decided that it was 'unworthy of an hospital professor to call on his pupil to believe anything in the absence of ocular demonstration' (J.F.S., 1836, p. 59). He and his students undertook a thorough quest for acari, but several days of intense effort failed to reveal the elusive parasite. Thereupon Lugol 'became ... a decided skeptic, and so fully was he convinced of the impossibility of finding the insect that ... he declared he would give a prize of three hundred francs to the first student who should extract an acarus in his presence'. Over the next six years, several persons sought the insect, but none was successful and the prize remained unclaimed. Then, in August 1835,

> a girl presented herself at the consultation room of the *Hôpital St. Louis*, to be treated for what she called the itch. Some doubt arising as to the exact nature of the eruption, M. Renucci, an Italian student, offered to remove all difficulty as to the diagnosis, by ascertaining the presence or absence of the acarus, which he said was so commonly found in cases of itch in his country, that the peasants extracted them from each other with pins or needles
> (J.F.S., 1836, p. 60).

Renucci quickly located a specimen that, to the delight of onlookers, 'exhibited the power of locomotion, scampering about with activity, unaware of the noise it might make in the annals of science'. Upon hearing of Lugol's challenge, Renucci claimed the prize. But Lugol had not witnessed the extraction of the acarus and remained unconvinced. Renucci offered to produce live acari in Lugol's presence and, if necessary, before the entire medical faculty. 'The affair now began to cause some excitement; nothing was talked of, or looked for, in the hospital, but the acarus; the wards allotted to itch patients, heretofore so quiet, were now thronged with students and visitors, anxious to discover or view the long-disputed insect.' On the appointed day, Renucci produced more acari. Moreover, under Renucci's tutorship, 'the searchers for acari soon produced them at last *en masse*, and during repeated sittings, and thus forced conviction on the unbelievers' (J.F.S., 1836, p. 60). Renucci was awarded the prize as well as a gold medal and, on 6 September 1835, his work was reviewed before the Academy of Science.

While existence of the acarus was no longer in doubt, its exact relation to scabies remained controversial. A British observer proposed that, instead of causing scabies, the acarus might 'show itself in the individual merely in consequence of the attraction produced by the itch matter or the filth attached to the person' (J.F.S., 1836, p. 62). A French physician wondered whether the insect might only be an accidental complication of the disease, and pointed out that, even if it were a cause, it might still not be the only possible cause (Biett, 1836, p. 547).

To clarify the relation between acari and scabies, Albin Gras, another medical student at St Louis Hospital,

> submitted his arm to a troop of these parasitical insects, and obtained a development of some characteristic vesicles. A subsequent intolerable itching, combined with the external characters, left little doubt as to the power of these insects to communicate the disease. But still the question is not decided, because the matter adhering to the insects may have been the cause of the vesicles, instead of the irritation simply produced by its presence. It has indeed been proposed by one of the professors (seriously?) to submit the insect to the action of a warm-bath before inserting it under the epidermis, and to pay particular attention to washing, brushing, and drying its feet!
>
> (J.F.S., 1836, p. 62)

According to the author of this account, experiments were still in progress.

A short time later, Gras reported the results of his self-inoculations (Gras, 1836). He claimed that acari appeared always and only in scabies, and that the insects were the only cause of the disease. In support of this claim, Gras reported that he had given himself scabies by inserting acari under his skin and that the ensuing disease had all the characteristics of ordinary scabies and could be further transmitted. On the other hand, he observed that the serous fluid associated with scabies could be introduced under the skin without effect. He judged that the insect was too complex and too perfect to have come about by spontaneous generation. This implied that scabies resulted only when living acari invaded a new host from an earlier one. If acari were not the cause of scabies, Gras asked, how could it happen that they were always present even in early stages of the disease. In the discussion of Gras's paper, respondents seemed willing to accept acari as one cause of scabies, but they questioned whether they were the only cause.

While some critics remained unpersuaded, to most, the central facts of the etiology of the disease seemed clear. In 1840, five years after publication of Renucci's first account, Jakob Henle concluded that scabies was the only disease in which human infection through a plant or animal parasite had been conclusively demonstrated (Henle, 1840, p. 971).

Agostino Bassi began studying muscardine, a fatal disease of silkworms, as early as 1807. Born in Lombardy on 25 September 1773, he worked as a civil servant in Lodi, but also managed his father's farm at Mairgo, four miles out of town. Bassi explained that, at the beginning of his research, he believed that the disease 'was due to some difference in the atmosphere, the food, or the method of breeding, or rather to the various fumes emanating from the fermenting litter'(Bassi, 1835, p. 4).[4] Bassi tried to produce muscardine by subjecting silkworms to various harmful influences. He reported breeding 'silkworms in all ways, even subjecting them to the most barbarous treatment: the wretched creatures died by thousands and in a thousand ways', but, when dead, none displayed the hard white crust that typified the disease. Bassi reported:

> I inflicted the cruellest treatment on [the worms], and used several kinds of poisons, mineral, vegetable and animal; I employed irritant, corrosive, and caustic substances, now simple, now compound; acids, alkalis, earths, and metals, in short the most noxious substances, deadly to the animal organism, in the solid as well as in the liquid or gaseous states; but everything proved useless for my purpose. There is no chemical substance nor any product of the perverted animal economy which can cause the terrible muscardine in the silkworm.   (p. 9)

Given existing beliefs about disease causation, one would have expected these measures to have provoked various disorders including muscardine. However, Bassi had no success. He reported that he continued these experiments for five years, from 1808 until 1813, 'wasting money and journeys and labor in vain, without ever in the least succeeding in my purposes'.

As he later described his work, Bassi seems then to have changed his approach: he began trying to simulate the symptoms of muscardine. Assuming that a disease is a group of symptoms, by producing the symptoms one could produce the disease. Bassi believed that the typical white crust consisted of an excess of 'earths and phosphoric acid', and he fed the worms these substances. His results seemed favorable: 'the corpses of the worms into which I had introduced these substances with their food were preserved from putrefaction or decayed much more slowly than the others' (p. 4). He found that by frequently soaking silkworms in liquified phosphoric acid and lime 'their corpses remained uncorrupted like the worms killed by *calcinaccio* and almost as white' (p. 5). But the dead worms were not as hard as those that died naturally; so the analogy was not yet perfect.

Then Bassi tried this procedure:

> I hung little paper bags, each containing a large silkworm near maturity, at various heights in the chimney of a fireplace in which a

fire was burning continuously. When, after several days, I opened the bags, ... I found several that were solid and hard like calcified worms. I maintained a given degree of moisture on the surface of these by putting some in the cellar and placing the others under small glasses, taking care to wet the surface of these last every day: under these conditions, some became covered with a white eruption exactly similar to that found on muscardined silkworms; and, since they were as firm and hard as these, they had all the appearance of true calcified worms, and a large number of silk worm experts to whom I showed them without saying anything of their origin, judged them all without exception to be true calcified worms.

(p. 5)

Bassi was encouraged, but he soon realized that these results were also imperfect: although the corpses were superficially indistinguishable from those of muscardine worms, they lacked 'the power of contagion'. Healthy worms exposed to these hard white corpses remained healthy, while worms exposed to true muscardine corpses died of the disease. Bassi saw this as a crucial difference between his artificial cases and real muscardine. Coming at the end of nine years of unsuccessful attempts to produce the disease, this realization was a major disappointment: Bassi tells us that he fell into 'the deepest dejection ... Humiliated in the extreme, silent and idle, I wept over my lost laurels and bitterly lamented the adverse fate which had put me to so much study, expense, and labor in vain' (p. 5).

Then came a turning point. Bassi described what happened:

It was the year 1816: oppressed by a terrible melancholy, which had already beset me for many months in various ways and from different directions,[5] I found the courage one day to shake off its yoke, and, challenging adverse fortune once more, I began to interrogate nature afresh in various ways, with the firm resolve never to abandon her until she had been tamed and answered my questions honestly. Having failed by so many different processes to produce muscardine in the silk worm except by the use of the true calcified worm, it occurred to me that it did not originate spontaneously in the insect, and that it needed an extraneous germ which entered the insect from outside and caused the disease.   (pp. 5f.)

Thus Bassi concluded that muscardine arose only when a germ was conveyed from a diseased worm to a healthy one. 'No product of the living body or of the perverted animal economy, no simple or compound substance, whether of the animal or vegetable kingdom, is capable of causing the disease. The organism that I am about to describe alone has the power of achieving this result' (p. 10). Bassi went on to describe what is now known as the fungus *Beauvaria bassiana*: 'This murderous creature is organic, living, and vegetable. It is a cryptogamic plant, a parasitic fungus.'

Bassi concluded that, after the fungus penetrated the skin of dead worms, it released germs that could infect new worms.

> The contagion is communicated by food, by inoculation, and by the mere contact of insects that have died of the terrible disease, of any infected object, and even of air contaminated by the disease-bearing germs. These are so abundant in a single calcified or efflorescent insect, and so minute, that they spread with extreme rapidity and in infinite numbers, cling fast even to the smoothest and most polished objects, such as glass, metal, etc., and even rise up into the air which they partially infect so long as they remain suspended in it.   (p. 8)

Bassi found that simply touching a healthy worm with a contaminated pin would usually (but not always) bring on the disease (p. 9). Especially in high temperatures or in high humidity, the disease did not always occur (pp. 31, 36). He also noted that other larvae were vulnerable to muscardine and that, in forests, one occasionally found dead worms covered with the same fungus; from these larvae he was able to infect healthy silk worms (p. 9). Later Bassi demonstrated that blood and tissue from diseased worms could also infect other worms. This proved that the internal tissues contained elements of the contagious fungus even before the appearance of the white excrescence.

Bassi's understanding of the role of the fungus enabled him to explain various facts about muscardine. The ease with which fungus germs were carried through the air or became attached to animals explained how the disease could spread to areas far from any known cases; the vast numbers of germs released from each corpse explained how the disease could suddenly destroy all the densely concentrated inhabitants of a silkworm facility; the growth of the fungus explained the hardening of the worm's corpse (p. 14). Bassi's discoveries also suggested practical ways of controlling muscardine. He recommended strict cleanliness to prevent the dissemination of germs. He found that, when exposed to fresh air, muscardine germs gradually became inert, so he recommended that breeding facilities be well ventilated. Bassi also identified chemical washes that could disinfect eggs and even live silkworms after contamination.

As Bassi recognized, his work hinted at the possible role of parasitic organisms in other diseases. 'My book ... may perhaps resolve some of the many anomalies which the doctrine of contagious disease in general contains' (p. 3).

> The germs of the various animal and vegetable contagions travel about, being transported hither and thither by so many bodies, dead and alive, organic and inorganic, and on the wings of the wind – especially the lightest germs and those that can live without a liquid or an animal mucus to envelop and preserve them. ...

> These are the effects produced in general by the contagions that afflict man and other animals, and that live for a long time, or at least over a year. (p. 34)

Bassi speculated that parasitic organisms could cause a variety of contagious diseases: 'Who knows whether some species of contagions that afflict man are not also vegetable? Indeed I suspect that the *Cholera morbus* is of this nature' (p. 39). In a later paper, Bassi compared the spread of muscardine to the spread of infectious human diseases. Such analogies suggested that several human diseases could also be caused by 'parasitic beings, either animal or vegetable, which germs pass from one individual to another and become more harmful and fatal to the poor patient whom they invade' (Major, 1944, p. 102). Bassi conjectured that smallpox, spotted fever, bubonic plague, gonorrhoea, rabies, and syphilis may be produced by minute vegetable or animal parasites.

Bassi's account, published in 1835, did not achieve immediate success. In 1836 the French naturalist Jean Victor Audouin reported further studies of muscardine. Audouin observed that when white excrement material from a muscardine worm was inoculated under the skin of a healthy worm, the inoculated worm invariably contracted a malady that resembled muscardine 'in its symptoms and consequences' (Audouin, 1836a, p. 231). But Audouin found it 'extraordinary' that a plant could parasitize a living animal, and he sought proof that the inoculated fungus actually developed within the living worm rather than simply remaining inert and flourishing only after the worm died. He examined worms microscopically at different intervals after they had been inoculated, and he described the stages by which the inoculated fungus spread through the living worm's body, gradually destroyed its tissues, and finally caused its death (Audouin, 1836a, p. 241). Audouin repeated his experiments several times, sometimes in the presence of observers, and published precise accounts of his work. In contrast to Bassi's rambling and impressionistic book, Audouin's publications satisfied existing standards of scientific proof.

Like some of Bassi's other critics, Audouin believed that muscardine could occur spontaneously under conditions that seemed to preclude any chance of contagion (Audouin, 1836b, p. 269). In allowing for spontaneous muscardine, Audouin seems not to have meant that the disease could occur independently of the fungus (because he identified victims of spontaneous muscardine by the characteristic excrescence on their corpses). Audouin tried to demonstrate the spontaneous origin of muscardine by maintaining silkworms at suitable temperatures and humidity in sealed, moss-filled containers; he found that such worms could become diseased, die, and produce a characteristic excrescence. Thus, Audouin believed that the fungus itself could arise by spontaneous generation. He reported that he caused true muscardine by inoculating healthy silkworms with fungus taken from such spontaneous cases of the disease. He also confirmed Bassi's conclusion that muscardine was not unique to silkworms but could attack other larvae (Audouin, 1836b, p. 265). The excrescence from these worms could also propagate the disease. This suggested that muscardine could arise spontaneously among the larvae indigenous to some location and then spread, by contagion, to any nearby silkworm facility.

In 1838 a commission reviewed the muscardine literature for the French Academy (Duméril et al., 1838). The commission concluded that inoculating healthy worms with pins that had been injected into muscardine worms, as Bassi had done, did not show that the fungus was the causal agent – perhaps body fluids adhering to such pins induced the disease by acting on the fluids of the inoculated worms as a ferment (Duméril et al., 1838, p. 90). Bassi had also failed to show that the fungus actually killed the worms by developing within them while they were yet alive. Thus Bassi had 'divined' many facts without proving them, but 'science does not consist of divinations' (Duméril et al., 1838, p. 100). The commission viewed Audouin's work more favorably. Audouin had established that the fungus actually caused muscardine and killed worms by growing within them. The commission also accepted Audouin's evidence that the fungus could arise spontaneously.

Two years later, Jacob Henle observed that 'one must agree with [the commission] that the facts that, according to Bassi's presentation, still permitted many objections – objections that Bassi actually experienced – were first proved by Audouin, who combined anatomic and microscopic studies with the experiments concerning contagiousness' (Henle, 1840, p. 945).

In 1839, four years after Bassi published his book on muscardine, Johann Lucas Schönlein, a Berlin physician and clinician, reported that favus was due to a minute fungus (Schönlein, 1839). Schönlein acknowledged Bassi's influence in his work. The fungus that Schönlein described is now known as *Achorion schönleinii*.

In July 1841 independently of Schönlein, and without knowing of his work, David Gruby also reported discovery of the fungus that causes favus.[6] Gruby was a Hungarian physician and microscopist who spent most of his professional life in Paris. His publication was more detailed and more accurate than Schönlein's, and, once he became aware of Schönlein's letter, he pointed out errors in the latter's sketchy account. Over the next few years, Gruby published reports on other human mycoses – reports still deemed substantially correct. We will review a sample of the brief causal arguments scattered through Gruby's publications.

In the first paper, which was on tinea or favus, Gruby argued that 'since we have not yet found any minute particle of the true tinea not being heavily loaded with this mycoderma, they constitute a true, essential characteristic of this disease' (Zakon and Benedek, 1944, p. 158). In his third paper, on thrush, Gruby argued for causality as follows:

> If one puts a small particle of this substance [of thrush] under the microscope, one sees it composed solely from a mass of cryptogamic plant ... Since we have not found ... in the white substance of the thrush anything but the vegetables and epithelial cells and no products of inflammation, we believe it is right to conclude that the thrush is nothing but a cryptogamic plant vegetating on the living mucous membrane.
>
> (Zakon and Benedek, 1944, p. 161)

In a fourth paper, Gruby described another human mycosis – probably *sycosis barbae*; he wrote:

> In previous communications I demonstrated that two diseases, the tinea favosa and the thrush of children, are due to development of certain cryptogams in the tissues of living individuals. Today I have the honor to submit to the judgment of the Academy my investigations on a third species of cryptogam which fixes itself in the hair sheath of the human beard causing a disease not yet sufficiently characterized up to this time. ... In examining the scales [of diseased tissues] under the microscope, one recognizes they are composed purely of epidermal cells; the microscopic examination of the hair, however, reveals its entire dermal portion is enveloped by cryptogams.
>
> (Zakon and Benedek, 1944, p. 162)

In the fifth paper, Gruby reported research on a disease he called *phyto-alopecia decalvans*. He observed that 'when one examines with attention this white dust under the microscope which covers the skin in porrigo decalvans, one will be surprised to find the whole formed entirely by cryptogams' (Zakon and Benedek, 1944, p. 164). He proposed naming the fungus '*Microsporum audouini*' in honor of Audouin's 'fine research work on muscardine [that] has contributed to direct attention to the vegetable parasites that destroy the live tissue of the animals'. Later, without having given any further evidence of causation, he observed: '*Microsporum audouini* which causes the phyto-alopecia (that is the name I suggest for distinguishing this affection) has many analogies with the cryptogams causing the disease I described under the name of phytomentagra' (Zakon and Benedek, 1944, p. 165).

Finally, in a sixth paper, Gruby observed, 'In examining with attention under the microscope hair fragments of the tinea tonsurans, one recognizes that their entire tissue is filled with cryptogams' (Zakon and Benedek, 1944, p. 166).

Gruby's reasoning in these passages is easy to characterize: in each case he inferred causality simply from finding a cryptogam to be present in (indeed to mostly constitute) the morbid materials of all of the observed cases of each disease. For six different diseases, he inferred causality after observing that disease products consisted mostly of the fungi.

Through the 1820s, English and German pathologists occasionally reported small, white specks in the muscle tissues of corpses. Pathologists speculated about the nature of the concretions, but were unable to associate them with any disease process or with any living organism.

On 2 February 1835 small, hard bodies – called bone spiculae – were found in the muscles of a corpse being dissected in St Bartholomew's Hospital in London. James Paget, a medical student at the time, reported that, in examining some of the structures under a lens, he 'found that they were cysts, and almost directly afterwards ascertained that nearly every cyst contained a small worm coiled up' (Paget, 1866).[7] The worms were called trichinae.

In 1852 a Göttingen physician, G. Herbst, made chance observations about the spread of trichinae. Herbst owned a pet badger that he fed partly with scraps from his dissecting table (Foster, 1965, p. 73). When the badger died, Herbst found that its muscles contained encysted worms indistinguishable from human trichinae. He fed the badger to three dogs, and later found that the muscles of all three contained encysted worms. Since worms were distributed throughout the dogs' muscles, he inferred that they were spread by the blood, but, apparently assuming that worms would already be encysted in the intestine, he was unable to imagine how they had entered the blood stream (Foster, 1965, pp. 72f). Herbst's feeding experiments, a novelty at the time, revealed much about how trichinae arrived in the muscle tissues of carnivores, but he reported his observations in a minor journal (Herbst, 1851–52) and his work was overlooked.

Through the 1850s there were isolated reports of trichinae, but the worms were believed to be harmless and rare. While there was interest in discovering how they arrived in the muscles and in tracing their subsequent development, these matters were thought to have no medical significance. One observer noted that, at this time, most physicians had never even heard of trichinae (Zenker, 1865, p. 103).

In 1859 Rudolf Virchow, the famous Berlin pathologist, fed to a dog human flesh infected with trichinae and, four days later, discovered unencysted sexually mature male and female trichinae in its intestine. At about the same time Rudolf Leuckart observed that, after tissues containing trichinae were digested, the worms were released from their cysts and matured in the intestine. He also saw that mature females were viviparous, which helped explain how worms entered the blood stream (Leuckart, 1860). These discoveries showed that the parasites could only enter a host through the consumption of encapsulated worms. With these discoveries, the essential steps of the life cycle of trichinae was clear. Leuckart noticed disease symptoms in a dog invaded by trichinae (Leuckart, 1860) and speculated that, instead of being mere harmless guests within the human body (as they were widely believed to be), trichinae may prove to be 'among his most dreadful enemies' (Foster, 1965, p. 74). However, pathologists were still unable to associate trichinae with any specific human or animal disease.

In January 1860 a young woman was admitted to the Dresden hospital suffering from fever, abdominal and muscular pains, oedema and pneumonia; the diagnosis was typhoid fever (Zenker, 1860, p. 563). She was expected to recover but soon died. Friedrich Alberti Zenker immediately began an autopsy looking for remains typical of typhoid; instead

> the first glance immediately revealed the astounding picture of the most thorough penetration of the muscles with unencapsulated trichinae. Because for several years I had often been occupied with trichinae and had already personally observed and thoroughly studied a series of cases of encapsulated trichinae and was familiar with all the associated questions, the uniqueness and novelty of these findings and their significance were immediately clear
> (Zenker, 1865, p. 104).

Zenker still assumed that the diagnosis had been correct and that trichinae were a coincidental complication. However, as the examination progressed, he found no morbid changes typical of typhoid, and he became persuaded that the multiplication and dissemination of the trichinae had itself caused the symptoms and the patient's death. 'The worms, which until then had been regarded as entirely harmless, were recognized as the cause of a horrible disease. Thus the almost purely zoological issue became an eminently practical and pathological one' (Zenker, 1865, p. 104). Zenker discovered free mature worms in the woman's intestine. He also learned that, one month earlier, she had assisted in slaughtering a pig. He visited her village, obtained samples of the pig's flesh and confirmed it was infested with trichinae. He could not establish that the woman had actually consumed raw pork, but this seemed likely. He found that other persons in the village, who had eaten raw meat from the same pig, had suffered similar symptoms but recovered (Zenker, 1865, p. 111).

As the clinical picture of the disease became clear, physicians began to recognize epidemics throughout Europe. It soon became obvious that infection was more common and the disease more deadly than anyone had guessed.

We now have a sense of the different paths by which independent lines of research culminated in the conclusion that several particular diseases had universal, sufficient, and necessary causes: Renucci may have conducted inoculation experiments (Ghesquier, 1999, p. 49), but his belief that acari caused scabies seems ultimately to have stemmed from a conviction widespread among the peasants of his homeland (J.F.S., 1836, p. 60). Bassi surmised that *Beauvaria bassiana* was necessary because he was unable to induce muscardine except by contagion. Gruby saw that the pathological materials typical of his mycoses were actually composed of fungi. And, in 1860, Friedrich Zenker abstracted the concept of trichinosis from the clinical and pathological picture presented by one patient infested with unencapsulated trichinae. Thus, by different paths and while dealing with mostly unrelated diseases, each of these lines of research pointed to a cause similar to those Henle called for.

However, while these innovative efforts approached Henle's ideal of universal necessary causes, they were all subject to a crucial limitation: no one of them clearly indicated how (or even if) universal necessary causes could be identified for other disorders. This was true for two reasons: First, on practical grounds, each of the paths reviewed above was dictated by the circumstances of the disease in question. For most diseases, common opinion did not point to a single cause; for most diseases, it would be impossible to subject healthy subjects to every conceivable trauma and note the results; most disease products were not composed of whatever was the cause; and for most diseases, research could not begin with a known organism whose presence could later be correlated with clinical and epidemiological observations. While each of these paths led to a universal necessary cause for one disease, no one of them was open to research on most other diseases.

Second, and more fundamentally, as diseases were typically characterized, they simply did not and could not have universal necessary causes. If hydrophobia is an extreme inability to swallow, it really can be caused by blows to the throat, by psychological factors, or by the bites of rabid dogs (Andral, 1832–33). As long as diseases were defined in terms of symptoms, different episodes of any one disease simply did not share a common necessary cause. And no research, however brilliant, can find what isn't there.

A universal necessary cause can be identified for a given disease only if the disease is characterized so that it has one. But how is this to be achieved? Not by defining the disease in terms of symptoms or of internal morbid alterations, since both approaches allow for various remote causes. How else might diseases be defined? By 1860 the first clear example had been given.

Notes

1. The most complete statement of Ricord's theory appeared in 1838 (Ricord, 1838), but he first announced his results in 1835 (Ricord, 1835). References are given below for Renucci, Bassi and others mentioned in this paragraph. I am grateful to Alex Dracobly for drawing my attention to Ricord (Dracobly, 2000).
2. Henle observed that his own thinking about infectious diseases was influenced by Bassi (Henle, 1844b, p. 302). He knew of contemporary studies of other parasitic diseases like favus and scabies (Henle, 1844b, p. 310). He discussed Gruby at a time when Gruby's work was almost universally ignored (Henle, 1844b, pp. 381f). He knew of the discovery of *Trichomonas vaginalis*, and speculated that it may be causally associated with syphilis (Henle, 1840, p. 969). Henle himself was among the first to report seeing the small structures in human flesh that Paget discovered to contain *Trichinella spiralis*, and Rudolf Leuckart's important observations about the life cycle of trichinae were published in a journal that Henle edited.
3. Danièle Ghesquier has recently examined this interesting story (Ghesquier, 1999). I agree with Ghesquier's conclusion that 'the reappearance of the itch-acarus was the very beginning of [the] change in concept from sufficient to necessary cause of disease' (p. 54). However, one must bear in mind that Bassi and Ricord also reported discovering universal necessary causes in 1835, the same year that Renucci persuaded the medical authorities of the cause of scabies.
4. Through this section, page numbers in parentheses are references to Bassi (1835).
5. Just at this time, Bassi was forced into early retirement from his government post because he was losing his sight.
6. For translations of Gruby's main articles and useful references, see Zakon and Benedek (1944).
7. William C. Campbell has given an account of the discovery of trichinae (Campbell, 1979).

CHAPTER THREE

Etiological Characterizations

The *only* way of characterizing diseases so that each disease will have a universal necessary cause is by defining them in terms of their causes. For example, the tubercle bacillus is universally necessary for tuberculosis only because 'tuberculosis' is defined as infestation by this bacillus. One cannot be certain that *no one* (perhaps Fracastoro, Paracelsus, Ugo Benzi of Siena, or Sinan ibn Thabit ibn Qurra) employed such characterizations before 1850 although, to date – loose talk about disease specificity notwithstanding – no textual evidence has been presented that anyone did. One reads that Fracastoro envisioned defining diseases in terms of what he called 'seeds'. But unambiguous evidence has yet to be provided and, even if this had been his intent, in the absence of any empirical means of distinguishing among seeds (or, indeed, even of demonstrating their existence) any such attempt would have been exactly as useless as defining diseases in terms of assorted evil spirits; vacuous definitions explain precisely nothing. However, this much is absolutely certain: Ignaz Semmelweis was the first person to have adopted such definitions in publications that are linked by citations directly into the etiological research programme. The only way to dispute this fact would be to exhibit citations in core works of the programme to writers *before* Semmelweis who used this approach, and there simply are none.[1] Semmelweis may or may not have been aware of the significance of what he did; others may or may not have consciously followed his example; it matters not. The facts are that Semmelweis employed this strategy clearly and unequivocally, he did so without any identifiable precedent (none of his teachers in Vienna ever proposed such characterizations and neither did any of the horde of marginally significant eighteenth-century English physicians who wrote on childbed fever), and his work figured in the etiological research programme. For these reasons we take his use of etiological characterizations to exemplify this approach – an approach without which the systematic identification of universal necessary causes is absolutely unthinkable.

Semmelweis's story has been told and retold many times (although usually by persons oblivious of the nature and significance of his contribution).[2] For our purposes only four claims require discussion:

1.   In the mid 1840s, typical accounts of the etiology of childbed fever

(also called puerperal fever) conformed to similar accounts for other diseases as discussed in Chapter 1 above.

2. At least by 1858, and probably as early as 1850, Semmelweis advanced an etiological definition of 'childbed fever' that guaranteed a universal and necessary cause.

3. This definition was the basis for a theory of childbed fever that, while seriously flawed, was unquestionably superior to any other existing account.

4. In spite of a persisting tradition to the contrary, Semmelweis's work was widely known and frequently cited between 1865 and 1890 by many of the very persons who actively contributed to the etiological research programme – the programme that ultimately replaced *chimbuki*-medicine.

Representative accounts of childbed fever from the 1840s

Childbed fever, a particularly horrible disease, was common in the eighteenth and early nineteenth centuries.[3] A few days after delivery, victims suffered a variety of symptoms, typically including abdominal pain and intense fever, and they usually died within hours of the onset. Pathologists tried to understand childbed fever by studying morbid remains in the corpses of victims. They gave particular attention to the uterus since the disease was associated with birth, and autopsies often revealed morbid changes there. However, no clear picture emerged. In some victims no morbid alterations were discernible and in others the changes took a variety of forms and did not always focus on the uterus. According to the principles of pathological anatomy, this implied that childbed fever was not a single disease, but a group of superficially similar diseases. Some obstetricians abandoned the term 'childbed fever' and fell back on anatomical concepts like endometritis, peritonitis, or metrophlebitis.

In 1842, Paul-Antoine Dubois, a leading French obstetrician, summarized his views about puerperal fever in a long essay in a French 'dictionary' (encyclopedia) of medicine (Dubois, 1842). Dubois discussed the inconsistent pathological remains. He acknowledged that some pathologists had given up looking for a primary alteration and had concluded that childbed fever was actually a group of several different but symptomatically similar diseases. Against this view, Dubois hypothesized that the victim's blood could be the site of a common primary alteration. If so, he reasoned, a given patient could die so quickly that other tissues could remain unaffected. On the other hand, if a patient lived long enough, secondary morbid changes could occur.

Thus, he speculated, in spite of the variations, puerperal fever could still be a single disease stemming from a common corruption of the blood. He could not identify or describe this supposed corruption, and he admitted that there may be cases in which other alterations came first (Dubois, 1842, p. 339).

Dubois believed the corruption of patients' blood could be initiated by a variety of remote causes, for example, by a miasm originating in a maternity clinic or by the putrefaction of blood clots retained in the uterine cavity after delivery. He also admitted that childbed fever could sometimes be contagious, and he urged physicians to prevent direct contact between sick and healthy patients and even indirect contact by way of healthy third persons such as physicians (Dubois, 1842, p. 343). Dubois knew that childbed fever sometimes occurred in epidemics. At the time, epidemics were usually ascribed to harmful atmospheric influences that could not otherwise be detected, and he concluded that childbed fever sometimes seemed to arise from such influences. He noted that these influences could provoke the disease in predisposed but otherwise healthy women. As predisposing causes, Dubois mentioned the disruption of pregnancy, the shock of labor,

> a soft and effeminate life, a milieu of luxury and abundance, the absence of exercise sufficient to induce physical vigor and complete vitality of the blood, ... weakness produced by poverty, an unhealthy place of residence, a diet inadequately restorative, the abuse of spirituous liquors, various kinds of grief, debauchery, and excessive work.
>
> (Dubois, 1842, p. 348)

Because of such predisposing conditions, Dubois observed, some women 'carry within themselves the disease rather than contracting it in the hospital'. Exciting causes of childbed fever included

> the length of labor, an abundant uterine loss, a grave eclampsia, various maneuvers and surgical operations, something attendant on parturition or the accidents that complicate it, more or less serious genital lesions ... the affect of cold air, the use of cold and humid linen, cold water lotions, departures from a [normal] regimen, exciting drinks ... , the imprudence of some women who rise in the first days [after delivery], ... and the emotional states of the newly delivered.
>
> (Dubois, 1842, p. 349)

Dubois observed that many of these causes had no effect except during an epidemic. Of course, Dubois's account of the causes of childbed fever was entirely consistent with contemporary beliefs about disease causation in general.

In 1843, one year after Dubois's essay appeared, the American physician Oliver Wendell Holmes published an essay entitled 'The Contagiousness of Puerperal Fever'. In 1855 the essay was reprinted with an introductory note and an appendix containing additional references but with no changes in the body of the text. The purpose of the essay was to show that 'the disease known as puerperal fever is so far contagious as to be frequently carried from patient to patient by physicians and nurses' (Holmes, 1843, p. 131).[4] Holmes' conclusions and most of his case histories were drawn from earlier British sources; he admitted, both in the essay and again in the later introductory note, that his was a majority view. 'A few writers of authority can be found to profess a disbelief in contagion – and they are very few compared with those who think differently' (p. 129). Indeed, one year before publication of Holmes's essay, *Lancet* reported a discussion of puerperal fever in the London Medical Society in which 'the chief apparent circumstance is the diversity of opinion ... as to the nature ... the symptoms and the treatment of the affection. ... One fact only respecting the disease was generally admitted, namely, its unquestionable contagiousness' (*Lancet*, 1842–43). But, while Holmes had little new to say about childbed fever, he felt that the existence of the minority, who questioned its contagiousness, justified his essay.

Holmes cited about twenty cases in which physicians examined or treated patients with puerperal fever or in which they performed autopsies on women who died from puerperal fever and in which their other patients subsequently contracted the disease. He warned obstetricians against taking 'any active part in the post-mortem examinations of cases of puerperal fever' and that 'on the occurrence of a single case of puerperal fever in his practice, the physician is bound to consider the next female he attends in labor ... as in danger of being infected by him' (p. 168). Holmes considered cases suggesting that puerperal fever could be produced 'by an infection originating in the matter or effluvia of erysipelas'. But he found the relation of puerperal fever to other diseases 'remote and rarely obvious'. Thus, while he mentioned reports that 'puerperal fever has appeared to originate from a continued proximity to patients suffering with typhus', these cases were so rare that they 'hardly attract our notice in the midst of the gloomy facts by which they are surrounded' (p. 165). Holmes never suggested that patients with other diseases or corpses of persons who died from other diseases constituted a risk to maternity patients. Indeed, he observed that

> the number of cases of serious consequences ensuing from the dissection of the bodies of those who had perished of puerperal fever is so vastly disproportioned to the relatively small number of autopsies made in this complaint as compared with typhus or

pneumonia (from which last disease not one case of poisoning happened), and still more from all diseases put together, that the conclusion is irresistible that a most fearful morbid poison is often generated in the course of this disease (p. 162).

Each time Holmes stated precisely his main point he claimed only that the disease is sometimes (or frequently) carried from one patient to another (pp. 112, 129, 131). He always allowed for the same range of other possible causes that all his contemporaries acknowledged: 'It is not pretended that the disease is always, or even, it may be, in the majority of cases, carried about by attendants; only that it is so carried in certain cases' (p. 123). Following the British, Holmes distinguished cases arising from infection from epidemic or sporadic cases. 'It is granted that the disease may be produced and variously modified by many causes besides contagion, and more especially by epidemic and endemic influences' (p. 133). In the chronologically later introductory note, he wrote that his theory 'makes full allowance for other causes besides personal transmission, especially for epidemic influences' (p. 107).

When Oliver Wendell Holmes' essay was published, Eduard Lumpe was an assistant physician in the first section of Vienna's charity obstetrical clinic. In 1845, two years after publication of Holmes' essay, Lumpe wrote a carefully documented and thorough survey of contemporary views of puerperal fever (Lumpe, 1845). It is a good sample of Viennese thinking about the disease.

Lumpe gave sympathetic attention to the view, dominant among pathologists, that what was called puerperal fever was actually a group of symptomatically similar but anatomically distinct disorders; for this reason, he acknowledged, many preferred the term 'puerperal diseases' rather than 'puerperal fever' (Lumpe, 1845, p. 342).[5] Lumpe also mentioned that, while inconsistent with the meaning of 'puerperal', women sometimes contracted these disorders even before delivery. He accepted the common view that puerperal diseases usually began in the uterus. This could be the point of attack even if autopsy disclosed only minor changes in the uterus itself. Lumpe recognized that the morbid remains in puerperal fever resembled those found when decaying organic matter was accidentally introduced into the blood of a healthy patient or of a surgeon or pathologist (pp. 350f.).

Lumpe gave considerable attention to the causes of puerperal fever. He felt that maternity patients may be vulnerable because 'lochial secretions, the purpose of which is to remove waste matter, can be retained or absorbed and thereby induce decay of the blood' (p. 345). The likelihood of absorbing harmful matter was greater following delivery because the epithelium of the womb had been discharged and was being regenerated and the veins were lacerated. Women were predisposed to the disease by general deprivation, worry, fear, shame, attempted abortion, and by the fear of death associated with admission to a hospital. Exciting causes included difficult delivery, damage to tissues through the use of mechanical devices, and the retention and decomposition of the placenta (p. 348). Lumpe was aware of the possibility that the disease could be contagious (pp. 345f.), and he mentioned an unnamed British physician who 'had gone so far as to claim that, through the contagion of childbed fever, non-maternity patients and even men could contract similar diseases' (p. 348). However, he discounted this possibility and seems to have regarded contagion as a minor problem.

Because of the accurate morbidity records of Vienna's General Hospital, Lumpe made several astute observations about the incidence of epidemic puerperal diseases. He felt the existence of epidemics was 'demonstrated by occasional increases and decreases in the number of cases without any change in the factors most commonly recognized as causes, by the simultaneous occurrence of numerous cases, and by the similarity of the course of simultaneous cases' (pp. 342f.). He observed that the disease was more prevalent in winter than in summer; this also suggested that the disease may be epidemic and caused by atmospheric conditions. He knew that the disorder was almost always associated with maternity clinics – women who delivered at home, or even on the street as they were on their way to the hospital, seldom became ill. He concluded, as others had before him, that the disease was usually caused by harmful miasms that, once generated, persisted in maternity clinics because of inadequate ventilation.

To Lumpe, the incidence of disease at Vienna's General Hospital also suggested a miasmatic origin. The hospital's maternity clinic was divided into two sections and patients were assigned to the sections according to the day on which they happened to arrive. Since 1840 all the male obstetrical students had been trained in the first section and female student midwives in the second. From then on, mortality had consistently been higher in the section for obstetricians than in the midwives' section. 'At the height of an epidemic, when ten to twelve patients die in the second section, the number of deaths in the first section will be four or five times greater' (p. 347). He could imagine only one explanation for this difference: since there were more births each year in the first section, the second could be cleared and ventilated more frequently. Thus, Lumpe supposed, the difference in mortality was due to local miasms that were dispelled from the second section but retained in the first. Lumpe wrote, 'let anyone who doubts the power of

local miasmatic influences explain this difference in any other way'
(p. 347).

Semmelweis's etiological characterizations

On 1 July 1846 Ignaz Semmelweis became assistant physician in the
obstetricians' section of the Viennese maternity clinic – the same section
in which Lumpe had served two years earlier.[6] At the time, mortality
from childbed fever averaged about 7 per cent in the first section and
about 2 per cent in the second. The Viennese maternity facility was
relatively healthy – even 7 per cent mortality compared favorably with
similar clinics around Europe. But medical personnel knew and were
troubled by the difference in mortality between the two Viennese
sections.

After a few months, during which Semmelweis was tormented by the
relatively higher mortality rate in his section, it occurred to him that the
difference could be due to contamination on the hands of students in
the first section. Student obstetricians in the first section, but not the
student midwives in the second, were required to perform dissections.
In May 1847 Semmelweis began requiring all the medical personnel in
his section to wash in a chlorine solution. The washings were intended
to destroy decaying organic matter from the morgue with which their
hands may have become contaminated. Mortality in the first section
immediately fell to about 1 per cent – a level at or below that maintained in the second section.

Other experiences soon convinced Semmelweis that decaying organic
matter capable of causing puerperal fever could also be generated within
the patients themselves. This could happen because of disease, because
of retained lochia or placental remains, or through the decay of body
tissues damaged in delivery. He estimated that these sources of decaying
organic matter caused fever in approximately 1 per cent of patients.
This explained the deaths in the second section and those that occurred
in spite of the prophylactic washings, and he regarded these cases as
beyond his control.

Word of Semmelweis's work gradually spread through Europe. This
came about partly by letters written by his students (Carter and Tate,
1991) and partly by two notices, written by Ferdenand Hebra, that
were published in a Viennese medical journal. Three years elapsed
before Semmelweis himself publicly reported his work. Finally, on 15
May 1850, Semmelweis delivered a lecture before a Viennese medical
society. Discussion of the lecture continued through three successive
meetings in June and July. Unfortunately, the lecture itself was not

published; we know it only from the secretary's summary, from the report of the ensuing discussions, and from a published critical response by Eduard Lumpe who attended the meetings.

According to the secretary's account, Semmelweis criticized earlier attempts to explain the imbalance in mortality between the two sections. He noted that the pathological remains in childbed fever bore 'the greatest possible similarity to those found in pyaemia as it occurs in anatomists and surgeons after [suffering accidental wounds while] dissecting corpses' (Györy, 1905, p. 49). He described how decaying organic matter could be conveyed on the hands of medical personnel, and he pointed out that the disease was rare in schools for midwives except where students also participated in dissections. According to the secretary's account, Semmelweis concluded that

> puerperal fever is neither contagious nor even a specific disease. Rather it develops when putrefied animal-organic matter, from any disease whatsoever, regardless of whether from a living organism or from a corpse, is taken into the blood system of a recently delivered woman and generates the puerperal (pyemic) disintegration of the blood. ... Thus, one can protect against this disease by cleaning the fingers, the utensils, and the air. If this is done, there will be only isolated cases of puerperal fever resulting from the retention of decaying remains, decidual or placental.
> (Györy, 1905, pp. 50f)

While less explicit than one might like, these sentences can best be understood as advancing a new definition of childbed fever (as we will see, this strategy becomes more explicit in later publications). The implication is that *every* case of the disease is due to decaying organic matter. However unclear the secretary's account may be, there was no question in the minds of those who responded to Semmelweis's lecture that this was his position.

In his response to this lecture, Eduard Lumpe criticized several of Semmelweis's claims. In his own paper, published five years earlier, Lumpe mentioned virtually all the evidence that Semmelweis now used to support his new concept of the disease. Yet Lumpe was astounded by Semmelweis's claim that every case of childbed fever had the same one cause. While granting that chlorine washings may be useful, Lumpe emphatically denied that every case of the disease was due to decaying organic matter:

> When one thinks how, since the first occurrence of puerperal fever epidemics, observers of all times have sought for its causes and the means of preventing it, Semmelweis's theory takes on the appearance of the egg of Columbus. I was myself originally overjoyed as I heard the fortunate results of the chlorine washings; ... However, during my two years as assistant in the first section, I observed

incredible variations in the incidence of illness and death. Because of this ... any possibility is more plausible than one common and constant cause.

(Lumpe, 1850, pp. 392f.)

At the conclusion of the discussions, Karl Rokitansky, who presided in the meetings, 'emphasized the incontestable utility of chlorine washings which is admitted even by opponents of Semmelweis's opinions' (Győry, 1905, p. 58). This sentence shows clearly that the usefulness of the chlorine washings was never in dispute. Everyone was more or less willing to accept the washings, and, of course, for years the British had advocated disinfection. However, there is no evidence in the minutes that anyone supported or even accepted Semmelweis's claim that childbed fever was *always* due to one constant cause. That claim was the focus of the dispute.

Before the 15 May lecture, those who responded to the second-hand accounts of Semmelweis's work objected only that it was unoriginal; after his lecture, no one complained of a lack of novelty – instead they attacked his remarkable claim that the disease had a universal necessary cause. In an editorial published in 1850, Joseph Hermann Schmidt, Professor of Obstetrics in Berlin, recommended that obstetrical students have ready access to morgues in which they could profitably spend time dissecting while waiting for the labor process (Semmelweis, 1861b, pp. 225f.). He asked how Semmelweis's hypothesis could be reconciled with the observation that childbed fever seldom occurred in normal deliveries. He then wrote that while the resorption of decaying organic matter could be 'one path that leads to childbed fever, it is certainly not the only path'. In an 1855 text, Friedrich Scanzoni, professor of obstetrics in Prague, rejected Semmelweis's opinion. He acknowledged that puerperal fever could originate as Semmelweis had described, and that chlorine washings may be useful in such cases (Scanzoni, 1855, vol. 3, p. 1010). Yet Scanzoni rejected Semmelweis's views on the grounds that the disease was usually caused by atmospheric or miasmatic influences or by emotional trauma. In medical texts published in 1855 and 1857, Carl Braun, professor of obstetrics in Vienna, gave extensive attention to the etiology of childbed fever (Braun, 1855, 1857). Braun identified 30 possible causes of the disease including conception itself, the general plethora of pregnancy, the shock of delivery, pressure of milk secretions, the individuality of the patient, emotional disturbances, errors in diet, defective ventilation, chilling, and the inappropriate arrangements of some maternity hospitals. Cadaverous poison is the twenty-eighth possible cause in Braun's list. Braun claimed, inaccurately, that Semmelweis regarded cadaverous poisoning as the main cause – perhaps the only cause – of childbed fever. While admitting that cadaverous poisoning could account for some cases of disease, Braun denied that it could have the significance that Semmelweis (supposedly) attributed to it. In an 1858 letter to Semmelweis, D. Everkin of the Paderborn maternity clinic wrote: 'I could not imagine that this circumstance is the universal cause, but I was led [by your communication] to avoid undertaking any procedures on maternity patients after examining corpses.' He then warned Semmelweis that nowhere outside medicine is one so frequently tempted by the *post hoc ergo proper hoc* fallacy (Semmelweis, 1861b, p. 228). In the same year, Paul-Antoine Dubois wrote that while 'one could not dispense with precautionary measures to guard against contagion, the contagious element is neither as effective nor as pervasive as Semmelweis has claimed, ... even before delivery other factors predispose women to the disease' (Semmelweis, 1861a, p. 458). Through the early months of 1858, the French Academy of Medicine hosted a series of 26 lectures on puerperal fever by prominent French obstetricians (l'Académie, 1858). Semmelweis was mentioned in six of the lectures, but there was little discussion of his work. Some speakers associated his views with those of the British (l'Académie, 1858, p. 228). Some acknowledged that chlorine washings may be useful. Only one speaker, M. Danyau, considered Semmelweis's claim to have identified a universal cause; Danyau rejected this claim but urged physicians to do everything possible to avoid infecting patients (l'Académie, 1858, p. 228). In 1859 Hermann Lebert, Professor at Breslau, wrote: 'It is questionable whether those who have died of this disease can have been directly inoculated by poison from corpses. Semmelweis has elevated this possibility into an entire system. In any case this would be only one of many possibilities of conveyance' (Semmelweis, 1861b, p. 221).

Thus, through the 1850s, several physicians acknowledged that chlorine washings could be useful; some mistakenly associated Semmelweis's concept of childbed fever with that of the British; some mistakenly assumed that Semmelweis was concerned only with cadaveric poisoning. However, Semmelweis's view that the disease always had one common cause was invariably either ignored or rejected. In this respect, there was greater agreement between Semmelweis's opponents and those he regarded as supporters than there was between Semmelweis and his supposed supporters. Those who realized that Semmelweis was making this strong claim, rejected it. The few who thought they agreed with Semmelweis did so only because they ignored what was unique and original in his position. There is no textual evidence that, as late as 1862, anyone in Europe had accepted Semmelweis's claim.

In 1858 Semmelweis published a short essay entitled 'The Etiology of Childbed Fever'; two years later he published a second essay entitled: 'The Difference in Opinion between Myself and the English Physicians

Regarding Childbed Fever' (Györy, 1905, pp. 61–83, 83–94). In October 1860 he published his book, *The Etiology, Concept, and Prophylaxis of Childbed Fever* (Semmelweis, 1861a). When his book did not have the impact he had expected, Semmelweis began publishing open letters explaining his opinions and bitterly attacking various prominent obstetricians (Györy, 1905, pp. 431–511). He also explained his views in a letter, written in English, that appeared in a British periodical.

The account of childbed fever in his publications rests on two crucial definitions. In his first essay and in his book Semmelweis defined 'childbed fever' as 'a resorption fever dependent on the resorption of decaying animal-organic matter' (Semmelweis, 1861b, p. 114). He also defined 'pyaemia' as 'disintegration of the blood through decaying animal-organic matter' (Semmelweis, 1861b, p. 117). Semmelweis used the uncommon word 'resorption' in the first definition because it precisely expressed his opinion that childbed fever occurred when decaying organic matter was resorbed – literally absorbed back – into a living organism.

Semmelweis's new characterizations of childbed fever and of pyaemia have several important consequences:

1. Given these characterizations, it is true, *by definition*, that *every* case of childbed fever is caused by decaying organic matter – there cannot be a single exception. Semmelweis was clear about this: 'In order for childbed fever to occur, it is a *conditio sine qua non* that decaying matter is introduced into the genitals' (Semmelweis, 1861b, p. 149). Semmelweis frequently asserted that, without exception, every case of childbed fever came about through resorption of decaying organic matter (Semmelweis, 1861b, pp. 114, 115, 120, 149). This, of course, was the claim to which everyone objected following his 1850 lecture, but at least by the time of his publications it was a matter of definition.
2. It followed that there were no spontaneous, epidemic, or miasmatic cases of the disease (Semmelweis, 1861b, pp. 120f, 201).
3. Given the characterizations, it is true, by definition, that every case of childbed fever is a case of pyaemia.
4. Given the characterizations, it follows that infected surgeons and maternity patients all died from the same disease, namely, from pyaemia or blood poisoning.
5. Given the definitions, Semmelweis could explain precisely how childbed fever differed from contagious diseases: 'Childbed fever is a conveyable but not a contagious disease. By "contagious disease" one understands a disease spread by material generated from and only from cases of that same disease' (Györy, 1905, p. 72). By

contrast, on his view, childbed fever could be caused by decaying organic matter derived from any source.

6. Finally, given the characterizations, Semmelweis could also explain precisely how his views differed from those of the British contagionists:

> The important difference between my opinion and the opinion of English physicians consists in this: I hold that every case of childbed fever, without a single exception, has only one cause, namely incorporation of decaying organic matter. Of this I am convinced. The English physicians, while they also believe that childbed fever can be caused by decaying matter, still recognize all the old epidemic and endemic causes that have been believed to play a role in the origin of the disease.
> (Győry, 1905, p. 94)

These etiological definitions and their consequences are the core of Semmelweis's theory of childbed fever. He himself emphasized that they alone made his teachings unique.

By the time Semmelweis published the *Etiology*, many accounts of his ideas had been circulated. Thus, by the time his own definitive accounts appeared, everyone had an opinion about his views and few bothered to read his book. There were only two published reviews. In 1862 Carl S.F. Crede reviewed the *Etiology* in a prominent German journal of obstetrics. According to Crede, Semmelweis called everyone who disagreed with him an ignoramus and a murderer. Crede wrote that Semmelweis's assertions

> go too far and are too one-sided. In any case Semmelweis owes his reader proof that only the one etiological condition he identifies is always responsible. Nearly every obstetrician is still of the opinion that a large number of cases of illness remain that originate from a different cause, a cause admittedly as yet unknown.
> (Crede, 1861, p. 407)

August Breisky, an obstetrician in Prague, published a more careful review of the *Etiology*, but even Breisky referred to Semmelweis's book as 'naive' and as 'the Koran of puerperal theology' (Breisky, 1861, p. 1). Breisky objected that Semmelweis had not proven that puerperal fever and pyemia were identical, and he insisted that other factors beyond decaying organic matter had to be included in the etiology of the disease.

The advantages of Semmelweis's account of childbed fever

There were substantial defects in Semmelweis's theory of childbed fever (Semmelweis, 1861b, pp. 42–46), and all things taken into account his critics were probably justified in remaining skeptical. However, his approach had two remarkable advantages, one practical and one theoretical. First, so long as the disease was defined to allow for various independent causes, measures that were effective in one case could conceivably have exacerbated other cases of the same disease.[7] This made prophylaxis and therapy so confusing it was virtually impossible to find effective measures for prevention or treatment.[8] An etiological definition meant that every case of the disease had the same cause, thus any prophylactic or therapeutic measures directed against that cause that were effective in one case would be effective in every case. Thus, the definition made possible consistent and uniform strategies for prevention and treatment.

Second, Semmelweis's approach provided a way of explaining an amazing range of facts. From his account, in spite of its weaknesses, Semmelweis drew explanations for dozens of facts many of which had already been observed and recorded but never explained. For example, Semmelweis explained why the mortality rates in the two clinics differed (Semmelweis, 1861b, p. 118),[9] why those rates had changed through history as they had (pp. 118f), why chlorine washings were effective, why disease was rare during pregnancy or after a week or more following delivery (p. 115), why the disease appeared to be contagious (p. 118), why it exhibited seasonal patterns (in summer 'the charming surroundings of Vienna [were] more attractive than the reeking morgue or the sultry wards of the hospital' so students spent comparatively less time dissecting corpses and examining patients) (p. 122), why the disease focused on teaching hospitals (p. 123), why some non-teaching hospitals had higher mortality rates than others (p. 125), why women who delivered prematurely or on the way to the hospital had a lower mortality rate (in order to delay labor, women who seemed likely to deliver prematurely were never examined by students) (p. 101), why the disease often appeared in particular sequential patterns among patients (p. 101), why infants seldom died of pyaemia while their mothers remained healthy (p. 99), and why the disease appeared with different frequencies in different countries and in different historical periods (p. 133). Semmelweis gave coherent explanations for all these observations and more.

In this respect, the difference between Semmelweis and everyone else who wrote on the disease – including Dubois, Holmes, and Lumpe – is the difference between day and night. In their essays, however astute and even beneficial, Dubois, Holmes, and Lumpe explained almost nothing. Holmes (like others before him) observed that medical personnel sometimes endangered their patients; he explained this by the hypothesis of contagion and recommended that physicians disinfect themselves before visiting patients. Lumpe observed that mortality in the first section was several times greater than in the second; he explained this by the hypothesis of local miasms and recommended that maternity clinics have adequate ventilation. Both observations were correct; both recommendations beneficial. However, appeals to undetectable contagions or miasms were inherently defective: the only evidence for the existence of either were the morbid processes that the hypothesized factors were intended to explain. Thus, both explanations were circular and vacuous – perfect examples of what a later nineteenth-century researcher referred to as 'the empty generalities of the past [that] only appeared, superficially, to satisfy the need for causes' (Strümpell, 1893, p. 22f). Moreover, everyone else, including Dubois, Holmes, and Lumpe, left almost all the observations unexplained. For example, they could not explain why women who delivered prematurely were safer than those who went full term or why the disease was especially prevalent in teaching hospitals. Finally, at least as the epidemic and miasmatic hypotheses were commonly stated, they were refuted by events in the Viennese clinic since atmospheric and miasmatic influences had to be the same in both sections (which were adjacent and even shared some rooms).

All of the explanations Semmelweis gave and that others couldn't give rested on the existence of a single universal cause. This is because, if the disease were so defined that its cases had many different causes, it would be impossible to provide a unified explanation (for example, of the reduced incidence of morbidity among premature deliveries) that would, in effect, cut across all the different explanations that contemporaries gave for each of the different individual cases. The superiority of Semmelweis's account was soon obvious to contemporaries: In 1868, one Berlin obstetrician noted that Semmelweis's theory 'provides a unified, clear, and entirely intelligible meaning for a whole series of anatomical and clinical facts and for the disinterested experiences and discoveries of reliable observers' whereas 'none of the earlier or alternative hypotheses or theories ... has this characteristic to the same degree' (Boehr, 1868, p. 403). That says it all.

In a recent book on childbed fever, Irvine Loudon criticizes Semmelweis's theory in several ways and, while some of the criticisms are valid, others are not. Some of Loudon's failed criticisms reflect a serious misconstruction of the logic of Semmelweis's position. Semmelweis's theory rests on *definitions* and, while empirical observations certainly motivated the definitions, such observations cease to have effect once the definitions are in place. Loudon wonders how Semmelweis would explain 'the awkward fact' that 'throughout Europe ... deaths from puerperal fever [were] between 20 and 30 per 10,000 births [i.e., 0.2

per cent to 0.3 per cent] – a much lower figure than the [1 per cent] rate in the early days of the Vienna Lying-in Hospital [that was the basis for Semmelweis's estimate of the rate of self-infection]' (Loudon, 2000, p. 98). Presumably, Loudon thinks Semmelweis would find this fact awkward because the discrepancy suggests deaths due neither to self-infection (which, according to Loudon's figures, could only account for a 0.2 per cent mortality) nor to contamination from external sources (which, according to Semmelweis, could only account for deaths above 1 per cent). So how would Semmelweis explain the other deaths? Very easily. Most likely Semmelweis would have admitted that his estimate of the rate of self-infection was too high (his figure, after all, was arrived at only empirically and even in the early days of the hospital *some* decaying organic matter would have been conveyed – for example, from patients with superficial infections or medullary carcinomas that generated decaying organic matter in his time as well (Semmelweis, 1861b, pp. 93f.). But he could also have simply *denied* that the excess deaths (any above 0.2 per cent but below his 1 per cent standard) were really childbed fever.[10] For example, suppose, from our present point of view, a woman contracted a fever from fomites bearing strep organisms and that no decaying matter was involved. Such a woman simply did not have childbed fever in Semmelweis's sense – nothing awkward about that at all.

Loudon also finds it 'extraordinary' that Semmelweis denied that 'puerperal fever was ever contagious, or that it ever occurred in the form of epidemics' (Loudon, 2000, p. 98). But clearly it all depends on what one means by 'contagious' and 'epidemic': Semmelweis never denied that the disease could spread from patient to patient (which, he agreed with the British, happened only rarely) or that it could be spread by way of other healthy persons such as medical personnel (which, he agreed with the British, was the means by which it was usually conveyed). Semmelweis also never denied that the disease occurred more frequently sometimes than others – that observation, after all, was the main basis for his argument. However, given his definitions, the only way the disease could spread at all or occur more frequently sometimes than others was through conveyance of decaying organic matter. If illness arose under other circumstances, once again, Semmelweis would simply deny that the cases were really childbed fever. But how could he deny that such other cases (which everyone *knew* to be childbed fever) really were childbed fever? In exactly the same way that, once Robert Koch had defined tuberculosis as infestation by the tubercle bacillus, he could deny that all other cases (which everyone *knew* to be tuberculosis) really were tuberculosis (namely, symptomatically and pathologically indistinguishable cases 'due to leprosy bacilli, brucella bacteria, histoplasma fungi, beryllium poisoning, or the unknown agent of sarcoidosis' (Taylor, 1979, p. 18) but lacking the tubercle bacillus). Or, to take a more obvious example but one from outside medicine, given current physics, glass is not classified as a solid (that is, it does not have a crystalline molecular structure) but rather as a highly viscous liquid (Schrödinger, 1969, p. 63). How could the initial advocates of this classification propose anything so contrary to what everyone *knew* as that glass isn't solid? In all such changes in scientific nomenclature, the justification is the explanatory power of the result. However, such recharacterizations inevitably leave a residue of cases that were included under the old concept but do not fall under the new one. That is why (as Foucault and others have emphasized[11]), the *reference* of disease names changes much more radically than one might suppose given that we continue to use the same names in spite of fundamental changes in their *sense* (to use Gottlob Frege's terminology). But that is what scientific progress is all about. 'Every scientific advance marks some departure from the common sense that preceded it' (Copi, 1979, p. 195). So, to summarize, given Semmelweis's definitions, if there were cases that resembled childbed fever but that were due neither to self-infection nor to contamination from external sources (and it is not clear to me exactly how we are to envision such cases), they were not really childbed fever after all.

Loudon also wonders whether Semmelweis simply failed 'to understand the British view of contagion, or [chose] to misrepresent them? [*sic*]' (Loudon, 2000, p. 99), and he thinks that, because James Young Simpson recognized that 'puerperal fever was [sometimes] transmitted to the patient by the fingers of the birth attendant', he somehow anticipated or simultaneously originated Semmelweis's theory (Loudon, 2000, pp. 85–87). But (excuse me, gentle reader, for saying it again and again) the issue is not chlorine washings or (what comes to *exactly* the same thing) contaminated fingers. Everyone from Semmelweis on has admitted that the British were first to recognize the danger of the latter and to extol the virtues of the former. The issue is: how are we to define diseases?[12] If we want the theoretical and practical coherence afforded by universal necessary causes, then diseases must be defined so that they have them. That is what the British contagionists failed to do, and that is what James Young Simpson failed to do; so, as they themselves were eager to admit, Simpson, like the British generally, continued to allow for other possible causes (as we saw, Holmes repeatedly emphasized this point) and they thereby excluded, *in principle*, the very possibility of systematic measures against the disease or coherent explanations of it. Yet, for all the defects in his theory (and they were legion), Semmelweis gave an etiological definition, and he recognized that the resulting theory was better than anything else around. Now, to be sure, the subtle shift in meaning that differentiated Semmelweis from the British would not have mattered much to the hundreds of thousands (possibly millions) of young women sacrificed in the maternity clinics, and it may not matter much today to physicians busy trying to keep their patients healthy. But if one claims to understand Semmelweis's *theory* (and especially if one undertakes to explain how it is wrong or unoriginal), one must, at the very least, be clear about this rather subtle but profoundly important distinction. Because, for the last 150 years, all those who have failed to grasp it end up either rejecting Semmelweis's theory for reasons that are totally irrelevant or saying that his theory wasn't all that original after all. Somehow, Loudon manages to do both.[13]

Semmelweis probably had little interest in the purely methodological significance of his definitions; he was interested only in saving lives. But methodologically they were singularly brilliant. The definitions effectively created a new disease, albeit one called by the same name and encompassing most (but not all) instances of what had previously been called childbed fever. The definitions excluded from consideration all cases that failed to have the one common cause, and that cause became, thereby, universal and necessary. By what could be seen as nothing more than a verbal trick – which Lumpe astutely, correctly, and precisely characterized as an egg of Columbus (Lumpe, 1850, pp. 392f) – Semmelweis made it possible, at least in principle, to identify reliable strategies against the disease and to give coherent explanations of disease phenomena. Semmelweis provided not merely new facts about the fever or practical advice for avoiding it; he offered a coherent and empirically verifiable explanatory theory. In this respect, his account was vastly superior to anything else that had been written on the disease. As Semmelweis's great contemporary Charles Darwin observed, in reference to his own (similarly flawed yet powerful) theory of evolution, it would be impossible for an altogether false theory to explain so much (Darwin, 1876, p. 239).

Semmelweis's influence in the research programme

There is a long-standing tradition that Semmelweis and his work were essentially forgotten from about the time of his death (1865) until about 1890 when his memory was, supposedly, resurrected in connection with an international medical conference in Budapest: 'In the twenty years after his death, Semmelweis's name was mentioned only on rare occasions, and usually in uncomplimentary terms' (Loudon, 2000, p. 108). This view is simply false. It has been refuted conclusively and repeatedly (Manninger, 1904, pp. 74–8; Murphy, 1946; Böttger, 1955; Carter, 1985a), but it dies hard. To appreciate the extent to which Semmelweis was tied to the etiological research programme, it is necessary only to look at the evidence.[14]

During the late 1860s, a year or two after Semmelweis was beaten and died in an insane asylum in Vienna (Carter et al., 1995), three important Viennese obstetricians converted to Semmelweis's views: Carl Mayrhofer, Joseph Späth and A. G. C. Veit. All three had initially opposed Semmelweis but each seems to have become converted by his own independent research (Carter, 1985a). Mayrhofer was particularly noteworthy; he sought, albeit without complete success, to trace childbed fever to infection by vibrions (microorganisms). As we will see, through the following decades, he was frequently mentioned together with Semmelweis.

In an 1864 paper, Späth noted that, whatever anyone might say, every obstetrician now believed that Semmelweis was correct and that even attempts to control childbed fever by improved ventilation were ultimately based on an awareness that Semmelweis was right (Späth, 1864, pp. 160f.). Späth continued, 'even Mayrhofer's theory, if it turns out to be correct, can only be regarded as a further confirmation of Semmelweis's view, because in that theory the vibrions that originate in decomposed animal matter are taken as the infective agents'. In 1865 A.C.G. Veit observed that in addition to confirming Semmelweis's findings, Mayrhofer's work refuted the view that ventilation significantly influenced the incidence of childbed fever (Veit, 1865, pp. 195f.).

Investigations of childbed fever were more prominent in the development of the bacterial theory than one might now think. Before 1880, studies of cholera, tuberculosis, the exanthemata, and most other infectious diseases produced only meager and equivocal results. In the early 1870s, surveys of literature on the role of vibrions in disease etiology usually focused on anthrax, relapsing fever, and especially wound infections (Steudener, 1872; Birch-Hirschfeld, 1872, 1875). Of these, wound infections received more attention in medical literature than anthrax and relapsing fever combined. Indeed, in this period more than half of all publications on the etiological significance of bacteria concerned wound infections.[15] Thus, it is not surprising that both German and French writers in the period regarded the bacterial theory of disease as having originated from the study of wound infections (Ravitsch, 1872; Jeannel, 1880). By the middle of the nineteenth century, childbed fever, and so-called surgical fever were the most frequently discussed forms of wound infections. Semmelweis was recognized as having been among the first to connect these two diseases; by 1860, even before publication of his book, the idea that childbed fever was a septic wound infection seems to have been generally associated with him (Roser, 1860). 'Before the time of Semmelweiss [*sic*], the idea of the identity of puerperal fever with pyemia was very far from the minds of the obstetricians, puerperal fever being regarded as something essentially inherent in the relations presented by the puerperal woman' (Hoag, 1887, p. 832). Perhaps because clinical cases of puerperal fever and surgical fever were readily available in nearly every hospital, discussions of these two diseases, and especially of childbed fever, became prominent in the literature on wound infections. Thus, given the historical situation and the knowledge available at the time, studies of puerperal fever were central to the development of the bacterial theory.

In 1865, Mayrhofer's views were mentioned in connection with a paper on epidemic puerperal fever which was presented by a doctor Kaufmann in the annual meeting of the *German Natural Scientists and Physicians* (Kaufmann, 1866). After mentioning Semmelweis, Kaufmann rejected the possibility of septic infectious matter, and endorsed, instead, a miasmatic explanation of childbed fever. However, according to the published report:

> *Veit* (Bonn), [Franz Ludwig Wilhelm] *Winckel* (Rostock), *Pernice* (Greifswald), and [Eduard] *Martin* (Berlin) were inclined to the infectious theory. ... *Martin* mentioned *Mayrhofer*'s theory of vibrions, and *Mankiewitz* (Mühlhausen) referred to the injuries to genitals, particularly in operations with forceps.
>
> (Kaufman, 1866, p. 424)

Thus all who are reported as having responded to Kaufmann's lecture favored the infection theory, and Mayrhofer was explicitly mentioned. This report appeared in the same issue of the periodical that contained Veit's article (cited above) in which Mayrhofer was associated with Semmelweis.

In 1866, F.L. Winckel published an important text on obstetrics. His detailed historical account of various theories of childbed fever included a summary of Semmelweis's position (Winckel, 1866, p. 264). Winckel mentioned that Lange of Munich had been among the first to adopt Semmelweis's views. He also discussed and agreed with Veit's conclusion that prevention of fever depended less on ventilation than on absolute cleanliness – a view Winckel had already supported in the discussion of Kaufmann's paper one year earlier (Kaufmann, 1866, p. 424). Near the end of his account, Winckel gave detailed and positive attention to Mayrhofer's work and to other publications based on it (Winckel, 1866, pp. 274f.).

Also in 1866 Leon Coze and Victor-Timothee Feltz mentioned Mayrhofer in an historical survey that initiated one of their series of highly influential studies of wound infections (Coze and Feltz, 1866,

p. 62). In 1866 and 1867, Semmelweis's animal experiments were cited by German scientists investigating infected wounds (Schweninger, 1866, pp. 591, 597; Roser, 1867, pp. 17, 20f). In one essay, W. Roser observed that Semmelweis's concept of childbed fever had become the accepted position among obstetricians and that even many surgeons had been converted to the doctrine (Roser, 1867, p. 20). In a long study of diseases of the female sexual organs, published in 1867, Veit noted that 'the old idea of miasmatic contagion was first challenged by Semmelweis. He taught that childbed fever was a resorption fever occasioned by infection with decaying organic matter. This view is penetrating ever greater circles and, in a short time, will find no more opponents' (Veit, 1867, p. 678). He also noted that, since childbed fever was the result of a septic infection, it was essential to establish the exact nature of the septic poison, and he mentioned Mayrhofer's work as a possible solution to this problem. In 1867 Mayrhofer was also mentioned in a general review of literature on the etiological significance of micro-organisms (Richter, 1867, p. 95).

In 1868, Max Boehr published an essay entitled 'On the infection theory of puerperal fever and its consequences for public health officials'. The paper, which was originally presented before the *Society for Obstetrics* in Berlin, drew heavily on Semmelweis's work and conclusions. Boehr noted that Semmelweis's theory

> has the characteristic of all good pathological and physiological theories; it provides a unified, clear, and entirely intelligible meaning for a whole series of anatomical and clinical facts and for the disinterested experiences and discoveries of reliable observers during epidemics. None of the earlier or alternative hypotheses or theories regarding the occurrence of childbed fever has this characteristic to the same degree.
>
> (Boehr, 1868, p. 403)

Boehr mentioned that in Semmelweis's *Etiology*, 'the superstitions of our predecessors, who believed in unknown cosmic-telluric-atmospheric influences, were dealt a severe blow, as was the belief in miasmata' (Boehr, 1868, p. 404). Boehr cited Veit, Späth, and Mayrhofer, as well as others who had supported the infection theory. The same periodical reported the discussion of Boehr's paper. The report included comments by Max Wegscheider, David Haussmann, Eduard Martin, and three other physicians identified as Scharlau, Krieger, and Ebell. Only Ebell is reported as having said anything opposed to the infection theory; his comment was that 'in addition to contagiousness, there are still other causes of puerperal fever' (Boehr, 1868, p. 433). According to the report, 'Boehr responded that in addition to artificial infection from external sources, he himself recognized only self-infection through foul matter from the patient herself' – which, of course, was exactly Semmelweis's view.

Over the next few years, Semmelweis and Mayrhofer were mentioned favorably in several publications (Ferber, 1868, p. 318; Haussmann, 1870, p. 46). Beginning in 1872 they were cited in papers, both French and German, that were among the most influential of the early contributions to the bacterial theory of disease. During the 1860s, Coze and Feltz conducted studies of infectious diseases that resulted in several publications and culminated in a book that was cited by both Pasteur and Koch. The chapter on puerperal sepsis began with a sympathetic and favorable discussion of Semmelweis (Coze and Feltz, 1872, p. 259). Friedrich Wieger and Franz Hektor Arneth, two of Semmelweis's students in the first clinic and eyewitnesses to his discoveries, published the first French accounts of Semmelweis's work; both were cited by Coze and Feltz (Coze and Feltz, 1872, pp. 259, 261). One page later, Coze and Feltz praised Mayrhofer as the first to identify vibrions in the lochial discharge of puerperal fever victims. Also in 1872, in an article in a German periodical on gynecology, Wilhelm Waldeyer of Breslau mentioned that Mayrhofer had been the first to identify bacteria in puerperal fever victims (Waldeyer, 1872, p. 294). Three years later, Felix Victor Birch-Hirschfeld identified Waldeyer's paper as one of four that had been most influential in awakening general interest in wound infections (Birch-Hirschfeld, 1875, p. 171). In 1873 Johannes Orth published an important discussion of puerperal fever in *Virchow's Archives* (Orth, 1873, p. 437). The paper began with a careful and sympathetic review of Mayrhofer's work. Orth mentioned that Mayrhofer had attempted to use pure cultures to show that the vibrions caused the disease. 'Remarkably enough,' Orth observed, 'this obvious and conclusive experiment was not sufficiently appreciated and in the next few years there was almost no subsequent research.' In the mid-1870s prominent French writers also mentioned Mayrhofer and Semmelweis favorably (Billet, 1872, pp. 20, 28; D'Espine, 1873, pp. 13, 139).

In 1874 Haussmann published accounts of animal experiments intended to confirm the results of the similar animal experiments conducted by Semmelweis and by Mayrhofer (Haussman, 1874, pp. 311f, 315). In the same year Carl Rokitansky, Jun., published a study of the microscopic constituents of lochial discharges. He mentioned Mayrhofer as the first to have examined the occurrence of bacteria in lochial discharges (Rokitansky, 1874, p. 172).

In 1877, Mayrhofer's results were mentioned in Birch-Hirschfeld's widely used textbook on pathological anatomy (Birch-Hirschfeld, 1877, pp. 1141f.). One year after the appearance of this textbook, Robert Koch published his essay on wound infections. Koch relied heavily on

Birch-Hirschfeld's review of the literature and on his textbook (Koch, 1878a, pp. 20–23, 27, 29). Koch also cited the papers by Waldeyer and Orth mentioned above (Koch, 1878a, pp. 22f.). In his studies of puerperal fever, Pasteur also cited Waldeyer and Orth (Pasteur, 1879a, p. 133). Thus, both Pasteur and Koch cited both French and German authors who discussed Mayrhofer's work. While neither Pasteur nor Koch ever mentioned either Semmelweis or Mayrhofer, Mayrhofer was mentioned in a history of bacteriology written by Friedrich Loeffler, Koch's associate and colleague (Loeffler, 1887, p. 89).

In 1888 M. Wertheimer wrote,

> The earlier theory of the miasmatic nature of [childbed fever], as taught and developed by Eisenmann, Helm, Litzmann, Kiwisch, Scanzoni, and others, was first put on the right track by Semmelweis. ... His theory was soon supported, expanded, and confirmed by a series of authors such as Hegar, Buhl, Winkel, Fischer, Veit, [and] Mayrhofer.
>
> (Wertheimer, 1888, pp. 5f)

Semmelweis and Mayrhofer continued to be cited in German, French, and English sources into the 1880s (Bar, 1883, p. 28; Lomer, 1884, pp. 366, 369; Jaggard, 1884, p. 443) although by that time (15 years after Semmelweis's death and Mayrhofer's publications), more recent developments in bacteriology were eclipsing the older work.

In 1882 – at the very time when, according to conventional wisdom, Semmelweis had been completely forgotten throughout Europe – Wilhelm Fischel wrote: 'although long contested, the opinions of the genial Semmelweis ... have become part of the common property of a whole generation of medical personnel' (Fischel, 1882, p. 1). The phrase 'the genial Semmelweis' – poignant in view of the treatment he received from his peers and of his ultimate fate – appears again in the same year in an obituary for Carl Mayrhofer (r, 1882).[16]

There is no reason to think Henle saw any relation between his call for a rational system of medicine built on universal necessary causes and Semmelweis's definition of 'childbed fever' in terms of decaying organic matter. For all we know, Henle, like most of his contemporaries, regarded Semmelweis as an aberration. Moreover, Semmelweis almost certainly never thought of his theory in terms of Henle's aspirations for rational medicine. Yet the two are inseparably linked: only by way of etiological characterizations can the range of human illnesses be systematized into diseases with universal necessary causes, and only in the creation of such a system can the potential strength of Semmelweis's innovation be realized. However, Semmelweis showed no interest in generalizing from his new approach – he was content to exploit the practical ramifications of his theory, and Henle never mentioned Semmelweis in print.

To be sure, even given the possibility of etiological definitions, there was a serious obstacle to reorganizing all of medicine in terms of necessary causes: it was first essential to find causes in terms of which all (or at least many) diseases could be defined. In this respect Semmelweis's theory was something of a dead end. Of course decaying organic matter did cause childbed fever and, given a suitable definition, it could be made into a universal and necessary cause. However, decaying organic matter – like acari, *Beauvaria bassiana* or trichinae – could be causally linked only to a limited variety of diseases. Where was one to look for causes in terms of which to define other diseases? Imagine a philosophical physician (1) committed to Henle's goal of making medicine an explanatory science, (2) aware of the universal necessary causes being identified for such unrelated diseases as scabies, muscardine, trichinosis, and childbed fever, and (3) sensing the power of Semmelweis's tactic as a potential tool for creating a rational explanatory system. Had such a person thought of all this in just the right way (and certainly no one ever did) that person could still have despaired of achieving a rational system of medicine on the grounds that there simply were no causes of the sort required to bring it all together.

Yet, at the very time Semmelweis was writing his book on childbed fever, Louis Pasteur was becoming fascinated with the enormous variety of natural organic processes caused by microscopic living organisms. Some of these processes – for example, different kinds of spoilage in wine (*diseases* of wine, as Pasteur called them) – were caused by a variety of different microorganisms. Moreover, Pasteur traced organic decomposition to the operation of germs and, as Semmelweis and others had recognized, childbed fever and other wound infections involves tissue decomposition. The possible connection was too striking to be overlooked: Pasteur's discoveries motivated *both* Carl Mayrhofer's search for microorganisms in the lochial discharges of childbed fever victims *and* Casimir Davaine's profoundly important investigations of anthrax.

Notes

1. Although, to be completely honest, some writers came close. For example, in one paper, David Gruby observed of a particular fungus that it constituted 'a true, essential characteristic of [favus]' (Zakon and Benedek, 1944, p. 158). It is a small step from this recognition to an etiological definition, and there are similar passages in Agostino Bassi's discussions of muscardine. However, as far as I can see, Fracastoro never came close to anything like this.

2. For references to some of the standard sources see Semmelweis (1861b, pp. 1–58).

3. For a fine study – informative, scholarly and yet moving – of the history of childbed fever see Loudon (2000). Below, I disagree with certain aspects of Loudon's discussion of Semmelweis. These points are crucial in the context of our investigation, but are less significant from the perspective of Loudon's purposes and so (in spite of the emphasis they here receive) they constitute at most a limited criticism of his book.

4. Through this sub section, page numbers in parentheses are references to Holmes (1843).

5. Through this sub section, page numbers in parentheses are references to Lumpe (1845).

6. The present account is based on the Translator's Introduction to Semmelweis's *Etiology* (Semmelweis, 1861b).

7. For example, like many other diseases, among other possible causes, childbed fever was ascribed both to eating too much and to eating too little. In cases of the first kind, physicians removed blood; in the second, they sustained patients with rich and nourishing foods. Letting blood in cases of the second kind would have been regarded as life threatening.

8. David S. Barnes has recently pointed out that one can also reduce the incidence of a disease by attacking causes that are not universal (Barnes, 2000, p. 438). Of course. One can prevent some house fires by insuring that wiring in new houses conforms to building codes even though other houses will still burn down if struck by lightning. I am not denying that the chlorine washings were beneficial. Some cases of TB can be avoided if we prevent people from breathing the miasms of TB wards, but other cases may still occur if people drink infected milk. By contrast, if we somehow block invasion of the tuberculosis bacillus, we avoid the disease altogether – end of story, no matter what one breaths or eats or drinks. But this latter possibility depends on having tuberculosis (or childbed fever, or any other disease) defined in terms of a cause that is universal.

9. Through this paragraph, page numbers in parentheses, such as this one, are references to Semmelweis (1861b).

10. Eight sentences further on I will return to and justify this dubious claim.

11. See Chapter 1, note 2.

12. The reader may wish to review the quotation on page 45.

13. As I wrote 20 years ago: 'The problem [with criticisms of Semmelweis's theory] is that no one bothers to determine what the theory in question is, before deciding [it is wrong or] that Semmelweis didn't originate it' (Semmelweis, 1861b, p. 52n). The situation has not changed appreciably.

14. What follows is an abbreviated version of one part of an earlier publication (Carter, 1985a). Here I include only a representative sample of sources that cited Semmelweis and Mayrhofer during the years from about 1865 through 1890 – there are many more.

15. For example, 46 of the 86 papers cited by Birch-Hirschfeld in his 1875 review of the role of bacteria in infectious diseases concerned infected wounds (Birch-Hirschfeld, 1875).

16. The author of the obituary was identified only as 'r' which suggests, at least, that this author was someone other than Fischel who used the same phrase in the same year.

CHAPTER FOUR

Microorganisms as Causes

In this chapter we will review some of Louis Pasteur's early attempts to prove that germs cause certain organic processes. Today, it seems obvious that microorganisms cause various natural phenomena such as fermentation, decomposition, and disease, but in the early nineteenth century this was not clear. There were inherent obstacles to accepting germs as causes, and overcoming some of these obstacles required more than simply making the right empirical observations. Causes are not discovered in the same way that one might discover shells on a beach.

As described by Imre Lakatos, a 'research programme consists of methodological rules: some tell us what paths of research to avoid (*negative heuristic*), and others what paths to pursue (*positive heuristic*)' (Lakatos, 1968, p. 132). Such rules are often left implicit. However, if stated, they may resemble very general claims about the world – claims that exceed any possible empirical confirmation.[1] Lakatos says that such principles are made '"irrefutable" by the methodological decision of its protagonists' (Lakatos, 1968, p. 133). However, strictly speaking, being *rules* and not empirical claims, they are neither true nor false and they are not subject to proof or refutation. Like any rules, they can be shown to be useful in achieving certain objectives (for example, in explaining and controlling nature) and, once seen as useful, they may become standard conventions (one might say made irrefutable) by the consensus of the researchers who adopt them.

Three such heuristic rules emerged in early work leading to the etiological research programme. We will refer to these rules as the Distinguishability, Dissemination, and Bacterial Hypotheses.[2] These hypotheses cannot be confirmed empirically yet they were required before microorganisms could be accepted as causes of the natural processes with which they are now universally associated. In this chapter we will encounter the first two of these, the Distinguishability and Dissemination Hypotheses; the third, the Bacterial Hypothesis, will appear at the end of the next chapter. In this chapter we will also examine several of Pasteur's early arguments to see how he attempted to prove that germs are causes.

The distinguishability and dissemination hypotheses

In 1854, Louis Pasteur, a chemist by training, was appointed professor of chemistry and dean of the Faculty of Sciences in Lille. The faculty at Lille had been formed, in part, to find scientific solutions to the technical problems challenging local industry (Geison, 1974, p. 361) – a task perfectly compatible with Pasteur's practical disposition. One important industry in Lille involved the production of alcohol from fermented beet roots. However, the process often failed because the beet pulp spoiled rather than fermenting. In seeking to avoid such failures, Pasteur began studying fermentation.

In the 1830s Charles Cagniard-Latour, Theodor Schwann and Friedrich Traugott Kützing had independently concluded that yeast was a living organism and that it alone could ferment sugar to produce alcohol. This implied that fermentation was essentially a biological process. Other scientists, including Jons Jacob Berzelius, Friedrich Wöhler, and Justus von Liebig, regarded fermentation as a chemical process having no necessary connection with living organisms.

Pasteur began publishing on fermentation in 1857; by the time his first papers appeared, he seems already to have been convinced that fermentation was always due to what he called living ferments. Gerald L. Geison argued that this conviction was likely a result of strongly held convictions that originated much earlier while Pasteur was still doing research in chemistry (Geison, 1995, pp. 95–103). By this time, Pasteur had become preoccupied with the life processes of microorganisms. From then on, except for occasional reports and special lectures, all his scientific publications related directly to what he later called the theory of organized ferments (Pasteur, 1875a, p. 43). As he conceived it, this theory encompassed a wide range of natural processes such as putrefaction and fermentation as well as many animal and human diseases. Pasteur observed that he had become fascinated with the immense role of microscopic organisms in nature (Pasteur, 1880a, p. 147), and all the activities of such organisms fell under the theory of organized ferments. In a letter written to Pasteur in 1874, Joseph Lister used the phrase 'theory of germs'. Pasteur included Lister's letter in a book published in 1876 (Pasteur, 1876a, pp. 40f). Pasteur himself first used Lister's phrase somewhat later in the same book (Pasteur, 1876a, p. 101). Thereafter, rather than 'theory of organized ferments', Pasteur used 'theory of germs' to identify his central research interests.

Although from an early period Pasteur seems to have been interested in human infectious diseases (Pasteur, 1863a, pp. 8f.), he did not conduct original research in this branch of the theory of germs until the early 1870s. But, as he himself explained, when he began studying human infections, his work was based on the same ideas and methods that had guided him in his earlier studies (Pasteur, 1873a, p. 415). In this chapter we will consider only Pasteur's early publications on the theory of germs – those appearing before 1870.

In his first paper on fermentation, Pasteur claimed that, just as a particular ferment is always present when sugar breaks down to form alcohol, so too a different ferment is always present when sugar forms lactic acid (Pasteur, 1857a, p. 6).[3] In his early papers, Pasteur frequently made assertions of this kind, and it is important to understand the nature of such claims. Asserting that the lactic ferment is present whenever sugar is converted into lactic acid is equivalent to saying that, in the absence of the ferment, no lactic acid forms, and therefore, that the ferment is *necessary* for the production of lactic acid. Having inferred from his own observations that the ferment was necessary for fermentation, Pasteur seems simply to have concluded that the ferment *caused* fermentation. Pasteur also reported seeding appropriate media with lactic and alcoholic yeasts. He reported that either ferment would multiply in the liquid in which it was seeded (Pasteur, 1857a, p. 9). This experiment suggested that, under suitable conditions, either ferment was *sufficient* for its fermentation products; it also persuaded Pasteur that the two ferments were distinct organisms. In this early paper Pasteur asserted that all fermentation was correlative with organic life (Pasteur, 1857a, p. 13).

By the end of 1857, as part of an attack on Justus von Liebig's chemical theory of fermentation, Pasteur reported growing yeast and sustaining fermentation in a medium free of organic nitrogen (Pasteur, 1857b). In 1861 Pasteur identified another ferment that he described as an animal that could live without free oxygen (Pasteur, 1861a). This ferment produced butyric acid. Again, Pasteur inferred causality from the observation that the ferment was always present in (and so necessary for) the production of butyric acid. He also reported that the organism produced butyric acid whenever it was seeded in a suitable medium.

Pasteur's early work on fermentation persuaded him that there were several different ferments. He later admitted that he was not always able to distinguish ferments morphologically and sometimes identified them physiologically (Pasteur, 1866a, p. 155). By this he can only have meant that he distinguished them by their metabolic byproducts, that is, by the different fermentation processes with which they were associated. By 1861 Pasteur was convinced that different forms of fermentation were associated with the life processes of distinct organized ferments

(Pasteur, 1861b, p. 142) and that these ferments could not be transformed into one another (Pasteur, 1862). Given that he could not always distinguish ferments other than by their fermentation processes, this conviction could not be confirmed universally without begging the question. However, it could be illustrated in some cases (since some organisms could be distinguished morphologically) and thereby made plausible, and it was an absolutely essential presupposition if one wished, as Pasteur did, to explain different fermentation processes strictly in terms of the ferments themselves. If, as some researchers then believed, all ferments were ultimately the same and transformable into one another (that is if they were not truly distinct), then different fermentation processes could not be explained simply in terms of the organisms themselves – such explanations would require an appeal to whatever other factors accounted for their different effects in different circumstances. Thus, insofar as the ferments themselves were to be the basis for explaining fermentation, it was essential to *assume* that different fermentation processes were due to distinct ferments. Of course the same assumption would be equally essential if one attempted, as Pasteur and others later did, to explain different kinds of spoilage or different diseases in terms of organisms. Here and throughout his career, therefore, Pasteur required a crucial assumption that could not be conclusively demonstrated – an assumption that would constitute part of what Lakatos would call the negative heuristic of his research programme. Pasteur had to assume that different organic processes, whether fermentation, spoilage, or disease, are caused by distinct organisms. As we will see later (p. 105) this assumption need not be understood as a claim about the world although it is natural to think of it in this way. As Imre Lakatos explained regarding other basic scientific hypotheses, this assumption may be best regarded as a rule that guides research: always suppose that different organic processes are due to distinct organisms. We will refer to this as the Distinguishability Hypothesis[4] and I will have more to say about it later on.

Pasteur's attempts to reduce failures in industrial fermentation led directly to the ancient problem of spontaneous generation. If, as Pasteur believed, fermentation and putrefaction depended on the multiplication of living organisms, one could prevent spoilage by excluding undesirable ferments. But how was this to be accomplished? The answer depended on knowing how organisms gained access to fermenting liquids. If organisms could arise spontaneously, there was little hope of preventing spoilage; but if there was no spontaneous generation, spoilage could only occur when fermenting liquids were contaminated from external sources. This meant that preventing contamination would in-sure consistent success. Of course, the question of spontaneous generation had broader significance than merely insuring the success of industrial fermentation. Joseph Balsamo-Crivelli and others argued that, given suitable nutrients and proper atmospheric conditions, *Beauvaria bassiana* could arise spontaneously and do so simultaneously with the onset of muscardine (Balsamo-Crivelli, 1839, p. 123). Even Henle felt that the possibility of such a miasmatic origin could not be ignored (Henle, 1840, p. 945). However, if this were to happen, even if the fungus and muscardine always occurred together (so each was necessary and suffi-cient for the other), the pre-existing materials together with the crucial atmospheric conditions, not the fungus itself, would be the cause. This possibility must be excluded if organisms are to be identified as causes of organic processes and thereby explain those processes. Thus, as Pasteur recognized, the question of whether living organisms could arise independently of antecedent organisms had profound implications for the germ theory.

In his early studies of fermentation, Pasteur occasionally used the term 'spontaneous generation' in reference to the unintended growth of organisms in a culture medium (Pasteur, 1857a, p. 9). However, he explained that he had too little evidence to determine whether such developments were truly spontaneous or were due to accidental con-tamination (Pasteur, 1859a, p. 628). Then, in about 1860, Pasteur began a careful study of the subject. Geison has shown that Pasteur's research on spontaneous generation, like his work on fermentation, was driven by deeply held convictions – preconceived ideas – that can be traced to his early work in chemistry (Geison, 1995, pp. 110–42), so, as he began this phase of his research, he was not really neutral with respect to the issue. By the time Pasteur began studying spontaneous generation, earlier scientists had already devoted considerable effort to the problem without conclusive results, and it was not clear that Pas-teur would have greater success. However, within a few months, he concluded that pure air and a suitable medium were *never* sufficient to generate living organisms, and that the organized corpuscles regularly found in airborne dust were 'the exclusive origin – the first and neces-sary condition – for life in infusions, in putrescible bodies, and in all bodies capable of fermentation' (Pasteur, 1860, p. 204). That is, the presence of living organisms is always due to their having spread from some source of contamination and is never spontaneous. Pasteur re-ferred to this idea as 'the hypothesis of the dissemination of germs' (Pasteur, 1860, p. 202). We can shorten Pasteur's title to 'the Dissemi-nation Hypothesis'. Thus, as we use this term, the Dissemination Hypothesis is the *denial* of spontaneous generation.

In 1861 Pasteur published an extensive study of spontaneous generation (Pasteur, 1861c). He criticized earlier attempts to exhibit the process; all such attempts, he argued, had failed to exclude contamination. He also reported his own research on the topic. Pasteur's experiments fell into two classes. In the first, he showed that ordinary airborne dust contained particles indistinguishable from the germs of living organisms. When fermentable liquids were seeded with such dust, colonies of living organisms soon flourished there. However, the same liquids remained sterile if exposed to dust-free air or even to dust that had been heated sufficiently to destroy living organisms (Pasteur, 1861c, pp. 238–59). Pasteur concluded that 'all organized productions of the previously heated infusions have no other origin than the solid particles which the air always carries and allows constantly to be deposited on all objects' (Pasteur 1861c, pp. 259f.) – the Dissemination Hypothesis.

Pasteur's second series of experiments involved the use of flasks with long contorted stems. Pasteur filled such flasks with milk, blood, and urine; he sealed the stems and sterilized the flasks and their contents. He then broke the seals and exposed the liquids to ambient air. However, air could reach the liquids only by passing through the contorted stems where it deposited all the dust it normally bore. The liquids remained sterile (Pasteur, 1861c, pp. 259–64). Indeed even today, more than a century later, some of Pasteur's flasks and their unaltered contents can be inspected in museums throughout France. As the months and years passed, without any change in the liquids, it became progressively less plausible to think that living organisms of any kind would ever arise spontaneously.

Partly because of Pasteur's great rhetorical skills, his experiments were psychologically compelling (Geison, 1995, pp. 132f.), but were they conclusive? Did he prove absolutely that life *never* arises spontaneously – that contamination is 'the *exclusive* origin' of living germs? He freely admitted that he did not:

> I must hasten to repeat here what I have often said: one cannot prove *a priori* that there exists no spontaneous generation. All one can do is demonstrate (1) that there have been unperceived sources of error in the experiments [of those who claim to have observed spontaneous generation], and (2) that by eliminating these sources of error, without affecting the basic conditions of the trials, the inferior beings cease to appear.
>
> (Pasteur, 1866b, pp. 354–5)

On another occasion, Pasteur wrote that 'in the empirical sciences, in contrast to mathematics, it is impossible to demonstrate a negative' (Pasteur, 1874a, p. 16). In fact, Pasteur's experiments were less compelling than he himself made them appear. One problem was that Pasteur's own experiments often failed, in some series of experiments, perhaps more than 90 per cent of the time, 'but rather than draw the seemingly obvious conclusion that this microbial life had originated spontane-ously, Pasteur refused to accept this experimental evidence at face value and pressed relentlessly toward an alternative explanation' (Geison, 1995, p. 130). On the other hand, of course, advocates of spontaneous generation could never prove, absolutely, that it had occurred, that is, that there had been no contamination. Thus, neither the Dissemination Hypothesis nor its denial were susceptible of strict empirical proof or confirmation: for either side, and for the public at large, it was a question of which experiments were to be taken as successful and which as having failed.[5] Pasteur's arguments 'ingenious and wonderfully theat-rical' (Geison, 1995, p. 118), carried the day; his opponents retired in confusion.

While Pasteur's theory of germs requires the absolute exclusion of spontaneous generation, this could never be accomplished merely by observation or experiments. At this point, one might despair of ever giving a rational justification for the Dissemination Hypothesis. And, in fact, Geison himself seemed to teeter on the very brink of this abyss: he invited his reader to share the 'liberating effect' of ceasing to pretend 'that we believe in the Scientific Method ... [for] it is not Pasteur who has fallen short; it is this Scientific Method' (Geison, 1995, p. 132). On a causal reading, these remarks suggest the pathos of a lost soul luring others to the illusory emancipation of the damned. However, by '*this* Scientific Method' (my emphasis), Geison may have been referring to (and so discrediting) only 'the simplistic and passé notion' that the impossibility of direct empirical confirmation means there is no rational justification whatsoever. That would still leave open the possibility of some other sort of justification (that is, of a more sophisticated and up-to-date understanding of how science works). Unfortunately, instead of going on to explain such an alternative justification, Geison cited Bruno Latour (the great bugbear who *does* seem to argue against scientific justification in general[6]) and then passed directly to an account of Pasteur's rhetorical and theatrical skills (which, obviously, could pro-vide no sort of justification whatsoever). This leaves the reader perplexed: can we or can we not justify the exclusion of spontaneous generation?

To be sure there was (and could be) no conclusive *empirical* justifica-tion for the Dissemination Hypothesis. And Geison made a persuasive argument that Pasteur's own rejection of spontaneous generation flowed, not from evidence, but from what Pasteur himself admitted were 'pre-conceived ideas'. However, this is no surprise. As explained above (p. 6) isolated laws, being universal in scope, can never be justified empirically (as we have seen, Pasteur even admitted this); at best they can be illustrated, made plausible, or shown to apply in certain cases. Laws are justified by being part of a theory which, in turn, is justified by its explanatory power. Who would be so foolish as to try to justify, in isolation from the kinetic theory as a whole, the law (which is one part of the kinetic theory) that molecules in a gas 'exert no forces on one another between collisions' (Oxtoby and Nachtrieb, 1990, p. 104) – stated like this, naked and alone, it doesn't even seem plausible, much less verifiable, no matter what or how many experiments one performs, but so what? *At this point in our story* (as in the historical context as presented by Geison) the Dissemination Hypothesis – the denial of spontaneous generation – stands as an isolated claim, and as such, it can not be fully justified by any means whatsoever. However, as we will see in Chapter 6, this hypothesis was soon assimilated to an explicit bacterial theory, and in that context it, along with the other laws comprised by the theory, was justified by the explanatory power of that theory as a whole. By the 1880s, everyone saw that the bacterial theory could better explain a whole range of facts than any other theory that was then (or is now) available (seeing this did not rest primarily on rhetorical or theatrical tricks), and the Dissemination Hypothesis was accepted as an indispensable part of that theory. Of course, as Geison brilliantly demonstrated, even in the 1860s Pasteur regarded the Dissemination Hypothesis as part of his own system of ideas (which he called the germ theory), but, at that point, it remained to be seen how successful Pasteur's system would ultimately be. Thus, his system could provide little or no help in justifying the hypothesis.

I agree that in the 1860s, when Pasteur advanced the Dissemination Hypothesis, it could not be justified – not by any means whatsoever (so its acceptance at that point can only be explained in terms of force), and, from a logical point of view, it remained an open question for some time whether the hypothesis would ever be justified. From one point of view, justification did not really begin until about 1876 when Klebs made the hypothesis part of an explicit bacterial theory of disease and it was completed only in the early 1880s when the bacterial theory, as a whole, finally won out. At that point, as Lakatos would put it, the Dissemination Hypothesis became 'irrefutable' by the consensus of the researchers who used it. But understanding things in this way does not expose a defect in the Scientific Method (whatever that may be) – instead it illustrates the poverty of arguments based on simplistic and passé conceptions of science.

Pasteur's early attempts to prove microorganisms are causes

In 1863 Pasteur began publishing papers on the spoilage of wine. In his earliest papers he assumed the Distinguishability Hypothesis, that is, he assumed different forms of spoilage, like different forms of fermentation, were caused by distinct organisms (Pasteur, 1864, p. 396).

As in his work on fermentation, Pasteur seemed not to have felt that establishing causality presented any particular difficulties. He did not identify causal criteria and occasionally simply asserted that a particular form of spoilage was caused by a specific organism without giving any justification whatsoever (Pasteur, 1864, p. 402). When he did give reasons, the reasons were usually of the form exemplified by this statement: '*Mycoderma aceti* causes the acidity that attacks the vats of red and white wine in the Jura. I have identified it on the surface of all the wines, a considerable number, that have been pointed out to me as acidic' (Pasteur, 1864, pp. 396f.). As in his work on fermentation, Pasteur seems to have assumed that finding a particular organism in all cases of acid wines proved that it was the cause. In discussing another form of spoilage, Pasteur wrote that a certain ferment 'determines the disorder known as bitterness of wine ... I have studied bitter wines from all the provinces, and have constantly recognized this curious vegetable in a quantity that varies according to the bitterness of the wine in question' (Pasteur, 1864, p. 401). He made similar observations for other forms of spoilage (Pasteur, 1864, p. 400). Here again we see the same kind of reasoning: Pasteur argued that, since a given organism was always present in wine that had spoiled in a certain way (that is, since the organism was necessary for that kind of spoilage), it was the cause of the disorder. The only evidence for causality one finds in these early essays is observational evidence of necessity.

In 1865, Pasteur concluded that 'the diseases of wine, at least all those presently known to me, are determined by the development of a microscopic vegetable of the nature of a ferment' (Pasteur 1865a, p. 409). One year later, in 1866, in his main work on wine spoilage, Pasteur claimed: 'there is never a souring of an alcoholic liquid except in the presence of the microscopic mushroom known as *Mycoderma aceti*' (Pasteur, 1866a, p. 125). He asserted that 'without exception' certain other wine disorders were due to the presence of other organized ferments (Pasteur 1866a, pp. 138, 161f.). In all this work, the sketchy evidence for causation Pasteur actually gave was of the form 'in the absence of the organism, there is no spoilage'.

While Pasteur continued to write on the spoilage of wine and to seek methods for preventing it, colleagues urged him to study a new problem: In the 1860s vast numbers of silkworms were dying throughout Europe from unknown causes, and the French silk industry was suffering serious losses (Geison, 1974, p. 372). Pasteur agreed to investigate. By 1865, when he began studying silkworms, a certain corpuscular structure had already been found in the intestines of many dead worms, and some researchers believed the structures were parasitic organisms that infected and killed their hosts. Pasteur began by confirming the existence of the structures (Pasteur, 1865b). He soon found that if healthy worms were exposed to dust containing the corpuscles they also became diseased (Pasteur, 1866c, pp. 442f.). Yet the situation was different from what he had found in spoiled wines because, while worms with corpuscles were always diseased, diseased worms did not always contain corpuscles – we would say that corpuscles appeared to be sufficient but not necessary for the disease. Thus, the situation was not the same as in his earlier research, and Pasteur was clearly reluctant to infer causality (Pasteur, 1866c, p. 447). Moreover, he found no evidence that the corpuscles reproduced (Pasteur, 1866d, p. 472) and was unsure they were alive. Instead, he suggested, they may be similar to corpuscles of blood or pus (Pasteur, 1866d, p. 472; Pasteur, 1866c pp. 442, 447). Pasteur suspected that, rather than causing the disease, the corpuscles may form in existing tissues as a result of the disease process (Pasteur, 1867a, p. 466). He also thought the disorder may be constitutional, and he compared it to tuberculosis (Pasteur, 1866c, p. 445). Given contemporary beliefs, this may have meant that Pasteur suspected the silkworm disease resulted from unhealthy environmental factors rather than from a specific cause.

In 1867 Pasteur reported several important new conclusions. First, he discovered that silkworms were dying from two distinct diseases. One disease, called *pebrine*, was associated with the corpuscles; the other, *flacherie*, involved no corpuscles, but was characterized by the appearance of ferments in the digestive tracks of the worms.[7] Of course, this way of thinking enabled Pasteur to hold that corpuscles were present in (and therefore necessary for) every case of *pebrine*. In other words, this change brought the situation into line with the kinds of experimental results he had found both in fermentation and in the spoilage of wine. This increased his confidence that the relation was truly causal. Second, he claimed to have discovered that the corpuscles reproduced by a kind of scission – a discovery that removed one obstacle to recognizing them as alive (Pasteur, 1867c, p. 499). Finally, he concluded that both diseases could be prevented, or at least controlled, by suitable breeding techniques. In several papers that appeared in the next few months,

Pasteur claimed to have mastered *pebrine*; he justified this claim on the grounds that he could 'give and prevent it at will' (Pasteur, 1868a, p. 528; 1869a, p. 19).

Pasteur soon identified two different species of ferments associated with *flacherie*. He described one species as a kind of vibrion and the other as having the structure of a string of grains (Pasteur, 1869b, pp. 591f.) – a form of organism already becoming familiar to microbiologists in some human diseases. However, he insisted that no one had, as yet, proved that these organisms caused *flacherie*, and he acknowledged the organisms could actually be a consequence of prior digestive disorders (Pasteur, 1868b, p. 568). Pasteur's reluctance to draw a causal conclusion – so different from the attitude displayed in earlier papers on fermentation and spoilage – may reflect the fact that, in contrast to what he had found in his earlier work and even ultimately in *pebrine*, neither species of ferment was present in all cases of *flacherie* (that is neither species was necessary).

By 1869, when his book on silkworm diseases appeared, Pasteur was convinced the corpuscles caused *pebrine*; however, he remained unsure about the significance of the ferments in *flacherie*. Pasteur identified four organisms that could often be found in the intestines of worms dying of *flacherie* and that did not appear in healthy worms (Pasteur, 1870, p. 205). Against the objection that the organisms may be a product rather than the cause of the disease, Pasteur wrote: 'if I can take very healthy worms and communicate *flacherie* to them by introducing vibrions, … is it possible not to relate the cause and first origin of the evil to the vibrions and to the fermentation they determine?' (Pasteur, 1870, p. 216) This argument, like the observation that organisms are never present in healthy worms, supports sufficiency rather than necessity. Thus, the evidence for causation in these studies is different from that in his earlier discussions and in his work on *pebrine*. This change was forced on him because, in *flacherie*, he was unable to identify a particular microorganism that was present in all cases.

Beginning with his studies of fermentation and spontaneous generation and continuing through his work on wine disorders and diseases of silkworms, Pasteur's arguments for causality took this form: he found some organism regularly present in an organic process and concluded it was the cause of that process. When he was unable to reason in this way, he fell back on experiments suggesting sufficiency, but he was clearly reluctant to infer causality from that relation.

From a logical point of view, Bassi, Gruby, Semmelweis, and Pasteur all reasoned in much the same way. Bassi concluded that a fungus was the cause of muscardine after becoming persuaded that the disease never occurred in the absence of the fungus. Gruby saw that the morbid remains he studied were actually composed of fungi; in their absence, therefore, there would be no morbidity. Once Semmelweis eliminated decaying organic matter by chlorine washings, childbed fever occurred only in cases he identified as self-contamination; thus, in the absence of the purported cause, there would be no disease. Pasteur inferred causality by observing that the same ferment was present in each case of each organic process and, therefore, in the absence of that ferment, the process would not occur. Bassi, Semmelweis, and Pasteur sometimes exposed test animals to the operation of purported causes, but they seem to have conducted these tests without much conviction and gave little emphasis to their results. The evidence that each seemed to find most compelling was evidence of causal necessity. So far as one can tell, each reasoned in this way without much awareness that doing so departed from the way physicians usually thought about causes. Yet the closer their work approached human diseases, the more vigorously they were opposed. Gruby was ostracized and his work dismissed as insignificant (*British Medical Journal*, 1898). Bassi and Semmelweis were immediately attacked by those who continued to think in terms of spontaneous disorders and of pluralities of possible causes. Pasteur's early work, which concerned problems relatively remote from human disease, seems not to have attracted much critical attention from contemporary physicians. However, after 1870, as he began studying human diseases using the same methods he had used earlier, physicians and pathologists criticized him in the same ways and with the same animosity experienced by Bassi, Gruby, and Semmelweis.

We now move into a new phase in the development of the etiological programme. Bassi, Gruby, Semmelweis, and Pasteur conducted their research and claimed to have identified causes, but they did so in the absence of clear and acknowledged standards for proving causality. Each seems to have assumed without justification (apparently without even sensing a need for justification) that one could demonstrate causality simply by identifying a factor always present in some organic process. The research we will now consider differs in two ways from what we have seen so far: First, we will find a growing awareness of, and interest in, the *concept* of disease causation. This interest is revealed in disputes about whether given sets of experiments are or are not adequate to prove causality. These disputes differ from those we have so far encountered. While critics of Bassi and Semmelweis challenged their claims that *Beauvaria bassiana* or decaying organic matter were the *only* causes of muscardine or of childbed fever, no one objected to the idea that each was *a* cause. Early in the century, causal concepts were sufficiently vague that virtually anything could be accepted as *a* cause of almost any pathological process. However, by the late 1860s there was a sense that causal claims required evidence, and by the 1870s disputes about how to prove causality were partly resolved with the elaboration and almost universal acceptance of explicit causal criteria. Thereafter, causal claims could be accepted only if they were supported by experiments intentionally organized to satisfy those criteria.

Second, whereas most of the research we have considered so far was conducted by scientists working alone, we now find research that builds on the work of predecessors and contemporaries. By the 1880s, in place of relatively independent research of relatively isolated scientists each following his own intuitions about proving causation, we find shared techniques, assumptions, and nomenclature, an interest in confirming the observations and in repeating the experiments of others, and research subordinated to the shared goal of finding specific causes of diseases. In short, by the 1880s, we find a full-blown research programme focusing on the identification of universal and necessary causes.

Casimir Davaine was a transition figure in this change. Rather than working in relative isolation, his work connected solidly into the research of others in the two ways just mentioned: he helped secure a consensus of expectations about how one could prove causation, and he frequently drew on and motivated the research of others. However Davaine's work never fully persuaded his contemporaries – a failure due, in part, to the very lack of the consensus he was helping to achieve. In particular, his work was an important step in securing acceptance of a vital heuristic principle, the Bacterial Hypothesis; but his contemporaries remained unconvinced by his work, in part, precisely because they did not as yet accept that principle.

Notes

1. For example, the first two Laws of Thermodynamics can be interpreted as stating that the total energy in the universe is constant and that entropy is always increasing. If understood as empirical claims about the world, neither could possibly be confirmed.
2. All three hypotheses are laws in the sense defined by Wim J. Van der Steen and Harmke Kamminga (Van der Steen and Kamminga, 1991) and they function within theories of disease in the same way that, say, the Laws of Motion function in Newtonian mechanics or the Laws of Thermodynamics function in thermodynamics. However, in common usage they are not referred to as 'laws', and 'hypothesis' would seem to be a suitable term.

3. Geison observed that this paper is 'astonishing in its audacity and scope' and that it introduced nearly all 'the basic convictions and techniques that would thereafter guide [Pasteur's] study of fermentation in general' (Geison, 1995, p. 90).

4. Geison wrote that, among the basic convictions introduced in Pasteur's first (1857a) paper on lactic fermentation was 'his notion of specificity, according to which each fermentation could be traced to a specific microbe' (Geison, 1995, p. 90).

5. This situation was made even more complex by the fact, recently unearthed by Geison, that Pasteur actually believed in a kind of spontaneous generation and conducted numerous (unsuccessful) experiments to verify it. However, Pasteur was not quite inconsistent; his view seems to have been that spontaneous generation could not come about using the ordinary techniques available in chemical or biological laboratories (Geison, 1995, pp. 136–42). This aspect of Pasteur's work does not concern us in the present context.

6. I will have more to say about Latour under 'Some Final Thoughts' at the end of this book.

7. Pasteur first reported this discovery in remarks before a special meeting of the *Comice agricole d'Alais* in 1867 (Pasteur, 1867b). *Pebrine* is now attributed to a protozoan, *Nosema bombycis*, and *flacherie* to a virus that predisposes the silkworm to infection by the bacterium, *Bacillus bombycis*, that Pasteur had observed (Lechevalier and Solotorovsky, 1975, p. 40).

CHAPTER FIVE

The Bacterial Hypothesis

During the 1860s, while Pasteur studied fermentation, spontaneous generation, and silkworm diseases, other French scientists were becoming interested in an infectious disease known as anthrax.

Anthrax usually attacks livestock, and especially sheep, in wet or marshy areas. Infected animals occasionally drop dead without any signs of disease, but, more commonly, over the space of a few hours or days, afflicted animals become progressively weaker until they are unable to walk. In the final stages of the disease, dying animals simply lie on the ground, panting and hemorrhaging through all body openings; death comes by asphyxiation. Anthrax spreads rapidly among livestock – within a few days of the first fatalities, entire herds can be lost; it can also attack humans who handle meat or skins from infected animals. Among humans, anthrax usually occurs either as cutaneous boils (known as malignant pustules) or as a gastro-intestinal disorder. Anthrax is sometimes fatal to humans, but livestock are at much greater risk: in early nineteenth-century Europe, a few hundred people may have died of anthrax in a given year, but deaths among livestock often numbered in the hundreds of thousands. Obviously the disease had profound economic significance.

By the end of the eighteenth century it was generally known that anthrax was contagious (Bollinger, 1875, p. 449), and by 1824 experiments had shown it could be conveyed by inoculating blood from diseased animals (Théodoridès, 1966, p. 157). However, it was still believed that animals could contract the disease if they were overfed, allowed to graze where the soil composition was inappropriate, or exposed to malarial poisons (Bollinger, 1875, p. 449). In addition to catching anthrax from animals, people were deemed vulnerable if they consumed indigestible or poor quality food, or were exposed to acid substances or to skin irritants. One writer reported having seen it 'several times in persons who had been attacked by mange or scaling and who had employed energetic repercussions to make the eruptions disappear' (Marjolin, 1833, p. 194). Another wrote that anthrax could occur in hot, humid weather, among the poor who had inadequate diet, after drinking corrupt water, by contagion, or spontaneously (Beaude, 1849, vol. 1, p. 129).

In the summer of 1850, Pierre-François-Olive Rayer conducted anthrax inoculation experiments on sheep in the region of Chartres (Rayer,

1850). In a footnote in his published report, Rayer noted that an associate, Casimir Davaine, had seen 'small filiform bodies about twice the length of a blood corpuscle' in the blood of anthracoid sheep. There is no indication Rayer or Davaine regarded the structures as having any particular significance. Five years later, in 1855, a German physician, Franz Aloys Antoin Pollender, reported finding immobile rod-shaped bodies in the blood of anthracoid animals (Pollender, 1855). Pollender noted that the bodies resembled bacteria and, in contrast to Davaine, speculated that they could be causally associated with anthrax. Pollender claimed to have seen the bodies as early as 1849, one year before Davaine, but his account was first published five years after Rayer's essay. Contemporary German writers generally credited Pollender rather than Davaine with discovery of the anthrax bacillus (Bollinger, 1875, p. 450; Birch-Hirschfeld, 1875, p. 205). Because anthrax was studied simultaneously by German and French scientists in the years surrounding the Franco-Prussian war, their efforts were animated by keen nationalistic rivalry.

In 1857 and 1858 Friedrich August Brauell published the results of inoculation experiments with the blood of anthracoid animals. Brauell confirmed Pollender's observations of rod-shaped microscopic bodies in anthrax blood. He reported the bodies did not result from the decomposition of blood after death because he had seen them in the blood of living animals. According to Brauell, before the death of an anthracoid animal, and even during the first two or three days after death, the rod-shaped bodies remained immobile. However, he reported that, about three days after an animal died, the rods began to move and gradually became active vibrions. He also reported finding similar vibrions in animals that had not died of anthrax (Brauell, 1857, pp. 142f.).[1]

In his 1858 paper Brauell claimed that the immobile rod-shaped bodies characterized, exclusively, anthracoid animals. He reported that the rods never appeared in the blood of healthy animals or of animals suffering from other diseases (Brauell, 1858, p. 462). Brauell continued to hold that, within three or four days after death, the previously immobile rods began to move and ultimately became active vibrions. He also found that, even if the blood of a pregnant anthracoid sheep contained the characteristic rods, the blood of its fetus may not, and inoculations with such fetal blood did not convey anthrax to healthy animals (Brauell, 1858, p. 466). Brauell was able to identify rod-shaped bodies in the blood of diseased animals only within the last few hours before they died, but he found that blood from anthracoid animals in which these bodies had not yet appeared could still convey anthrax. From these observations he inferred that, while the rods indicated the imminent death of diseased animals, they were neither the contagium of anthrax nor even the bearers of the contagium (Brauell, 1858, p. 463). Given that Brauell relied on visual inspection to determine whether blood samples contained rod-shaped bodies, he may simply have overlooked isolated organisms. Since he did not distinguish anthrax bacilli from ordinary decomposition organisms, it is also possible that some of his test animals died from other diseases. In any case while Brauell believed the rod-shaped bodies conclusively indicated that a diseased animal was about to die, he was not persuaded that they caused anthrax.

In 1863 Davaine resumed his study of anthrax. He later explained that, in 1850, when he first saw the rod-shaped bodies, he had intended to confirm his observations and to determine whether the development of the bodies could cause animals to deteriorate and die. However, he had not found the time for these studies (Davaine, 1863a, pp. 220f). He wrote that 'the opportunity had still not presented itself, and other concerns had not permitted me to seek it actively when, in February 1861, Pasteur published his remarkable work on the butyric ferment, a ferment consisting of small cylindrical rods possessing all the characteristics of vibrions or bacteria' (Davaine, 1863a, p. 221).

Davaine wrote that the similarity between the butyric ferment and the bodies he had seen in 1850 revived his interest in anthrax. He conjectured that the rod-shaped bodies could play the role of a ferment in the blood. This would explain, he wrote, 'the rapid infection of the blood mass of an animal that had received into its veins, accidentally or experimentally, a certain number of these bacteria, that is to say, of this ferment' (Davaine, 1863a, p. 221). Although his interest in anthrax was revived, two more years passed before Davaine obtained a sample of anthrax blood. He then resumed inoculations.

In his first report on anthrax, Davaine described the rods in detail and emphasized that they were incapable of independent movement. He also observed that they disappeared completely once blood began to decompose. This, he wrote, provides an easy way of distinguishing anthrax infusoria from those involved in ordinary putrefaction (Davaine, 1863a, p. 222). Davaine did not specifically mention Brauell, but the implication was obvious: Brauell had mistakenly believed he saw immobile anthrax rods changing into moving organisms, whereas in fact he had seen anthrax rods replaced by putrefaction vibrions. Davaine was unable to decide whether anthrax bacteria functioned as minute animalcules that poisoned their host or as ferments that decomposed the host's blood, but he hoped future research would shed light on such questions. 'For the moment', he concluded, 'I limit myself to announcing one fact I believe to be new. The examination of six animals suffering or dead of anthrax has six times revealed in their blood the same microscopic beings. These corpuscles evidently develop during the life of the infected animal, and their relation to the disease that leads to death cannot be in doubt' (Davaine, 1863a, p. 223).

Whether he realized it or not, Davaine's reasoning followed a familiar pattern. It was like Pasteur's arguments that various organisms cause fermentation and wine spoilage, it was like Gruby's arguments that various fungi cause human mycoses, and it was like Bassi's argument that *Beauvaria bassiana* causes muscardine: having observed a particular organism regularly present in some process (fermentation, putrefaction, disease), each inferred that the organism caused the process. Each author inferred causality from observational evidence of necessity. Partly in response to his critics (whom he identified as pathologists), Davaine soon provided other evidence of causality. However, in the preceding argument, which was his first attempt to prove a causal connection, and in others that came later, the evidence that Davaine seems to have found most compelling was evidence of necessity. Like Bassi, Gruby, Semmelweis, and Pasteur, Davaine began by thinking in terms of necessary causes. Given Davaine's interest in Pasteur's work, it is possible that this preference reflects Pasteur's influence.

In his second paper Davaine confirmed his earlier findings and reported new experiments in which he inoculated rabbits with fresh blood containing anthrax bacteria. He reported the organisms were present in the rabbits' blood before the onset of morbid changes and that very small quantities of infected blood could kill healthy rabbits. Davaine also found that anthrax blood, after being rapidly dried, could be heated to 100 degrees without losing its contagious powers. On the other hand, putrefied blood from which the organisms had disappeared was incapable of conveying anthrax. Davaine concluded that there was no reason to seek some further 'contagious element, mysterious and unknown', that presumably developed and destroyed when and only when the bacterium was also present. The bacterium 'is visible and palpable; an organized being, endowed with life, that develops and propagates as a living being. By its presence and rapid multiplication in the blood, it brings about, in the constitution of this liquid, without doubt after the manner of a ferment, those modifications from which the infected animal quickly dies' (Davaine, 1863b, p. 387).

In 1863, apparently thinking he was confirming Davaine's work, a French physician named Signol reported his own investigations of the blood of diseased livestock. Signol reviewed French and German literature on anthrax and mentioned particularly the work of Pollender and Brauell. He confirmed Davaine's claim that blood from anthracoid sheep contained bacteria, and he reported that, if infected blood was inoculated into healthy animals, the blood of those animals soon contained large numbers of bacteria. However, Signol also reported that the same bacteria could be found in the blood of horses with non-anthracoid diseases. Thus, he concluded, the bacteria were not unique to anthrax (Signol, 1863).

By 1864 when he presented his next paper, Davaine had conducted inoculation experiments on more than 150 animals; his experiments consistently confirmed his earlier results. Davaine was convinced the anthrax rods differed from the organisms Signol and others found in other diseases and, to help mark the distinction, he proposed calling the anthrax rods *bacteridia* (Davaine, 1864a, p. 393). Without mentioning Brauell's similar experiments, Davaine reported that the blood of a pregnant anthracoid sheep did not infect its fetus, and that inoculating healthy animals with blood from the fetus did not convey anthrax. He found that anthrax blood that had been rapidly air-dried and then conserved for as long as 11 months was still infectious. He also confirmed that anthrax could be induced by the consumption of contaminated food. These arguments were intended to provide experimental evidence that, if animals were suitably exposed to bacteridia, they could contract anthrax – that is, under certain conditions, bacteridia were sufficient for anthrax. Davaine argued that the contagious element of anthrax is completely different from the toxic element of putrefaction: 'the toxic agent of putrid matter does not regenerate itself as does that of anthrax blood. In a word, putrefaction acts on the animal economy as a poison whereas anthrax acts as a virus' (Davaine, 1864a, p. 396).

In another paper given later in the same year, Davaine reported that bacteridia were also prominent in cutaneous boils, known in human victims as malignant pustules, and that, if tissue fragments from these boils were placed under the skin of test animals, the animals soon died of anthrax (Davaine and Raimbert, 1864). Malignant pustules had long been associated with anthrax, and they were widely believed to follow from exposure to the blood and hides of anthracoid sheep. By showing that bacteridia were present in both diseases, Davaine supported the claim that bacteridia caused both.

Davaine also proposed using the presence of bacteridia as a diagnostic criterion for use in classifying questionable cases of anthrax (Davaine and Raimbert, 1864, p. 431). Although Davaine did not make this explicit, this proposal amounted to a redefinition of 'anthrax' in terms of its causal agent because, given this criterion, the presence of bacteridia, rather than any symptomatic or pathological considerations, became the ultimate criterion for deciding what was and what was not anthrax. Four years later, convinced that anthrax and malignant pustule both depended on the presence of bacteridia, Davaine just assumed that malignant pustule was simply a form of anthrax (Davaine, 1868a, p. 145). Davaine was now assuming that anthrax was to be defined in terms of the presence of its necessary cause.

Davaine's research was soon challenged by two French physicians, Emile-Claude Leplat and Pierre-François Jaillard (Leplat and Jaillard, 1864). Leplat and Jaillard cited Signol's paper as well as research conducted in Italy suggesting that bacteria were sometimes found in non-anthracoid disorders (Tigri, 1863). They criticized Davaine for using whole blood in all his experiments. Blood was a complex liquid containing many ingredients that could not be identified by microscopic examination. Thus, they reasoned, if one conveyed anthrax by injecting infected blood, it was impossible to decide whether the contagious element was the bacteridia or some other ingredient.

Like Davaine, Leplat and Jaillard saw no hope of isolating bacteridia from the blood. Instead they proposed inoculating vibrions contained in other media. Their idea was this: assuming the vibrions were the same regardless of the medium in which they flourished, if inoculating vibrions from different cultures produced different results, the differences had to be ascribed to the media rather than to the vibrions. 'Nothing is easier', they wrote, 'than to provide these small microscopic beings, that have the greatest resemblance to one another and, without doubt, the same properties' (Leplat and Jaillard, 1864, p. 251). In place of anthrax blood, Leplat and Jaillard injected 'certain vegetable infusions, some liquids charged with decomposing animal matter, putrefied urine, [and] the serum of decomposed blood'. In each case, before carrying out the injections, the authors determined 'the identity and the vitality' of the vibrions by microscopic examinations (Leplat and Jaillard, 1864, p. 251). Most of the injected animals remained healthy; deaths occurred only when the medium containing the vibrions was putrid and was injected in quantities so large that the animals died of septic poisoning. Leplat and Jaillard concluded that the vibrions themselves did not cause anthrax and were harmless. This was clearly intended as an argument that bacteridia (assumed to be the same regardless of their origin) were not *sufficient* for anthrax whereas, at least as he himself stated it, Davaine's position was that the organisms were *necessary* for the disease. Thus, to some extent, Davaine and his critics were speaking past one another. Of course, there were other enormous differences as well.

To many of Davaine's contemporaries, these and other criticisms seemed persuasive. In 1865, when Davaine was awarded a prize for his research, the citation stated that 'either the bacteridium is the transmitting agent of anthrax or else it is the corpuscle which invariably accompanies the necessary condition for inoculation and development of the disease' (Théodoridès, 1966, p. 161). Even the author of this citation, while honoring Davaine for his work on anthrax, was unwilling to accept without reservation Davaine's view that the organism was the only active agent in anthrax blood.

Davaine responded quickly to Leplat and Jaillard. He reported research indicating that even vibrions that appeared to be identical could have significantly different properties. Vibrions that are visually indistinguishable could require totally different media and may quickly die if introduced into an unsuitable medium. 'It follows', Davaine concluded, 'that these species cannot be substituted for one another. Thus researchers seeking to elucidate certain pathological questions, must not hope to determine identical phenomena by the introduction of vibrions drawn from different sources' (Davaine, 1864b, p. 633).

In 1865 a German physician named Huppert reviewed the anthrax literature in an essay in a prominent periodical (Huppert, 1865). Huppert was enthusiastic about Davaine's research; in his opinion, it conclusively demonstrated that bacteridia cause anthrax. He claimed that Brauell's work anticipated Davaine's results and had been inadequately appreciated only because, when Brauell conducted his studies, Pasteur had not yet shown that each fermentation process was associated with a unique ferment.

Brauell immediately responded to Huppert; he wanted, as he put it, to defend German soil from the encroachment of French theories (Brauell, 1866, p. 292). Brauell insisted the causal role of the anthrax bacillus had not yet been established: 'ignoring the fact that nothing is known about the development and spread of the rod-shaped bodies, I find no logically compelling reason for the opinion that these bodies cause anthrax' (Brauell, 1866, p. 293). Brauell pointed out that, even given Davaine's experiments, it was still possible that some other component of anthrax blood was the true contagium. He mentioned that Leplat and Jaillard had raised similar objections in France. According to Brauell, the only way to prove causality would be by inoculating isolated vibrions. However, he doubted that such a test could ever be conducted because, as he insisted, one could never insure that the bacteridia had been completely freed from every other ingredient in blood. Thus it would always be possible that the real cause was some other entity – an otherwise unknown virus – that was regularly associated with bacteridia.

Brauell reported that blood from anthracoid animals sometimes contained no trace of rod-shaped bodies, and he also confirmed that inoculations with such blood could sometimes induce anthrax. He mentioned other researchers, including even Davaine himself, who had acknowledged similar results. Thus, he concluded, far from proving causality, the research Huppert cited actually contained evidence against it (Brauell, 1866, p. 294). Brauell wrote that he would be pleased if Pasteur's theory of fermentation could be applied to the contagious diseases and if the rod-shaped bodies could be shown to cause anthrax by blood fermentation. However, he regarded this as unlikely: he doubted that all fermentation was due to living organisms, but even if it were, he observed, it would still be doubtful that anthrax was a kind of fermentation. Brauell wrote that, even if Pasteur's work had been available when he had conducted his own study of anthrax, his conclusions would have been precisely the same.

In 1868 Davaine published a paper intended to establish, once and for all, the role of bacteridia in anthrax. He began by observing that for more than five years his research had revealed that

> bacteridia are found in all anthracoid disorders and in all victims of the vulnerable species; the appearance of these small beings in the spleen, the liver, and in the blood precedes the onset of morbid phenomena; finally, anthrax blood ceases to be contagious once bacteridia disappear. These facts, and several others it would take too long to review, appear to me to be adequate reasons for affirming that the development of bacteridia is the cause of anthrax. However, these facts do not have the same value in the eyes of all pathologists, and in recent times, some very esteemed authors have expressed reservations in speaking of the role of the bacteridia in producing anthrax.
>
> (Davaine, 1868a, p. 144)

In this passage Davaine listed three reasons for accepting the causal role of bacteridia: First, the organisms were always present in the disease (this, of course, is the same observational evidence of necessity that he mentioned in his first argument for causality). Second, the organisms are in the blood before the onset of morbid alterations. Third, blood ceases to be contagious once bacteridia have disappeared (in other words, absence of bacteridia is associated with absence of the disease – further evidence of necessity). Davaine felt this evidence justified the claim of causality, but he acknowledged that some pathologists remained unpersuaded.

After emphasizing the importance of the issue, Davaine explained that, in the present paper, he intended 'to establish in a definite way, the role of bacteridia in anthrax'. He proposed to do this, first, by answering the objections his critics had raised, and second, by advancing an additional new argument. He considered three objections. First, that bacteridia were sometimes found in non-anthracoid animals (if true this would show bacteridia are not sufficient for anthrax). In response, he pointed out that those who made this claim were confusing bacteridia with other organisms. Second, bacteridia were not always found in the blood of animals that died after inoculation with anthrax blood (this would show that bacteridia are not necessary). He wrote that these observations could be explained either by assuming the animals in question had died of some other disease before the bacteridia had incubated or by assuming the observers were looking for bacteridia only in blood from the major arteries whereas bacteridia often collected 'in rather small fibrose clots, either white or semi-transparent, that one may neglect to examine' (Davaine, 1868a, p. 145). The third objection was this: 'it has been claimed that the vibrions are the effect and not the cause of the alteration of the blood' (Davaine, 1868a, p. 146). Recent observers had maintained, Davaine continued, that the only way of establishing that bacteridia are the anthrax virus would be by filtering bacteridia from anthrax blood and by inoculating the isolated organisms into healthy animals. However, he doubted that any man-made filter could achieve this result, so he repeated his earlier experiments using blood filtered through the placenta of a pregnant guinea-pig. He found (as he and Brauell had both reported earlier) that blood from the pregnant guinea-pig conveyed fatal anthrax while the blood of its fetus did not (Davaine, 1868a, pp. 146f).

After responding to these three criticisms, Davaine gave a new indirect argument in support of the causal role of bacteridia. Davaine observed that 'the invasion and subsequent destruction of an animal by an infusorium is, as yet, a fact without analogue, and because it is so singular, one requires a multitude of proofs before it can be admitted' (Davaine, 1868a, p. 147). Davaine supported his claim by an analogical argument based on his discovery that certain plants could also contract bacterial diseases. His discovery had some inherent interest, but there is no evidence his critics found it persuasive.

Later in the same year Davaine reported further experiments with anthrax blood. He demonstrated that even minute quantities of infected blood could be fatal. He also reported that the time required for the onset of symptoms varied inversely with the quantity of inoculated organisms (Davaine, 1868b). Both results made it appear that anthrax was not simply a consequence of physical or chemical poisoning, and he concluded that the cause of the disease had to be a living organism that could multiply within the victim.

In 1870 Davaine published yet another important paper on anthrax. The paper was read before the French Academy of Medicine and both the paper and the ensuing discussion were published. In this paper Davaine addressed one of the main problems raised by Brauell, namely, if one assumed bacteridia cause anthrax, how could one account for the spread of the disease. He began by listing various observations about the spread of anthrax that seemed difficult to explain – for example, anthrax sometimes appeared to spread without direct contact between diseased and healthy animals, anthrax epizootics sometimes ended when herds moved from one pasture to another, and changes in the weather sometimes affected the course of an epizootic. He then criticized a few of the inconsistent hypotheses that had been advanced to explain these facts. Finally he presented his own hypothesis: while acknowledging that other means of transference were possible, he proposed that anthrax was often conveyed by flying insects carrying minute traces of bacteridia-bearing blood from diseased animals to healthy ones (Davaine, 1870a, p. 219). He supported this claim with several experiments, and he showed the hypothesis could account for some observations that were otherwise difficult to explain (Davaine, 1870a, p. 225). He suggested how farmers could curb the effect of flying insects and, thereby, protect their herds.

The discussion following Davaine's paper provides insight into medical thinking in 1870 – seven years after he had begun arguing that bacteridia cause anthrax. Of the eight persons whose comments are reported, five specifically insisted that epizootic anthrax could better be explained by the assumption that anthrax was often spontaneous (Davaine, 1870a, pp. 231–5). The comments of a physician named Leblanc were typical. Leblanc allowed that anthrax could be contagious and could perhaps spread as Davaine had hypothesized, but he was convinced that 'the more usual cause of the great epizootics is the spontaneous development of anthrax under the influence of [un]hygienic and morbid influences' (Davaine, 1870a, p. 232). Judging from the reported discussion, even in 1870 many French physicians still accepted the idea that diseases could originate spontaneously and most were skeptical of the claim that anthrax had a single universal cause.

In a subsequent meeting of the Academy, Davaine defended his account of the spread of anthrax. He observed that the concept of 'contagion is sufficient to explain the indefinite transmission of anthracoid afflictions without appealing to the outdated doctrine of heterogony'

(Davaine, 1870b, p. 490). He insisted that, whenever possible, medicine should learn from its sister sciences. Without mentioning Pasteur by name, he observed that recent work in natural history had shed new light on the role of microscopic parasites and had so thoroughly discredited the notion of spontaneous generation that the doctrine could now be taken to apply, at most, to amorphous leukocytes – entities without identifiable characteristics that seemed to be neither plants nor animals. By contrast, he insisted, bacteridia had a fixed nature and could be precisely classified among other living beings. Davaine observed that, in the face of all that was known about bacteridia, it was impossible to believe they arose spontaneously. Those who still accepted this possibility were forced into the impossible situation of explaining how bacteridia or their germs could suddenly appear in malignant pustules, in anthracoid tumors, and in the liver, the spleen, and the blood of every anthracoid animal (Davaine, 1870b, p. 491). It seemed more plausible, he concluded, to regard them as spreading from one host to another and as multiplying in the hosts' bodies. Given this point of view, the only remaining question was how they spread, and this, he insisted, was usually by way of flying insects.

Davaine admitted that liquid anthrax blood quickly putrefied and, once putrefaction began, it no longer contained bacteridia. However, even if anthrax blood dried rapidly before the onset of putrefaction, it continued to be contagious for months and possibly even for years. This explained why anthrax occurred again and again in the same areas even though the outbreaks were separated by long periods (Davaine, 1870b, p. 492). In conclusion, he pointed out that, on his theory, one could understand how a drop of anthrax blood could dry and remain protected in a stable for years until it happened to be deposited in the open wounds of an animal, how this one animal could become ill and die, and how, by way of flying insects, the diseased animal could be the source of infection for a murderous epizootic. One could understand how, among all the herds grazing in a given pasture, the animals sheltered in a given stable might become diseased while those in other stables might not. One could understand how the disease could be controlled by measures that would prevent this from happening. Moreover, he insisted, 'this way of thinking was compatible with experimental results and with current knowledge of the nature of organized ferments and of their means of generation either within or outside the animal economy' (Davaine, 1870b, p. 496). Davaine was convinced he was right because his account could explain the facts and was compatible with other current scientific beliefs; other accounts did not meet these conditions.

In spite of Davaine's emphatic defense, respondents continued to insist that there still remained cases that could most plausibly be accounted for in terms of spontaneous generation (Davaine, 1870b, p. 497). Thus, while acknowledging that the spread of bacteridia could explain some cases of anthrax, they continued to believe that the disease did not always depend on the dissemination of bacteridia and their germs.

Even after all of Davaine's work, both French and German critics remained unpersuaded. In their minds, he had not excluded the possibility that anthrax could arise spontaneously or through some combination of factors not involving bacteridia (that is he had not proven causal necessity), and he had not proven that bacteridia, when isolated from every other ingredient of anthrax blood, would themselves bring on the disease (that is, he had not proven causal sufficiency). A German writer observed that Davaine had been unable to perform 'the one experiment that would have overcome all objections to his opinion on the significance of bacteridia: namely, freeing the blood from bacteridia by filtration through clay and inoculating the filtrate' (Steudener, 1872, p. 304). Explained in this way, the deficiency in Davaine's argument appears to have been purely technical – he seems only to have needed a more reliable way of isolating bacteridia from the other ingredients in anthrax blood. Indeed, Davaine and other researchers devoted considerable effort to progressively more rigorous methods of separating bacteridia from every contaminant that could have been causally relevant. However, no such effort could be completely successful until there was agreement as to exactly which potential contaminants *could be* causally relevant. In the absence of such agreement, no matter what steps were taken to insure the purity of a given culture, skeptics could always maintain there could still be some unknown substance that had not been excluded and that could be the true cause of anthrax.

The only way of silencing this objection would have been by appealing to some hypothesis such as this: every disease is caused by bacteria. We will call this the Bacterial Hypothesis, and we will defer until the next chapter the objection that it is obviously false. No one questioned that bacteridia were the only *bacteria* involved in anthrax. Thus if Davaine's critics had accepted something like the Bacterial Hypothesis, they would clearly have accepted the bacteridium as the cause, rather than continue holding out for some possible unknown entity. This is like saying (1) if Davaine's critics had accepted what Pasteur called the Dissemination Hypothesis – the assumption that bacterial cultures never arise spontaneously but only from antecedent bacteria – they would not have taken seriously the idea that anthrax could occur spontaneously, or (2) if Leplat and Jaillard had accepted the Distinguishability Hypothesis they would not have attempted to induce anthrax by injecting 'certain vegetable infusions, some liquids charged with decomposing animal matter, putrefied urine, [and] the serum of decomposed blood' (Leplat and Jaillard, 1864, p. 251). Regardless of whether the Bacterial Hypothesis is defensible, this suggests that Davaine's problems could have been due as much to the lack of a shared theoretical framework as to technical imperfections in his experiments.

Causation is ultimately a theoretical relation, so causal claims can never be justified in the absence of a theory. To say a set of conditions causes an event is to say our theories connect the conditions with the event in certain ways – it does not mean the event is somehow, once and for all, bonded to those conditions by 'cosmic glue' (Hanson, 1969, p. 64). Without a theoretical context to warrant these connections it is impossible even to conceive of causation, and it is impossible, in principle, to advance beyond such empirical correlations as necessity or sufficiency to justify a causal claim. Regardless of how much empirical evidence Davaine may have accumulated, in the absence of a shared theoretical framework his critics could never have been persuaded.

Davaine's problem is suggested by the following passage from a prominent and sympathetic nineteenth-century researcher, Otto Bollinger:

> From the almost constant presence of the characteristic bacteria (or bacterial germs) in the blood of anthracoid animals, in view of the inoculation experiments ... and of the unmistakable character of anthrax as a blood disease, if one succeeds in explaining the clinical and pathological appearances in terms of the properties and operations of the bacteria, one could attempt to regard these small organisms as the anthrax poison.
>
> (Bollinger, 1875, p. 461)

In this summary, Bollinger mentioned nearly all the empirical evidence one could imagine having for causality. But, the most Bollinger was willing to hazard was that, given this evidence, 'one could attempt to regard' bacteridia as the causal agent. Even given such evidence, in the absence of what we have called the Bacterial Hypothesis (or something like it) Bollinger was unwilling to conclude, categorically, that bacteridia cause anthrax.

The purpose of the Bacterial Hypothesis is to certify that, given some case of disease, of all the infinitely many conditions that could conceivably cause it (evil spirits, yesterday's cauliflower salad, miasms, astrological configurations, gazelles grazing on the Serengeti), only bacteria must be taken into account. By appealing to such a principle, and only by such an appeal, empirical evidence can finally amount to a proof of causation.

Note

1. French observers later dismissed these last two observations as resulting from a failure to distinguish immobile anthrax bacilli from mobile organisms that flourished in putrefying blood (Davaine, 1863a, p. 222).

CHAPTER SIX

A Bacterial Theory of Disease

Edwin Klebs was born 6 February 1834 in Königsberg. Klebs completed his medical studies in 1858 at the University of Berlin and, after graduating, he practiced medicine for one year in Königsberg. Perhaps because of an interest in Semmelweis's work (Röthlin, 1962, p. 6), Klebs was initially attracted to obstetrics but, in response to Rudolf Virchow's encouragement, he turned to pathology (Hirsch, 1935, p. 539). Klebs worked for a time as Virchow's assistant and, in the early 1860s, published several unexceptional essays on pathology in a journal edited by Virchow.[1] In 1866, he accepted a position at the University of Bern. Five years later, in the first volume of a periodical he founded and edited, Klebs reported investigations he had conducted on anthrax and on infected gunshot wounds (Tiegel, 1871; Klebs, 1871). These papers mark a significant and permanent change in his research orientation.

At the outset of his work he had followed Virchow's general research approach (Röthlin, 1962, pp. 6–7). In his early essays, like Virchow and other pathologists, he focused on internal morbid processes and displayed little interest in remote causes. His discussion of an outbreak of epidemic meningitis was typical: Klebs described in detail the sequence of pathological changes characteristic of the disease, but regarding causes he observed only that 'the local influence of cold and the pressing together of the population into a small area must be taken into account' (Klebs, 1865, p. 379). However, his studies of anthrax and wound infections seem to have persuaded Klebs that these diseases occurred only under the influence of microorganisms. Thereafter he became progressively more interested in parasitic organisms as causes of disease. Within a few years, Klebs was vigorously criticizing the pathologists for their narrow concern with internal disease processes and their indifference to what, in his opinion, mattered most about disease causation. Klebs noted that, in his later years, Henle 'recognized, as causes of disease, only general physical and chemical influences, the life impulses, the same factors that have often been identified by others who wrote before and after him. The concept of a specific cause of a disease, which is absolutely destructive of life, is alien to him as to most other pathologists' (Klebs, 1878a, p. 46). Klebs also objected to Rudolf Virchow's uncritical adoption of antiquated and fruitless causal notions (Klebs, 1878a, p. 46; Klebs, 1878b, pp. 133f.) and Virchow's few scattered remarks about remote causes suggest that this criticism was entirely justified.[2] In response to his former student's telling criticisms, Virchow admitted that pathologists were less interested in external remote causes than in internal disease processes, but he also warned that, by ignoring internal dispositions, Klebs risked falling into the opposite error: 'evidently Klebs is ... of the opinion the internal arrangement of the tissues is irrelevant [in determining the effect of a remote cause], or, expressed in terms of universal pathology, that the external cause is an *Agens Causa sufficiens* for all the consequences' (Virchow, 1880, p. 9). Klebs ignored this feeble response. Because the pathologists had limited their attention to internal phenomena, in his opinion, they were unable to contribute significantly to practical medicine. Klebs wrote that he had abandoned Virchow's interests and devoted himself to the 'progressive expansion of those teachings that seek to find the causes of many diseases outside the cell boundaries and thereby make into scientific truth the opinions of Schönlein, Remak, and Henle (in his earlier years)' (Klebs, 1874a, p. 207).

Through the late nineteenth century, Klebs published important studies on the etiologies of a variety of diseases; an excerpt from Fielding H. Garrison's history of medicine shows the breadth of his interests:

> He saw the typhoid bacillus before Eberth (1881), the diphtheria bacillus before Löffler (1883), used solid cultures of sturgeon's glue (1872), and investigated the pathology of traumatic infections before Koch (1871). The priority of his inoculations of syphilis in monkeys was recognized by Metchnikoff (1878), and, in his experiments on anthrax (1871) and other diseases, he was the first to filter bacteria and to experiment with the filtrates. In 1874, he invented the fractional method of obtaining pure cultures of bacteria ... which was followed by Lister's method of dilution (1877) and prepared the ground for Koch's work. He wrote two textbooks on pathology (1869–76, 1887–89), monographs on the bacteriology of gunshot wounds ... (1872), on tumors (1877), and gigantism (1884), made many investigations on tuberculosis, and he was, with Gerlach, the first to produce bovine infection or *Perlsucht* by feeding with milk (1873). In his studies on gunshot wounds (1872) he showed that the filtrate of the wound-discharges is non-infectious, whence he reasoned that traumatic septicemia is of bacterial origin.
>
> (Garrison, 1929, p. 581)

Garrison also mentioned that Klebs probably did more than any other single researcher to win the pathologists over to the bacterial theory of infection – no mean accomplishment (Garrison, 1929, p. 580). It was typical of Klebs that he gave cursory attention to many common diseases, but made thorough studies of few – this inevitably led to mistakes: Garrison does not mention that Klebs also claimed to have identified bacterial causes of smallpox, malaria, and goiter. On the other hand, the very breadth of his interests gave Klebs a perspective from which to approach philosophical issues. He gave more extensive and more explicit attention to causal criteria than any of his contemporaries, and he stated explicitly some of the basic assumptions underlying the bacterial theory of disease to which he was contributing. These are the two aspects of his work that will be of interest to us, but before we examine Klebs' views, we must briefly review some developments in bacteriology that provided the context of Klebs' own investigations.

Bacteriology in the 1870s

Since the late eighteenth century, pathologists had discussed the morbid alterations typical of infected wounds. In infected tissues one found soft gray spots the size of pin heads. In advanced cases the spots became larger and more numerous, they merged, and their centers degenerated into a substance resembling pus. These spots seemed to be new sites to which infection was spreading, and they were called metastases. In 1866 Eduard Rindfleisch, a German pathologist, found that metastases did not contain pus corpuscles, but rather microorganisms (Rindfleisch, 1867–69, pp. 183, 204). In harmony with existing terminology, he identified the organisms as vibrions. Rindfleisch reported that metastases originally contained vibrions densely packed between strands of muscle tissue; later the organisms spread into surrounding tissues and the muscle fibers decomposed. Another common morbid product of wound infections was a gray film that gradually spread over wound surfaces. Similar structures developed in the throats and lungs of diphtheria patients. As early as 1868 researchers reported finding clusters of small spherical organisms in these gray films. These organisms were called micrococci. However, finding living organisms in infected wounds did not prove they caused the morbid processes, and the exact role of the organisms remained a matter of dispute.

By the beginning of the 1870s, many different observations of microorganisms had been reported, but the reports were of uneven quality and, in the absence of photographs, they were supported at best by freehand drawings of the organisms in question. Under these conditions there was confusion about who had seen what and this uncertainty was compounded by the lack of a consistent nomenclature. Many writers followed Christian Gottfried Ehrenberg's 1824 taxonomic system, but as new organisms were discovered, this scheme became progressively less adequate and researchers simply made up names of their own (like Davaine's 'bacteridium'). Often there was considerable variation in terminology even within the works of a single author.

In 1872, Ferdinand Julius Cohn, a German botanist at Breslau, noted 'anyone who studies the literature, even from recent years, knows there is nearly chaotic confusion in the names of the bacteria' (Cohn, 1872, p. 128). In 1872 Cohn published an extensive review of the literature and recommended a new nomenclature and scheme for classifying bacteria. This scheme was widely adopted and became especially popular in Germany. Cohn characterized bacteria as 'cells lacking chlorophyll whose shape is spherical, oblong, or cylindrical, occasionally twisted or stunted, which proliferate exclusively by division and which vegetate either in isolation or in cell families' (Cohn, 1872, p. 136). He distinguished spherical, rod-shaped, thread-like, and spiral-shaped bacteria. Each group included various organisms. However, Cohn mentioned only those that were clearly documented in the literature, and he himself confirmed the existence and characteristics of most of the organisms he described.

Cohn's spherical bacteria included the smallest organisms that had then been observed; all were incapable of independent movement. Because they were so small, some were difficult to locate and to identify. However, small spherical bacteria were obviously important since they were the organisms most frequently associated with human diseases, and Cohn gave them more attention than those of any other group. The spherical bacteria included some of Pasteur's ferments and the micrococci commonly observed in diphtheria and in puerperal fever. Rod-shaped bacteria were also small, but they differed from spherical bacteria in that they were capable of independent motion. This group included the organisms usually associated with putrefaction as well as the ferments to which Pasteur ascribed the souring of milk and the creation of vinegar. None of the rod-shaped bacteria that Cohn identified were known to be pathological. Thread-like bacteria included the anthrax bacillus and Pasteur's butyric ferment. According to Cohn, all the organisms in this group were filaments that could, under suitable conditions, be seen to form extended cylindrical elements. Bacteria in this group varied in length, in thickness, and in flexibility. Spiral-shaped bacteria included, as separate subgroups, the organisms Ehrenberg referred to as the spirillum and the spirochaete.

At the time of Cohn's work, micrococci were regularly reported in a variety of diseases especially in several forms of wound infections. In 1871 Friedrich Daniel von Recklinghausen found micrococci in the kidneys, veins, urinary tracts, and lungs of childbed fever victims (Recklinghausen, 1871). In further studies of puerperal fever, Wilhelm Waldeyer found spherical bacteria in the kidneys and heart muscles (Waldeyer, 1872) and Felix Victor Birch-Hirschfeld observed micrococcal masses in vaginal ulcers, in paravaginal cellular tissues, and in victims' blood, spleens, and livers (Birch-Hirschfeld, 1872, p. 105). In

France, Gustave Nepveu found micrococci in the blood of erysipelas patients; he reported that the organisms were more numerous in blood drawn from the area of infection than in blood drawn from remote body parts (Nepveu, 1872).

In 1864, while studying an epidemic of relapsing fever, Otto Obermeier noticed fine thread-like structures in the blood of some victims. The epidemic ended at about the time he first observed the filaments, and, having no opportunity to confirm his discovery, he did not report it (Obermeier, 1873, p. 33). A few years later, in a new epidemic of relapsing fever, Obermeier found the same structures in the blood of new patients. In an 1873 paper, he reported that the structures were present only during the fever stage of the disease or within a short time before or after the fever stage. He also established that, while filaments could be found in the blood of most patients, they were not present in the blood of four healthy persons or of three persons suffering from other diseases (Obermeier, 1873, p. 34f.). The filaments moved vigorously and could most easily be detected by looking for certain irregular movements among the blood corpuscles. In his published report he drew no conclusions about whether the filaments had pathological significance or were simply modifications of normal body tissues. Obermeier reported showing blood samples to two professors in his clinic, Carl Westphal and Rudolf Virchow, and to several colleagues; each was able to identify the living filaments in the samples (Obermeier, 1873, p. 35). Within a few months of his discovery, in connection with further research, Obermeier contracted cholera and died.

Two years later, in a paper reviewing the literature on bacteria, Ferdinand Cohn wrote that Obermeier's discovery was 'clearly the most important fact [discovered] in recent times about the occurrence of fermenting organisms in the infectious diseases' (Cohn, 1875, p. 196). According to Cohn 'the discovery has been confirmed, without exception, by all later observers'. Cohn classified Obermeier's structures as spirochetes. He pointed out that, prior to the discovery, only one species of spirochete was known – a species observed in swamp water by Ehrenberg and later by Cohn himself, but it was difficult to find and had rarely been reported. According to Cohn, 'the most important fact about the spirochete of relapsing fever ... is that the threads are found exclusively in the blood of relapsing fever victims – never in their secretions or in other organs – and only during the paroxysm or a short time after the attack ... , but never during the interval between fevers' (Cohn, 1875, p. 197). The regular occurrence of the spirochetes in the blood seemed so clearly associated with the onset of symptoms that, even in the absence of other evidence for causality, most observers seem to have accepted the spirochetes as the cause of relapsing fever. In several papers Klebs cited Obermeier's work and seems to have taken it for granted that Obermeier had proven causation (Klebs, 1878a, p. 51). Thus, relapsing fever became the first disease widely believed to be caused by a spirochete.

Klebs on causal criteria

Klebs' first bacteriological publication was an 1871 paper on anthrax coauthored with his student, Ernst Tiegel. Tiegel and Klebs reported new experiments with anthrax blood; the goal was to determine whether bacteridia were the cause of anthrax (Tiegel, 1871). Tiegel filtered anthrax blood through clay to remove the bacteridia. He then showed that injecting the filtration residue, which included bacteridia, produced anthrax while injecting filtered blood did not. In a note at the end of Tiegel's paper, Klebs explained that 'Davaine wished to isolate the bacteria [from body fluids] while we undertook to free the liquids from the bacteria. Given our method, the latter is quite easy, but the former remains absolutely impossible' (Tiegel, 1871, p. 280). Tiegel and Klebs sought to answer objections to Davaine's work, but their paper seems not to have had much impact. Neither Otto Bollinger nor Felix Victor Birch-Hirschfeld cited the Tiegel-Klebs article in their thorough reviews of the anthrax literature that appeared only four years later (Bollinger, 1875; Birch-Hirschfeld, 1875).

Klebs' work on wound infections attracted more attention. Klebs studied infected gunshot wounds while serving in a military hospital, the *Bahnhofslazarette*, in Karlsruhe during the Franco-Prussian war. In his first paper on the topic, Klebs reported that a particular minute spherical organism, which he called *Microsporon septicum*, seemed to cause both fever and wound putrefaction (Klebs, 1871). He observed that wounds did not putrefy simply because tissues were damaged or even because they contained foreign matter; instead the health of a wound seemed to vary inversely with the quantity of *Microsporon septicum* it contained. He also reported that body fluids that had been filtered to remove the organisms did not cause fatal diseases in rabbits whereas unfiltered fluids produced local festering and death. Klebs obviously believed that specific organisms had unique causal roles in anthrax and in wound infections; the organisms were not simply one possible remote cause among many.

Klebs' work in Karlsruhe culminated in a book entitled *Contributions to the Pathological Anatomy of Gunshot Wounds* (Klebs, 1872), a work frequently cited by later researchers. Koch praised it as 'the first attempt to demonstrate a causal connection between bacteria and infected wound diseases' (Koch, 1878a, p. 22). In *Contributions* Klebs first stated explicit criteria for disease causality. He observed that 'tracing the invasion and the course of microorganisms can make causality probable, but the crucial experiment is isolating the efficient cause and allowing it to operate on the organism' (Klebs, 1872, p. 105). We can state these conditions as follows:

E1.   The presence of the organism correlates with disease phenomena.
E2.   Inoculation of isolated organisms is followed by the disease.

It is unclear exactly how E1 is to be understood. Klebs could have meant, starting with disease phenomena, always find organisms to be present (which was Pasteur's approach and would suggest the organisms are necessary), or, starting with advancing organisms, show that disease phenomena always follow (which would suggest sufficiency); most likely actual practice would have involved a combination of the two. In any case, E2, which Klebs regarded as more conclusive, clearly provides evidence of sufficiency. Bassi, Semmelweis, Davaine, and Pasteur all reported what happened when healthy hosts were exposed to purported causes, but they all seem to have been most persuaded by evidence of necessity. Perhaps Klebs' different preference reflected his background as an experimental pathologist – as we saw in Chapter 1, the general orientation of pathology favored thinking in terms of sufficient causes.

In 1872 Klebs moved to Würzburg and shortly thereafter gave a lecture on micrococci as causes of disease (Klebs, 1874b). Klebs noted that examination of blood samples revealed that micrococci, while normally absent from healthy tissues, were present in all cases of certain diseases. He observed that the next task was proving these bodies were alien parasites. Klebs described a new method for isolating and culturing microorganisms, a method that reduced the possibility of accidental contamination; he called his new technique fractional cultivation (Klebs, 1874b, p. vi). Body fluids from diseased animals were filtered and the residue washed in distilled water. Organisms from the residue were then purified by passing them through a series of cultures each of which was seeded with a minute sample from the preceding culture. By passing the organisms through numerous subcultures, Klebs sought to remove every possible disease product except the living organisms that multiplied in each successive medium. Davaine had used similar methods to study anthrax, but Klebs carried the approach to new levels of technical sophistication. He reported that inoculations after fractional cultivation still produced new artificial cases of certain diseases. He concluded 'that specific disease processes were due to various specific organisms' (Klebs,

1874b, p. vii). Klebs' process of fractional cultivation received favorable attention from Koch and others.

In 1874 Klebs was appointed a professor of pathology at the University of Prague. In Prague he was a founding editor of another journal, and he published a series of essays on microorganisms as disease agents. His first essay reviewed some of the reasons for associating microorganisms with specific diseases. He wrote that, if a disease could be induced by exposing an animal to fully isolated microscopic bodies, 'their significance as causes of disease could no longer be doubted' (Klebs, 1873, p. 33). Thus, satisfaction of E2 is conclusive. He discussed examples of research that approached this ideal including Davaine's work on anthrax.

In 1875 Klebs wrote that if one can show 'inflammation and other reactive changes follow, step by step, the spread of the schizomycetes, it is logical to infer a causal relation rather than a simple coincidence' (Klebs, 1875–76, p. 321).[3] The criterion Klebs here identified for proving the schizomycetes are pathological is E1, but as here described it seems clearly to support sufficiency, not necessity. Klebs noted that experimental evidence could yield the same conclusion. To obtain such evidence, he wrote, one must 'isolate substances from the body and use them to induce further cases of infection' (Klebs, 1875–76, 321). Klebs reported following both approaches and obtaining mutually supporting results. In the conclusion of the paper, Klebs observed that the goal now was to identify more external causes and to characterize them precisely just as, in Virchow's cellular pathology, one characterized cellular morbid changes (Klebs 1875–76, p. 324).

On 20 September 1877, Klebs delivered a controversial address to the Society for German Natural Scientists and Physicians entitled 'On the Revolution in Medical Opinions in the Last Three Decades' (Klebs, 1878a). Klebs observed that pathology had contributed almost nothing to practical medicine, and that recent advances resulted from associating particular diseases with specific remote causes. He identified three areas of research as relevant to demonstrating disease causation: the study of diseased organs, the isolation and cultivation of germs, and the generation of new cases of disease by exposing healthy animals to germs (Klebs, 1878a, p. 49). Near the end of his lecture, he described, in more detail than usual, two criteria for establishing the causal significance of germs: '(i) If organisms are identified that are well characterized and that are found exclusively in the given disease process, anatomical evidence can be conclusive. (ii) If the form of the organisms provides no certain point of departure, it can be decisive to convey the disease by means of organisms that have been isolated and cultivated outside the body' (Klebs, 1878a, p. 51). These criteria correspond to E1 and E2 respectively. Klebs' remarks suggest that correlating disease phenomena with advancing organisms can prove causation, but only for organisms that are conclusively identifiable and found exclusively in the given disease. Thus, as here stated, the first way, E1, requires the satisfaction of three conditions: (1) the organisms must be distinguishable from other organisms; (2) given the parasitic organism, one always observes the disease process; and (3) the presence of the organism must correlate with disease phenomena. Supposedly, the second method, E2, can work even if the organisms in question are not conclusively distinguishable from organisms associated with other diseases. Klebs' lecture was reported in medical periodicals (for example, *Berliner klinische Wochenschrift*, 1877), and was widely known in German medical circles. As we will see later (pp. 141–2), it may have been the immediate source for the first version of what we now know as Koch's Postulates (Carter, 1985b).

In 1878, Klebs responded to Louis Pasteur's claim to have been the first to have established conclusively the cause of anthrax (Klebs, 1878c). Klebs discussed 'the beautiful work of Davaine' that made it 'extremely probable that anthrax is caused by bacteridia'. He noted that 'the conclusive proof of this opinion is provided by the ineffectiveness of anthrax fluids that have been deprived of bacteridia', in other words, proof that inoculation of liquids not containing the organisms is not followed by the disease. Satisfaction of this test provides evidence the organism is necessary (but not that it is sufficient) for the disease. This passage is the closest Klebs ever came to stating that evidence of necessity was relevant to proving causation, and here he suggested that such evidence was conclusive. However, surrounded as it was by repeated appeals to evidence of sufficiency, this passage should probably be discounted as anomalous. According to Klebs, in showing that fluids deprived of bacteridia have no effect, Pasteur had merely repeated the experiments that he and Tiegel had reported in their 1871 anthrax paper.

In a long paper published in 1879, Klebs argued that a specific bacillus may cause malaria. He wrote that 'to convert this hypothesis into a scientific theory one must decide, first, whether the bacillus occurs in malarial soils or in the surrounding air, and second, whether this organism itself, without the support of any other disease causing agent, can cause true intermittent fever' (Klebs and Tommasi-Crudeli, 1879a, p. 326). In a summary of the paper, Klebs explained that the second of these steps consisted of propagating bacilli through fractional cultivation and then inoculating both filtered liquids and the cultivated organisms to determine the effect of each (Klebs and Tommasi-Crudeli, 1879b). Thus, once again, the crucial test is E2 – isolation and inoculation.

In an 1881 paper on abdominal typhoid fever, Klebs observed that 'in every carefully examined case, one and the same form of schizomycete has been identified in the fresh and intensively developed changes' (Klebs, 1880, pp. 232f.); here Klebs is invoking E1. Later in the same year, in another paper on typhoid, he observed that 'obtaining the same results in repeated attempts gave us a certain confidence that the result was not merely accidental. ... In the meantime I have provided experimental proof the organism is the carrier or the cause of typhoid poison. I now regard the question of the cause of typhoid fever as closed (Klebs, 1881, p. 381). The experimental proof Klebs provided was isolating and inoculating the organism.

Between 1872 and the early 1880s, Klebs consistently invoked one or both of E1 and E2: these two approaches to causality require, respectively, establishing that the advance of certain clearly identifiable organisms corresponds to disease phenomena, and isolating and inoculating a possible causal agent. Many of Klebs' contemporaries deliberately patterned their experiments on these causal criteria. In 1877 Felix Victor Birch-Hirschfeld discussed these strategies in his widely used pathology textbook. He observed that Klebs and others tried to explain the pathological significance of microorganisms by correlating advancing parasites with the sequence of morbid changes (Birch-Hirschfeld, 1877, p. 233). According to Birch-Hirschfeld, recognition that this was inconclusive led to experiments in which 'bacteria were isolated in various ways from the liquid constituents of infectious substances. One then compared the results of inoculating isolated bacteria and the other liquid materials' (Birch-Hirschfeld, 1877, p. 234). Birch-Hirschfeld called Klebs' use of these approaches 'epoch making' (Birch-Hirschfeld, 1872, p. 98). Other early bacteriologists who deliberately adopted Klebs' methods included Friedrich Steudener (Steudener, 1872, p. 300), Leopold Landau (Landau, 1874, p. 529), and Max Schüller (Schüller, 1876, p. 160).

A bacterial theory of disease

In 1875 and 1876 Klebs wrote a series of papers summarizing his research on the pathological schizomycetes. The last of these papers contains at least part of an explicit theory of disease.[4] As when Henle approached similar fundamental questions, Klebs drew on an analogy with 'the exact sciences'. According to Klebs, these sciences (and, by following their example, pathology and physiology) make progress 'by simplifying conditions before one puts questions to nature' (Klebs, 1875–76, p. 376). The answers one obtains through such simplifications,

Klebs continued, are valid even if later experiments, conducted under more realistic conditions, yield unexpected results. Klebs' idea is that in studying etiology one must adopt similar simplifications. Here is an example of what he may have meant. Scientific theories typically involve basic assumptions from which explanations can be derived; for example, in a kinetic theory of gases one makes assumptions such as the following:

> (1) A pure gas consists of a large number of identical molecules separated by distances that are great compared with their size. (2) The gas molecules are constantly moving in random directions with a distribution of speeds. (3) The molecules exert no forces on one another between collisions, so between collisions they move in straight lines with constant velocities. (4) The collisions of molecules with the walls of the container are elastic; no energy is lost during a collision.
>
> (Oxtoby and Nachtrieb, 1990, p. 104)

Some or all of the assumptions associated with a particular theory may be literally false. For example, molecules are not identical; and, like all physical bodies, they exert gravitational forces on one another so they do not move in straight lines or with constant velocities. However, such false assumptions are justified because, by simplifying calculations, they enable us to predict (within ordinary requirements for accuracy) what will happen in the physical world. Without such assumptions, if one sought to take account of the actual shape of each molecule, of gravitation and other forces, and of all other distorting influences, the calculations necessary even for relatively simple problems would be impossibly complex. This may be what Klebs meant in writing that in the exact sciences one simplifies conditions before putting questions to nature. Klebs also wrote that the answers obtained in this way are still valid even if later experiments, conducted in the complex conditions of the physical world, yield unexpected results. Suppose, by using the simplified properties of an ideal gas, one calculates what will happen if one heats a sealed container. Perhaps Klebs meant there is a sense in which this prediction is still valid even if it turns out to be incorrect (perhaps the container explodes or dissipates heat more quickly than one expected).

What does this mean for etiology? Klebs identifies four *Grundversuche*.[5] On a superficial reading the *Grundversuche* may appear to be yet more causal criteria (Carter, 1987b), but this is surely incorrect. In this context Klebs does not mention E1 or E2, the criteria that consistently appear in his other papers, both before and after this one, and in none of the papers in which he uses and discusses causal criteria does he mention the *Grundversuche*. Moreover, in this context his interest is different. He is not arguing that some particular organism causes some disease (an argument that would require E1 or E2); instead, he is addressing the fundamental and more general issue of establishing a context within which *any* causal demonstration can be given. He is asking: what are the basic conditions on which any such demonstration depends? Rephrasing the question in terms of his analogy with the exact sciences, Klebs is asking: what conditions must be met in order successfully to ask nature (by applying E1 or E2) whether a particular schizomycete causes a certain disease? Read in this way, the *Grundversuche* are ideal or simplifying conditions basic to any investigation of disease causation.

Klebs writes:

> In respect to the pathological influence of the schizomycetes, as such fundamental tests [*Grundversuche*], I give heed to the following: first, the proof that they never occur in the body fluids or in some part of the secretions of a healthy organism; second, that they do not develop spontaneously in liquids appropriate to their nourishment ... third, the fact that with the mechanical separation or the natural death of the schizomycetes, the potency of the liquids that contained them ceases; and fourth, the fact that local or general infections of the [different] individual forms of pathogenic schizomycetes, which have now been at least partially characterized, bring forth changes that are precisely characterized, uniformly similar, and adequately distinguishable from [those associated with] the operation of schizomycetes of other forms.
>
> (Klebs, 1875–76, pp. 376f.)

As an idealized basis for a theory of disease, the *Grundversuche* tell us schizomycetes have these properties: first, they are absent from the body fluids and secretions of healthy animals; second, they never arise spontaneously, not even in fluids that satisfy their nutritional needs; third, once removed (artificially or otherwise) from some liquid, the liquid alone has no pathogenic effect; and fourth, distinct schizomycetes cause different pathological processes. In this passage, Klebs speaks of the third and fourth *Grundversuche* as 'facts' and of the first as 'a proof'. However, the second resembles what we have called the Dissemination Hypothesis (p. 66 above), and as Pasteur realized, this hypothesis can be neither proved nor disproved. While such principles can be illustrated and made plausible, strictly speaking they cannot be proven and they are not facts in the ordinary sense of the word. It seems most plausible to refer to all four as hypotheses, and this is consistent with Klebs' idea that the *Grundversuche* are simplifying conditions under which one can 'put questions to nature'.

Four hypotheses emerge from the *Grundversuche* that are of particular interest. In stating these, we use the more common term 'bacterium' in place of Klebs' term 'schizomycete'.

1. The first *Grundversuch* assures us that *healthy animals are free from all bacteria*. This hypothesis is basic to the use of test animals in inoculation experiments because it insures that any organisms found in a test animal, after inoculation, are the result of the inoculation. We will see in Chapter 7 that Pasteur gave explicit attention to this hypothesis.

2. The second *Grundversuch* insures that *bacteria never arise spontaneously*. This differs from the Dissemination Hypothesis only in being restricted to bacteria (or schizomycetes) rather than being about all microorganisms.

3. The third *Grundversuch* stipulates that any liquid that is free from bacteria has no harmful effect; in other words, pathologicality is always due only to bacteria. Thus, in general, *every pathological process is caused by bacteria*. In discussing Davaine's research, we called this the Bacterial Hypothesis.

4. The fourth *Grundversuch* tells us that distinct bacteria cause different pathologies. As stated, this hypothesis is inessential: many distinct organisms can cause the same pathological processes (as for example the common cold). However, the converse of this hypothesis (which Klebs, an unclear and sometimes imprecise writer, could have had in mind) is more important; it tells us that *different pathological processes are caused by distinct bacteria*. By virtue of being limited to bacteria (or schizomycetes) this is a special case of the more general Distinguishability Hypothesis that we encountered in Pasteur.

A few explanatory observations are necessary: First, the *Grundversuche* or the hypotheses we have derived from them, are clearly laws in the sense discussed by Wim J. Van der Steen and Harmke Kammingaa (Van der Steen and Kamminga, 1991) and, given their definition of 'theory' as a set of interconnected laws, the *Grundversuche* clearly constitute a theory – so far as I know, the first, and perhaps the only, explicit theory of disease in the history of medicine.

Second, a complete theory may require additional assumptions, and these four may require modification; they are intended only as a first approximation to illustrate how a bacterial theory of disease looks and works.

Third, the Bacterial Hypothesis refers to the *cause* of pathological processes. For use as a technical term within the theory, one can define the word 'cause' as anything within the domain specified by the Bacterial Hypothesis (that is, any bacterium) that satisfies acceptable criteria (perhaps E1 and E2) and explains disease phenomena. Given this definition, if some bacterium (say Davaine's bacteridium) satisfies the causal criteria in respect to a pathological process and explains the disease phenomena, then, by this definition, it is the cause of that process. Thus, we see how this *theoretical* assumption warrants inferences from *empirical* evidence to causal claims.

Fourth, these hypotheses do not exclude the possibility that more than one bacterium will satisfy the causal criteria with respect to the same pathological process and, therefore, qualify as its cause. In other words, these hypotheses do not insure that causes are universal and necessary. Universal necessity is achieved by defining each disease in terms of its cause. Having first established that some bacterium causes a given pathological process (in the sense of 'cause' just defined), one characterizes a particular disease as infestation by that bacterium. This definition comes *after* one has identified a *sufficient* cause for at least some cases of the process. By such a definition, one insures that the cause of each disease, as so defined, is universal and necessary even if two or more etiologically defined diseases are symptomatically indistinguishable. For example, different instances of the common cold may be symptomatically indistinguishable, but, once defined in terms of distinguishable organisms, they count as different diseases. Then since, by definition, every case of each disease has the same one cause, disease phenomena can be consistently explained in terms of that cause and one can seek means for controlling the disease by manipulating the cause.

Fifth (and finally), the phrase 'pathological process' in the last two hypotheses can mean either internal organic lesions or collections of signs and symptoms. However, once a disease is defined etiologically – say as infection by a certain bacterium – strictly speaking, the phrase 'pathological process' cannot be understood in the sense of a bacterial infection. Otherwise, we end up saying that bacterial infections cause bacterial infections; but nothing can cause itself. This means (again, strictly speaking) that we cannot both define a disease in terms of a causal factor and continue to hold that the disease is caused by that factor. However, both in technical medical treatises and in everyday conversation, we ignore this problem and slip between 'disease' in the sense of 'a collection of symptoms' and disease in the sense of 'infection by a particular organism'. For example, a medical text might define 'leprosy' as infection by *Mycobacterium leprae* and yet identify *Mycobacterium leprae* as the cause of leprosy (and sometimes even add that a certain percentage of cases are clinically inapparent).[6] However, this ambiguity is useful and there is no point in trying to avoid it.

We have already discussed the Dissemination and Distinguishability Hypotheses in connection with Pasteur's early studies. No further comments are required for the Dissemination Hypothesis. We will now consider the Bacterial Hypothesis and then return briefly to the Distinguishability Hypothesis.

The Bacterial Hypothesis tells us that each disease is caused by some bacterium; as it stands, understood as a claim about the world, this is obviously false. As we saw in discussing Davaine's research, the purpose of the Bacterial Hypothesis is to limit the field in which causes are to be sought. The need for such limitations is clear from nineteenth-century etiological discussions. At about the same time that Klebs wrote the *Grundversuche*, another prominent researcher, Julius Cohnheim, observed that existing etiology is 'an unbounded domain' including 'cosmic physics, meteorology and geology no less than the social sciences and chemistry as well as botany and zoology'. He observed that etiological discussions in common texts include everything 'from temperament to beds, from air electricity to fungi and fleas, from inheritance to drinks' (Cohnheim, 1877a, vol. 1, pp. 8f.). Only the imposition of limitations, such as those insured by the Bacterial Hypothesis, could produce order in this chaos. However, one might object that the Bacterial Hypothesis is *too* limiting – there are certainly causes of disease besides bacteria, and some (for example, acari, trichinae, and various poisons) were known before Klebs wrote the *Grundversuche*. Robert Koch criticized unnamed contemporaries for assuming that all diseases were bacterial (Koch, 1881a, p. 119), and it is imaginable that Koch had Klebs in mind. On the other hand, as Klebs himself made clear, the *Grundversuche* are only a simplification or an idealization and, as this suggests, he may not have regarded them as literally true.

Ultimately, it matters little what Klebs himself believed. A more serious question is: what is the value of adopting an assumption that is factually false? In line with Lakatos's account of research programmes, all four Hypotheses should probably be regarded, not as factual claims, but as strategic directives or rules of method. Taken in this sense, the Bacterial Hypothesis tells us: when confronted by some new and unexplained disease, assume it is caused by a bacterium. If understood in this way and if addressed to researchers who have techniques for studying bacteria but who are unprepared to study anything else (as would have been true of Klebs' intended readers), this directive not only makes good sense, it is absolutely indispensable. And this is true even if one knows in advance that, as a claim about the world, the Hypothesis is literally false – that is, even if one knows some diseases are non-bacterial. To act otherwise would be to begin by refusing contemporary researchers access to the only tools they were prepared to use. Rational inquiry must begin with the expectation that new problems can be solved by existing methods – that the unknown is homogeneous with the known. Only when this expectation is defeated is it rational to abandon proven methods and look for a new approach. From this point of view, understood as an idealized strategic rule, the Bacterial Hypothesis is entirely reasonable.

Now we return to the Distinguishability Hypothesis. Davaine, Koch, and Pasteur were all forced to rebut the idea that all bacteria were ultimately of one species – that, given suitable conditions, any bacterium could assume the characteristics of any other. Suppose this were true; what would it mean for a germ theory of disease? We have already seen (in Chapter 3) that organisms must be distinct if they are to explain different organic processes, but in the context of theories of disease it is worth sharpening that claim by considering two ways in which organisms could fail to be distinct in the sense required. First, even if bacteria were indistinguishable, it could happen that animals exposed to doses of bacteria usually contract some disease or other. Given such experiences, one might conclude that bacteria are a general health hazard (like malnutrition or smoking) and that one should minimize exposure to them as far as possible. However, it would clearly be impossible to regard bacteria as causes that could, themselves, explain different particular disease phenomena. Second, suppose bacteria were *only* distinguishable in respect to their pathogenic effect. It could then happen that animals exposed to bacteria from a particular culture regularly contract one disease while animals exposed to different (but physically indistinguishable) cultures regularly contract other diseases. This one difference among bacteria (their pathogenic effect) could not *explain* the differences in the diseases they provoke because these differences would be one and the same, and nothing can explain itself. Thus, if bacteria are to explain diseases and their differences – that is, to be their causes – then one must assume that differences in diseases can be explained by differences in the bacteria that cause them. Bacteria can qualify as causes of different diseases only if the bacteria themselves are distinct.

Here is a possible counter-example to the Distinguishability Hypothesis: it is currently impossible to distinguish directly between the spirochetes that cause syphilis, yaws, pinta, and endemic syphilis.

> The pathogenic treponemas cannot be distinguished by morphology, biochemical capabilities, physiologic criteria, or DNA homology. Specific antigenic differences have not yet been identified, and serologic reactions positive for one disease are also positive for the other three. Differentiation of the treponematoses is based on geographical location, modes of transmission, and clinical manifestations.
>
> (Fitzgerald, 1991, p. 496)

Since the diseases are distinguishable, and since the causal bacteria must somehow explain these differences, one must *assume* that the organisms themselves are also different, and they are given different names. It is reasonable to assume that they are distinct because other distinguishable bacterial diseases are known to be caused by organisms that are distinguishable in one way or another. Thus, one assumes there are relevant (although unknown) differences between the causal organisms of these four diseases and that one's inability to distinguish between them is only a temporary and technical inconvenience. As this example shows, 'distinguishability' in the phrase 'Distinguishability Hypothesis' means distinguishable *in principle* not necessarily in fact. If one believed the four causal organisms were really identical, one would probably be forced to regard syphilis, yaws, pinta, and endemic syphilis as different manifestations of the same underlying disease – just as we regard systematic anthrax and malignant pustule (or what were once called scrofula and phthisis) as different manifestations of the same disease.

Thus we see that systematic explanations of disease phenomena depend on accepting the Distinguishability Hypothesis. There is another way of making this point. The purposes of any scientific theory are explanation and control. In a theory of disease, achieving either purpose requires universal necessary causes, and such causes depend on etiological characterizations. But etiological characterizations are possible only if the causes in terms of which different diseases are defined are themselves distinct. Thus, the formulation of etiological definitions (and hence the adequacy of any theory of disease) requires distinguishability.

In logical terms, the Bacterial and Distinguishability Hypotheses insure that 'the cause of disease X' is a partial function whose domain is species of bacteria and whose range is all diseases; given the first *Grundversuch*, which implies that all bacteria are pathogenic, the function would be total and one to one.

Through the last five chapters we have traced the beginnings of an etiological research programme based on the quest for universal and necessary causes. We are now in a position to appreciate this development from a slightly different point of view. As we saw in Chapter 1, early nineteenth-century physicians distinguished between remote and proximate causes. So far, our entire discussion has involved only what would *then* have been thought of *remote* causes. As they each became prominent, acari, *Beauvaria bassiana*, and decaying organic matter were all thought of as remote causes, and bacteria would have been classified in the same way.[7] Given this continuity in *content*, it is natural to think that, insofar as any aspect of the earlier doctrine of causes has survived, it was remote causes. In fact, this is false.

Early in the nineteenth century, *proximate* causes were typically defined as original and internal morbid alterations from which the symptoms of each disease were thought to follow (Watson, 1858, p. 76). All talk of remote causes, now regarded as a vestige of earlier medical thinking, was rejected by contemporaries as 'scholastic and repulsive'. One problem was that such language implied that the disease itself (the essence of the disease: the morbid alteration) was its own (proximate) cause. And this made no sense since nothing can cause itself (Watson, 1858, p. 76). However, the increased explanatory power of pathological anatomy was due precisely to the use of morbid alterations – proximate causes – to explain the sequence of symptoms associated with each disease. This was possible because, given pathological definitions, every case of any one disease had the same one cause. And everyone recognized that such explanations raised medical theory to a new level of sophistication.

The introduction of etiological definitions simply made what had been specific *remote* causes into new *proximate* causes: whenever possible the essence of each disease became infection by a certain organism (say, tubercle bacilli) instead of a morbid alteration (for example, the formation of tubers). And the new proximate causes achieved *in spades* the same benefits as the old ones. Instead of merely explaining symptoms in terms of lesions (as the pathologists had done), researchers were now able to explain the lesions themselves (and thereby symptoms and everything else lesions could ever explain) as well as many clinical and epidemiological facts that the pathologists could never begin to account for. This is exactly what we saw in contrasting Semmelweis's account of childbed fever with the pathologically based accounts of Dubois, Holmes, and Lumpe. The new proximate causes also provided much more effective targets for therapy and prophylaxis than did internal lesions.

However, thinking of bacterial infections as proximate causes, brings into prominence certain similarities between earlier causal thinking and our own – similarities one might otherwise overlook. First, the 'scholastic and repulsive' problem of identifying the essence of a disease with its own cause has not gone away: it now shows up in the tendency (noted on p. 103), to define diseases as bacterial infections while continuing to speak of the bacteria themselves as causing those diseases. Second, the old proximate causes were universal and necessary in exactly the same way as the new ones, and their universality and necessity were achieved in exactly the same way as in the case of the new ones – namely, by redefining diseases in terms of causes. At the beginning of the nineteenth century, whenever possible, diseases (which had earlier been construed as collections of symptoms) were redefined in terms of specific lesions; with the rise of the etiological standpoint, whenever possible, diseases (then construed as lesions) were redefined in terms of bacterial infections. In both cases, the new definitions created proximate causes that were universal and necessary.

We no longer use the term 'proximate' and we are now interested, almost exclusively, in universal and necessary causes rather than in explaining the onset of particular instances of disease (which was the whole point of nineteenth-century talk about remote causes). This makes it easy to overlook the fact that, in respect to how causes function in the logic of disease explanations, the one aspect of earlier etiology that has vanished is actually remote causes and not proximate causes. Misled by the superficial similarity in *content* between earlier remote causes and the causes we now identify, and oblivious of how remote causes actually functioned in earlier medical thought, historians get this exactly backwards. For example, Christopher Hamlin portrays what he sees as Thomas Watson's increased emphasis on 'single exciting [remote] causes' as a kind of transition to 'the kinds of specific agents that we think of as causes' today (Hamlin, 1992, pp. 51f.). But there was no transition – there could be none: one either accepted new etiological definitions or one did not.[8] As with any true revolution in science, the change is all or nothing.

In spite of obvious shortcomings, the *Grundversuche* were (and still remain) elegant, powerful, and amazingly bold. Bassi, Mayrhofer, Davaine, Obermeier, and others argued that all cases of a few particular diseases were caused by specific microorganisms; Bassi and Henle speculated that several other diseases may also be caused by germs. So far as one can tell from the literature, they all regarded such diseases as *exceptional*. No one made claims about *all* diseases. And even their relatively guarded claims about particular diseases were strenuously opposed by contemporary physicians. Few researchers would have seriously entertained, even as a working hypothesis, the idea that *every* disease was caused by a bacterium.

With the *Grundversuche*, Klebs adopted as a new norm what everyone else regarded as exceptions (a few diseases believed to be caused only by specific bacteria); and what had been the recognized norm (diseases believed to be attributable to almost any chance trauma) thereby became new anomalies. The implicit challenge to contemporary bacteriologists was to assimilate these new anomalies (the old norm) to the new norm (the old anomalies). It was as though Klebs had seized on wound infections, anthrax, and relapsing fever, and by pulling on them, turned the entire world inside out.

Notes

1. Klebs' papers appeared in volumes 16, 32, 33, 34, and 38 of *Archiv für pathologische Anatomie, Physiologie, und klinische Medizine (Virchows Archiv)*.

2. For example, in an 1861 discussion of puerperal fever, Virchow insisted that 'just as a man who is overheated will contract facial erysipelas if he exposes his face to a draft, so too the puerpera, overheated by the process of delivery, can become ill if her uterus is chilled' (*Monatsschrif für Geburtskunde* ... , 1861, p. 380).

3. The term 'schizomycete' was coined by the Swiss microscopist Carl Naegeli, as a generic term including both bacteria and fungi. Ferdinand Cohn objected to the term as implying a false connection between bacteria and fungi (Cohn, 1872, p. 191; 1875, p. 201), but Klebs seems to have liked the term and used it regularly.

4. For an enlightening discussion of the nature and possibility of theories and laws in the biological sciences see Van der Steen and Kamminga (1991).

5. The roots of this compound plural noun are *Grund* (ground, basis or foundation) and *Versuch* (test, trial or attempt); literally, the word means something like 'basic tests'. However, the combination itself is uncommon, perhaps unique to this context, and Klebs does not explain what he means.

6. For another example, in discussing phenylketonuria (PKU), F. Kräupl Taylor writes: 'From such ambiguity, there is only a small step to apparent self-contradiction. The parents of PKU patients, being heterozygous for the pathological gene, can have PKU (the clinical sign) after a meal rich in phenylalanine, though they do not have PKU (the [disease] or the morbus). Similarly, a PKU patient, when on a diet poor in phenylalanine from his earliest days, still has PKU (the morbus) without PKU (the illness or the clinical sign) (Taylor, 1979, p. 84).

7. For example, as early as 1855 Semmelweis's bitterest enemy, Carl Braun, speculated about the possible causal role of Henle's 'botanical parasites' in childbed fever – he even mentioned *Beauvaria bassiana* (then called *Botrytis bassiana*) in muscardine as a possible analogy. Braun classified 'botanical parasites' among 30 kinds of possible remote causes of the disease (Braun, 1855, pp. 477–85).

8. In the same way, glass is either a solid or it is a viscus liquid – there is nothing in between, and there can be no possibility of gradually moving from one definition to the other. See p. 53 above.

CHAPTER SEVEN

Proving Disease Causation

Causes are made universal and necessary by adopting suitable disease characterizations. However, in discussing Klebs' *Grundversuche*, we noted that such characterizations require the prior identification of sufficient causes – one can only define diseases in terms of causes after causes have been found. But identifying causes requires a shared theory including (among other things):

a. a hypothesis – such as the Bacterial Hypothesis – specifying a domain of entities that can count as causes (Davaine's inability to convince opponents was due, in part, to the absence of such a hypothesis),

b. other assumptions as may be needed to insure that these entities can explain the diseases in question (disputes such as those between Davaine and Laplat-and-Jaillard, and between Bassi and Andouin were due to the absence of these hypotheses), and

c. criteria whose satisfaction establishes that some particular entity from the domain of possible causes generates the morbidity in question. Of course Klebs gave considerable attention to identifying such criteria.

Thus definitions to establish universal necessary causes, and the control and explanatory power that stem from such definitions, require shared acceptance of a theory of disease with at least these elements.

As we have seen, Pasteur started out inferring causality from the mere fact that distinguishable and non-spontaneous bacteria were found in different organic processes. However, in the mid-1870s, when he used similar reasoning to identify causes of infectious diseases, his contemporaries were unconvinced, and he was forced to broaden the evidence he provided. As we will see in the first part of this chapter, Pasteur came to rely most heavily on evidence of sufficiency of the sort required by Klebs' criteria. Then, over the next few years, Pasteur became involved in a bitter dispute with Robert Koch. Each claimed to have been the first to complete Davaine's proof that bacteridia cause anthrax. The second part of this chapter concerns this dispute. We will see that Pasteur and other contemporaries criticized Koch's arguments for the same reasons that Pasteur's own arguments had initially seemed inadequate. Koch sought to correct this deficiency by using causal criteria (his so-called Postulates) that seem to have been based directly on Klebs' E1 and E2. In this way, Pasteur and Koch ended up using essentially the same criteria for establishing causation. Finally, in the third part of this chapter, we will consider developments that, in the early 1880s, led to general acceptance of the bacterial theory (including, of course, the causal criteria that Koch and Pasteur were, by then, sharing). As explained in the preceding paragraph, general acceptance of the bacterial theory cleared the way for the systematic characterization of diseases in terms of bacteria and for the understanding and control of bacterial diseases that we associate with modern medicine.

Pasteur's changing arguments for causation

By 1859 Pasteur had become interested in infectious diseases, and he believed that many such diseases were caused by microorganisms (Pasteur, 1859b, p. 481). Through the 1860s he occasionally discussed issues relating to human infectious diseases: In 1865, at about the time he began studying silkworms, Pasteur reported and commented on the anthrax research conducted by Leplat and Jaillard (Pasteur, 1865c)[1]; and three years later he discussed the nature of vaccine (Pasteur, 1868c). However, Pasteur did not begin a systematic study of human infectious diseases until the early 1870s. The delay was partly because his attention had been focused on other projects, but Pasteur himself explained that he had been reluctant to study human diseases since he had never been trained in medicine (Pasteur, 1878a, p. 197; Geison, 1974, pp. 384f.).

When Pasteur did turn to human diseases, his work was based on the same principles that had guided his earlier research.[2] And, as one would expect, his approach to disease causation was similar to that exemplified in his earlier work. In the 1870s, Pasteur seems to have assumed that each infectious disease – like each disorder of wine or each disease of silkworms – would have a distinct cause present in every case of the disease. By contrast, contemporary French physicians continued to think in terms of sufficient causes that could vary from case to case. As Pasteur began lecturing on human infectious diseases, he did not demonstrate that the causes he identified were sufficient and he assumed that they were universal; in both respects he failed to meet contemporary expectations.

In March 1873 Pasteur was elected to the French Academy of Medicine. In the following month, in his first published comments before that body, Pasteur actively defended some of his causal claims. He discussed the spoilage of beer – a topic to which he was then giving attention – and ascribed the commonest form of beer spoilage 'to the presence of a microscopic filiform organism':

> This fact is so true, the relation of cause and effect is so evident, that it is absolutely impossible to produce an alteration of beer when it does not contain the germs of this inferior organism. On the other hand, I can demonstrate that no beer, whether from England, France, or Germany, can be conserved beyond a certain time; beer always becomes altered because it contains the germs of the organized ferments of which I speak. The correlation between the disease and the presence of the organism is certain and indisputable.
>
> (Pasteur, 1873b, p. 5)

Members of the Academy objected to Pasteur's claim that fermentation could only occur because of a living ferment. Pasteur responded sarcastically that only physicians could take seriously the possibility of putrefaction without a putrefying agent, he demanded proof that such a phenomenon had ever been observed, and he immediately associated spoilage without organic agents with spontaneous generation (Pasteur, 1874b, pp. 6–7; 1874a). He responded to critics by reviewing his arguments for the Dissemination Hypothesis; however, this response was not quite to the point. One could maintain, as his critics apparently did, that spoilage could result from a suitable combination of inert factors *without* regarding those factors as sufficient to generate living organisms. For some time Pasteur and his critics argued at cross purposes: Pasteur recounting his contributions to science and denouncing spontaneous generation; his opponents insisting that putrefaction could occur without living organisms (Pasteur, 1922–39, vol. 6, pp. 90–99, 20–26, 26–8, 28–37, 37–58 and vol. 5, pp. 344f.). The debate ceased in 1879 when other members of the Academy finally pointed out that most physicians had given up spontaneous generation even before Pasteur's experiments, and that he could not answer his critics by this evasion (Pasteur, 1879b, pp. 235–7). In these discussions Pasteur effectively assumed that the cause of spoilage must be universal; his opponents did not share this assumption.

In 1874 and 1875, Pasteur gave more lectures on putrefaction, and he began reporting studies on ammoniacal urine. He continued making assertions exactly in line with his earlier research and he continued to encounter opposition. Pasteur's opponents rejected his claim that an organism was 'the *sine qua non* of ammoniacal urine' (Pasteur, 1875b, p. 78) and insisted the disorder could occur without a living ferment.

Perhaps because of these discussions, in the second chapter of his 1876 book on the spoilage of beer, Pasteur gave increased attention to establishing causality. Pasteur insisted that 'all the alterations to which wort and beer are subject have as their exclusive cause the development of organized ferments whose germs are carried by dust' (Pasteur, 1876a, p. 21). Pasteur's argument for this claim fell into two parts, the first of which begins with the assertion that: 'all undesirable alterations of beer coincide with the development of microscopic organisms that are alien to yeast properly called' (Pasteur, 1876a, p. 22). Because the phrase 'coincide with' is vague, it is unclear exactly what Pasteur intended. He could have meant that whenever there are alterations there are organisms (organisms are necessary), or that whenever there are organisms there are alterations (organisms are sufficient), or both. His ensuing discussion does not clarify matters. Pasteur recounted having heated some bottles of beer while leaving others unheated. He found the unheated bottles spoiled while the heated ones did not. Moreover, the spoiled beer contained alien organisms.

The second part of the causal argument begins with the assertion that 'the absence of alterations in wort or beer coincides with the absence of the alien organisms' (Pasteur, 1876a, p. 26). This claim is ambiguous in exactly the same way as the earlier one, and again, the discussion does not remove the obscurity. In this section, Pasteur considered the possibility that germs were the effect rather than the cause of spoilage. He tried to dispose of this possibility by showing that, regardless of temperature, beer never spoiled when exposed to pure air, and he used experiments similar to those he had used against spontaneous generation. Pasteur summarized the chapter as follows:

> the absence of microscopic organisms alien to the yeast corresponds invariably to a beer that remains healthy indefinitely, even in contact with pure air; ... on the other hand, the presence of these organisms corresponds always to a disordered beer ... It would be difficult to go further in proving a correlation between the organisms and the alterations of beer ... No proof can more decisively establish a relation of cause and effect in the succession of physical phenomena.
>
> (Pasteur, 1876a, p. 31)

For all the ambiguity of the preceding arguments, two facts are clear: first, in comparison with his earlier studies on wine spoilage, Pasteur now recognized the need for explicit arguments and experiments to demonstrate causality; he no longer inferred causation simply from having regularly observed organisms in altered substances. Second, he was now using a concept of causation that included both necessity and sufficiency. While it may not be clear exactly how each of the halves of his argument is to be understood, several times Pasteur claims that beer becomes disordered *if and only if* it contains organisms. Thus, as a whole, Pasteur saw his argument as supporting the claim that organisms are both necessary and sufficient for spoilage.

In the summer of 1876 – just months after publication of his book on beer – Pasteur suddenly adopted a new strategy for demonstrating causality, one which dominated most of his subsequent writings on infectious diseases. This strategy first appeared in an essay on ammoniacal urine that began with the observation that outside the bladder, urine can only be converted into ammonia through the influence of organized ferments. 'It remains to be seen,' Pasteur continued, 'whether things are not similar in the bladder' (Pasteur, 1876b, p. 82). Pasteur then described the following strategy for proving causation:

> When one seeds the pure organized ferment in question in a nutritive liquid, ... the ferment multiplies. One filters and precipitates it with alcohol. The collected precipitate contains the soluble ferment ... ready to transform a solution of urine and water into carbonate of ammonia. The conditions of this experiment permit one to demonstrate that urine is not essential for production of the organized ferment, and that the ferment can form in a medium completely different from urine. ... It is difficult to go further in an experimental proof of the facts we have announced.
>
> (Pasteur, 1876b, pp. 85f.)

The method that Pasteur here outlined is a way of showing sufficiency: one isolates the ferment by growing it in an artificial medium and then introduces it into a new solution where it produces ammonia.

In the course in his early papers, Pasteur occasionally reported seeding experiments: he introduced dust containing organized corpuscles into culture media or into healthy silkworms. But these earlier experiments were different in two respects: they involved no attempt to insure that only pure strains were used and Pasteur did not use them to justify causal claims. Only when one wishes to establish that an organism itself causes a disease – that the organism is sufficient – must one isolate it from contaminating influences in a pure culture. Pasteur's 1876 paper on ammoniacal urine contains his first explicit description of isolation and inoculation, and his first clear use of these techniques to prove causal sufficiency. This contrasts sharply with his earlier seeding experiments and also with the confused and ambiguous causal arguments in his book on beer – a context in which such experiments would have been exactly appropriate.

A few months later, in 1878, in discussing diseases of silkworms, Pasteur observed that 'when *flacherie* occurs, one finds organisms in the digestive track of the immense majority of sick worms' (Pasteur, 1878b, p. 692).[3] This is evidence of necessity. Next Pasteur described the same experiment he had recently used in studying ammoniacal urine: 'Conversely when one makes leaves ferment in the intestinal canal by introducing germs or adult organisms, one induces *flacherie*.' Pasteur observed that 'two phenomena are in a relation of cause and effect if when one of the two exists the other follows. This is the case here; if the ferments are present in the intestinal canal, there is *flacherie*, and if there is *flacherie* there are ferments in the intestinal canal' (Pasteur, 1878b, p. 692). These remarks show clearly that Pasteur sought to establish necessity and sufficiency, that he understood the difference, and that he recognized his inoculation test as a means of demonstrating the latter. Pasteur's concept of causality and his account of how to prove necessity and sufficiency are more explicit here than in any of his earlier publications on *flacherie*.

The Pasteur–Koch dispute regarding anthrax

Through the late 1870s anthrax was studied extensively by several researchers including Louis Pasteur and Robert Koch. All of these studies were based on Davaine's research and, in turn, the work by Pasteur and Koch provided models for those seeking to trace other diseases to parasitic organisms. Koch claimed to have been the first to prove causality, and he is sometimes supposed to have done this in his 1876 anthrax paper using the criteria later known as Koch's Postulates (Susser, 1973, p. 23). However, Pasteur denied that Koch ever proved causality and claimed that he himself had been the first to do so in a paper published in 1877. These contradictory claims initiated an acrimonious dispute that quickly took on nationalistic overtones and was never clearly resolved (Geison, 1974, pp. 397–400; Dolman, 1974, p. 424; Mollaret, 1983). Only anthrax was a major research interest for both Koch and Pasteur and this was the only area of investigation in which they came into direct competition. Our interest in this dispute focuses on the arguments Koch and Pasteur used to show bacteridia caused anthrax.

The circumstances of the publication of Koch's 1876 anthrax paper have often been recounted (Brock, 1988, pp. 38–53); it is sufficient to note that Koch's research was carried out under primitive conditions and in virtual isolation from others who were studying the disease. Koch introduced and exploited technical innovations including the suspended-drop method for studying cultures. Using this method Koch was able to trace the complete life cycle of the bacteridium which he called *Bacillus anthracis*. He showed the bacillus formed spores that remained viable for long periods even in hostile environments. The discovery of spores removed some of the obstacles to recognizing bacilli as the cause of anthrax; in particular, it explained Davaine's observation that quickly dried anthrax blood could remain infectious for long periods.

Koch's conclusions were based almost exclusively on artificially induced anthrax in test animals. He claimed he had often examined animals that died of natural anthrax (Koch, 1876, p. 1), but of those examinations, he reported only that he found bacilli in the spleen of one anthrax horse – the only horse he had examined (Koch, 1876, p. 13). Koch cited earlier researchers who identified bacilli in natural cases, but he also mentioned that other researchers had been unable to find them. As Koch explained in the introduction to his paper, his study grew out of Davaine's research that was widely accepted as presenting the strongest evidence that anthrax was caused by bacteria. However, Koch did not have access to Davaine's papers (Koch, 1878a, p. 51); he knew Davaine's work only from abstracts in which Davaine's arguments were described as supporting the necessity of the anthrax organism (Steudener, 1872). In harmony with the abstracts, Koch noted that Davaine 'asserted that the rods were bacteria and that [anthrax] could occur only when these rods from anthrax blood were present' (Koch, 1876, p. 1). One objection to Davaine's view was that anthrax sometimes seemed to have been caused by inoculations with bacteridia-free blood. Koch answered this objection by arguing that the bacilli were often difficult to find and could easily be overlooked.

However, explaining away apparent counter evidence did not constitute a proof that the bacilli caused anthrax and, in spite of what Koch himself later claimed, his paper contained remarkably little direct evidence of causation. Moreover, the evidence it did contain was not persuasive to contemporaries. Koch's argument for causation appears toward the end of his paper. He observed that anthrax and septicemia bacilli were distinct because the latter never caused anthrax (Koch, 1876, p. 11) – an argument that presupposes the Distinguishability Hypothesis. He mentioned he had been unable to cause anthrax by injecting hay infusion bacilli or a species of bacillus resembling the anthrax bacillus that developed accidentally in one of his cultures. On the other hand, he reported that animals inoculated with spore masses 'derived from entirely pure cultures of *Bacillus anthracis* ... invariably died of anthrax' (Koch, 1876, p. 11). However, at this point Koch's inoculation cultures were grown in liquid media, as Davaine's had been, and his only evidence that the cultures were pure was that microscopic examination revealed no contamination. For more than a decade, Davaine had tried, unsuccessfully, to persuade critics with arguments at least as strong as these. Yet Koch insisted his argument was conclusive: 'Anthrax substances, whether they are fresh, decayed, or dried, can only cause anthrax if they contain *Bacillus anthracis* or its viable spores. This fact removes all doubt that *Bacillus anthracis* is the actual cause and contagium of anthrax' (Koch, 1876, p. 13). In an 1881 paper, Koch claimed he had established causality *by this argument*. In that later paper, after reviewing the earlier argument and without any additional evidence, he concluded 'thus, anthrax never occurred without viable anthrax bacilli or spores. In my opinion, no more conclusive proof can be given that anthrax bacilli are the true and only cause of anthrax' (Koch, 1881b, p. 64). However, this argument failed on two counts: first, it was not clear that Koch had truly isolated the bacillus; and second, while the argument provided evidence that the absence of the bacilli was followed by the absence of the disease (necessity), his audience expected inoculation experiments showing that the presence of isolated bacilli insured the presence of the disease (sufficiency). In spite of his brilliant technical innovations, which everyone acknowledged to be of major value, critics were unpersuaded (Bert, 1876). Koch's argument was judged to have failed for precisely the same reason that Pasteur's earlier arguments were inconclusive – both presented evidence of necessity and both assumed universality. In spite of his impressive technical innovations, there is no documentary evidence that, at the time, anyone found Koch's causal argument conclusive.

A few months later, in the spring of 1877, Pasteur published his first major paper on anthrax (Pasteur, 1877a). After mentioning that Davaine had preceded Pollender in reporting anthrax bacteridia, Pasteur claimed that he himself, while studying diseases of silkworms, had been the first to identify spores and to recognize that they remained viable for long periods.[4] Pasteur mentioned Koch's paper favorably and acknowledged that Koch had been the first to trace the life cycle of the bacteridium and to describe the formation of anthrax spores. However, he pointed out that Koch's work had not persuaded the skeptics, and stated that his own goal was to provide a conclusive proof. As Pasteur explained it, the main problem was showing that, of all the components of anthrax blood, the bacteridia themselves were the causal agent. Pasteur observed that the body of a healthy animal is closed to all bacteria – having reached this important conclusion, which is equivalent to Klebs' first *Grundversuch*, in a paper published several years earlier.[5] Thus the bodies of healthy animals provide sterile media in which one can produce successive cultures of anthrax bacteria. He observed that, if no other organisms show themselves, one could be sure the original culture was pure. He also produced subcultures in inorganic media and filtered the remains to remove impurities. The isolated and filtered bacteridia consistently caused anthrax. Toward the end of his paper, Pasteur considered some possible alternative interpretations of his results: the true cause of anthrax could be (1) virulent matter adhering to bacteridia even after isolation and filtration, (2) a substance secreted by the organisms rather than the bacteridia themselves, or (3) some organism other than bacteridia that also multiplied in culture media (Pasteur, 1863b, p. 170). Pasteur felt the first alternative could be eliminated by using numerous successive subcultures to eliminate all extraneous material from the diseased animal. He discounted the second alternative on the grounds that, if it were true, the bacteridia would still be necessary for the onset of disease. He tried to counter the third alternative by using a medium (urine) in which other organisms could easily be detected. Of course, ultimately, this argument rests on the Bacterial Hypothesis – the hypothesis that only bacteria are possible causes of disease.

In a second 1877 anthrax paper, Pasteur claimed that 'the experiments I have reported ... have demonstrated without reply that there is a microscopic organism, the unique cause of ... anthrax; it is the bacteridium, first perceived by Davaine in 1850' (Pasteur, 1877b, p. 172). He claimed Davaine had come closest to proving causality but had been unable to provide a conclusive argument. The issue could only be resolved by passing bacteridia through numerous subcultures and by filtering the remains to remove all other materials. Pasteur claimed to have been the first to have done this. This argument for causality obviously conformed more closely to contemporary expectations than did Koch's and some critics found it conclusive.[6]

Pasteur continued to study anthrax: seven more publications appeared in 1878, six in 1879, and five in 1880 (V.R. Pasteur, 1922–39, vol. 6, pp. 197–270, 452–512). Most of these reported new results. Pasteur found one could induce anthrax in chickens by artificially lowering their body temperatures (Pasteur, 1878c), and that spores from buried cadavers could be carried to the surface by earthworms where they could infect grazing animals (Pasteur, 1880b). Although Pasteur believed he had conclusively proven causality in 1877, he continued to refine his argument. In one paper he claimed to have passed bacteridia through more than 100 subcultures to insure they had been completely isolated from all extraneous disease products (Pasteur, 1878a, pp. 197f.).

In 1878 Pasteur observed that his research on anthrax 'left the etiology of the putrid diseases or septicemia less advanced than the etiology of anthrax' (Pasteur, 1878d, p. 112). He described his techniques for isolating bacteridia, and observed that 'in the current state of science' this procedure is the only way to prove 'the organism is the real agent of disease and of contagion' (Pasteur, 1878d, pp. 112f.). He proposed undertaking similar studies of septicemia. A few months later, in reporting research on plague, Pasteur again outlined the strategy of isolation, purification, and inoculation, and observed that, in the current state of science, the only conclusive proof of causality was passing an organism through successive animals and inert media and showing that isolated organisms could produce disease and death (Pasteur, 1879c, p. 494). He also claimed to have used this method to study a disease called chicken cholera (Pasteur, 1879c, p. 495), and he discussed the applicability of the method to puerperal fever (Pasteur, 1879d, pp. 498f). On two occasions during these months, Pasteur observed: 'everything is hidden, obscure, and open to discussion when one ignores the cause of some phenomena, but everything is clear when one possesses it' (Pasteur, 1922–39, vol. 6, pp. 110, 114).

In contrast to Pasteur, after his initial paper, Koch seems not to have continued studying anthrax. Apart from incidental references, between 1876 and 1880 Koch discussed anthrax in only one paper – his long 1878 work on wound infections (Koch, 1878a, pp. 46–48).[7] The only new result Koch announced was his use of methyl violet as a stain.

Having observed that anthrax was not recidivous, in 1880 Pasteur began looking for a vaccine (Pasteur, 1880c). This observation, together with similar results for other diseases, suggested what Pasteur called 'the general law of the non-recidiviousness of virulent diseases' (Pasteur, 1881a, p. 339). Early in 1881, Pasteur reported he could attenuate the virulence of the bacilli of chicken cholera; this led to his important discovery that one could also attenuate anthrax bacilli (Pasteur, 1881b).[8] Pasteur began using a vaccine in tests on thousands of livestock in various European countries. His results, along with other findings, were announced in a series of papers. Like many of Pasteur's earlier studies, his anthrax inoculations promised profound economic benefits and were widely publicized.

In 1881, Koch published a detailed criticism of Pasteur's work (Koch, 1881b) – this was only Koch's second major paper on anthrax. According to Koch, Pasteur's work had contributed nothing to the etiology of the disease. 'Only a few of Pasteur's beliefs about anthrax are new, and they are false' (Koc, 1881b, 65).[9] He accused Pasteur of confusing anthrax bacilli with unrelated contaminants (p. 62) and wrote that Pasteur had probably never observed anthrax uncomplicated by other diseases (p. 60). Koch rejected some of Pasteur's experiments as worthless and naive (p. 70) and ridiculed his work with chickens and earthworms. Koch also reviewed his own argument for causality and asserted that 'no more conclusive proof can be given that anthrax bacilli are the true and only cause of anthrax' (p. 64). In respect to the demand to isolate bacilli from every contaminant – the condition that most observers then expected in any proof of causality – Koch wrote: 'this is impossible ... no one can take seriously such an undertaking'. Koch acknowledged that, even in the face of his experiments, 'one could still object that ... some other substance associated with the bacteria, rather than the bacilli themselves, causes the disease'. But, he continued, 'for all practical purposes, this objection is meaningless'

(p. 64). However, critics did not find the objection meaningless. In reviewing Koch's paper, a Professor Zuber observed: 'how opinions can differ! We think, and much of the world with us, that this objection has a capital importance and we reproach precisely those authors who ... subject complex liquids to complicated procedures and thereby reach dubious results'. Zuber praised those who tried to isolate the bacillus by subcultures (Zuber, 1882, pp. 104f).

In September 1881 Koch and Pasteur met in an international medical congress in London. Pasteur had not yet seen Koch's recent scathing criticism and veiled insults, and their relations were cordial (Geison, 1974, p. 397). Pasteur praised some of Koch's new techniques. In a plenary session, Pasteur summarized the results of his inoculation programme (Pasteur, 1881c).

In March 1882, in the midst of his debate with Pasteur, Koch announced discovery of the tuberculosis bacillus (Koch, 1882a) – the announcement created an immediate sensation throughout Europe. After reporting he had identified a specific organism in hundreds of natural and artificial cases of tuberculosis, Koch turned to the question of causality. He began by explaining that in order to prove causality,

> it is necessary to isolate the bacilli from the body, to grow them in pure culture until they are freed from every disease product of the animal organism, and, by introducing isolated bacilli into animals, to reproduce the same morbid condition known to follow from inoculation with spontaneously developed tuberculosis materials'.
> (Koch, 1882a, p. 87)

Koch's paper was organized around attempts to meet these conditions. His proof of causality by isolation and inoculation is remarkable for two reasons. First, it is his earliest use of the causal criteria later known as Koch's Postulates. Second, by claiming that this strategy was *essential* for proving causality – a strategy he had rejected as impossible just a few months earlier – Koch was effectively admitting the inadequacy of his own attempt to prove causality for anthrax. Moreover, his claim implies that Pasteur's demonstration, although conceivably inexact or even unoriginal, at least followed the general procedure that Koch now described as essential for proving causality. Of course, Koch never explicitly admitted either that endorsing the new strategy undercut his earlier claims or that Pasteur's work had been more relevant to proving causality than his own, yet both conclusions follow from claims he made in the tuberculosis paper and in several papers that followed. Koch's adoption of isolation and inoculation probably resulted from a combination of factors: his dispute with Pasteur; discussions with his friend, Edwin Klebs, during the 1878 meetings of the *German Natural Scientists and Physicians*; and his introduction of solid culture media that enabled him to isolate bacteria much more reliably than had been possible using only liquid media.[10]

Pasteur answered Koch's criticisms in a lecture at a medical congress in Geneva in the fall of 1882 (Pasteur, 1882). Pasteur pointed out that critics had rejected Koch's initial work on anthrax as inconclusive. He explained that he himself had followed the only method for proving causation that satisfied existing standards, and he mentioned Paul Bert who had rejected Koch's argument but had been persuaded by his own. He also answered some of Koch's specific objections. Given the tone of Koch's attack, Pasteur's response was remarkably restrained. Yet Koch, who attended Pasteur's lecture, took offense and registered a formal protest (Schwalbe, 1912, vol. 1, pp. 207f.; Ellenberger, 1970, p. 269).

Koch responded quickly with a long and polemical attack on Pasteur's inoculation programme (Koch, 1882b). Koch insinuated that Pasteur was falsifying results (Koch, 1882b, pp. 106, 111), and he misrepresented Pasteur's work. Near the beginning of his paper he explained how his methods differed from Pasteur's. Koch claimed he first became oriented by undertaking a thorough investigation of all the diseased tissues of the body to determine the distribution of the organism.[11] Koch then claimed to use isolation and inoculation, which he described as 'the only method that meets current scientific standards' (Koch, 1882b, p. 98). As usual, he did not mention that Pasteur had preceded him in using this strategy or that his initial papers on anthrax, in which he still claimed to have proved causality, were defective for not using it.

This time Pasteur responded to Koch in an emotional open letter (Pasteur, 1883). Pasteur expressed surprise at the virulence of Koch's attack. He reviewed his contributions to medicine and to science generally and mentioned that several prominent researchers, including both Davaine and Joseph Lister, had based their studies on his own early work. Pasteur summarized earlier research on anthrax, reiterated his claim to have been the first to have identified spores (while admitting Koch had first seen anthrax spores), and reviewed his argument for causality. He again cited researchers who had rejected Koch's causal argument but had been persuaded by his own.

One year later, in 1884, Koch published another long criticism of Pasteur's attempt to attenuate anthrax bacilli (Koch, 1884a). In 1887 he again criticized Pasteur's inoculation program (Koch, 1887). However, by this time, Pasteur's programme had achieved significant success and had been dramatically corroborated by his work on rabies; he responded to Koch's criticism with a brief note (Pasteur, 1887). These were the last publications by either Koch or Pasteur on anthrax.

One can appraise the controversy between Koch and Pasteur in different ways. On a personal level, Koch comes off poorly: his arguments were sarcastic, polemical, unfair, and often included personal attacks. While Koch regularly minimized the significance of Pasteur's work and misrepresented his opinions, Pasteur's appraisals of Koch were fair and consistent with opinions expressed by others.

In respect to their arguments for causality, Pasteur's work obviously came closer than Koch's to satisfying existing expectations. Since most contemporary researchers expected evidence of sufficiency, Koch's arguments were not seen as compelling, in spite of his technical achievements. He seems to have tried to obscure the perceived inadequacy of his argument by *ad hominem* attacks on Pasteur. From what we have seen, there is a certain irony in using the phrase 'Koch's Postulates' to refer to the causal strategy that Koch ultimately adopted and that continues with us today. If one takes the strategy to focus on isolation and inoculation, both Klebs and Pasteur used it before Koch and both applied it to a wider range of diseases than Koch ever did. Moreover, Koch's early work was deemed inconclusive precisely because he was slow to adopt this approach.

In any case, by the mid-1880s, in France and in Germany, a consensus had emerged as to how one must go about proving that specific bacteria cause particular diseases. From this time on, everyone accepted isolation and inoculation as crucial to proofs of causality.

General acceptance of the bacterial theory of disease

In proving that some factor, say, bacteridia, causes some pathological process, one requires consensus as to what sorts of things must be taken into account as possible causes (that is, one requires something like the Bacterial Hypothesis) and consensus as to how one proves that some particular factor of the appropriate sort causes the morbidity in question (that is, one requires causal criteria). We have seen how a consensus emerged with respect to causal criteria. We now turn to what was, in some degree, a more basic problem: establishing a consensus among medical researchers with respect to the fact that bacteria were the sorts of things that could cause disease in the first place. Of course, Klebs, Pasteur, Koch, and other contributors to the research programme were already committed to the pathologicality of bacteria – the problem was converting skeptics.[12] To see how this was achieved, we must review another dramatic development that emerged from Pasteur's laboratories: discovery of a vaccine against rabies.

Rabies has never been a common disease, but it is so terrible and, once symptoms begin, death so certain that nineteenth-century physicians were willing to attempt almost anything by way of treatment. During the course of the century, *Lancet* reported the use of more than 300 assorted drugs and chemicals to treat victims; these included ammonia (as an ointment, orally, and injected into the blood stream 'until the patient begged that treatment might be discontinued'), antimony, arsenic, fresh blood (orally), Spanish fly, carbolic acid (orally and by injection), chlorine (applied to the wound and taken orally), chloroform (inhaled, rubbed on the skin, and orally), creosote, curare, ether (inhaled or injected), hydrochloric acid, iodine, lead, mercury, strychnine, prussic acid, rhubarb, steel, sulphurous acid, nicotine, turpentine (orally or by enema), viper's poison, vinegar, and zinc.[13]

Conventional wisdom dictated that a bite by a rabid animal should be cauterized as quickly as possible. Usually this was done by applying a strong acid such as nitric acid or sulfuric acid, but some physicians recommended physical cauterization by boiling oil or by a red-hot iron. Once the wound was attended to, various methods of treatment were employed. In England, sea dipping was common, and in some areas fishermen advertised their expertness in dipping – dippers used long poles to hold patients underwater for three or more minutes at a stretch. In some respects, strychnine poisoning resembled hydrophobia; Marshall Hall, a respected British physician, observed that frogs injected with strychnine died if they were agitated, but recovered if left in peace. He recommended that rabies patients be placed on spring beds and surrounded by gauze curtains in a dark and quiet room. By contrast, one patient seemed to have been greatly benefited by escaping from a hospital and running around the town; this suggested exercise and the use of tonics. Another physician recommended excision of the uvula as an excellent shock to the system.

Some writers attributed rabies to inadequate sexual release or, by contrast, to sexual incontinence in dogs. This led one physician to recommend castration as a radical but effective treatment. Other physicians advocated hot air baths with temperatures as high as 200°F, or vapor baths in which patients were wrapped in blankets or flannel and placed on a wicker chair over hot bricks, live coals, or a spirit lamp. Others advocated cold effusions, large doses of ice, or the application of ice along the whole length of the spine. Some combined warm baths with immersion in cold water. 'To reduce to a lesser or negative state' the great excitement under which the victim labors, one physician recommended wrapping the patient in blankets and dashing the spine with cold water every 15 minutes. Another physician reported that electrocution cured patients of hydrophobia but that they occasionally died of exhaustion in the process. Yet another recommended that patients be fed massive doses of asparagus; he reported trying this on a patient who went mad and died, but the patient seemed to have been cured of hydrophobia. Some writers noticed that rabies is spontaneous only in animals that do not perspire; to them, vigorous perspiration seemed to offer hope. Others wrote that in animals that do not perspire, saliva must carry off large quantities of effete matter; they advocated vigorous salivation. One physician recommended that patients be poisoned by curare – the South American arrow poison – and then be revived by artificial respiration. For a time it was believed that lead, mercury, and turpentine would cure rabies, but that victims were sometimes poisoned in the process. One case was reported in which massive doses of croton oil and prussic acid had apparently converted hydrophobia into a fatal case of typhoid fever. Some physicians recommended that patients be kept in a constant state of nausea or given small but continuous enemata. One physician tried soaking a rennet in water, saturating it with savanilla and forcing it down the patient's throat; after being placed in the sun and sleeping for 48 hours the patient awoke completely recovered.

For several reasons nineteenth-century research on rabies was particularly frustrating. First, it is difficult to convey rabies reliably among test animals. Even deep bites by rabid animals produce new cases of rabies only infrequently. Second, when the disease is conveyed, there may be an incubation period of several weeks or even months (Pasteur, 1881d, p. 574). Finally, while many physicians were fairly confident that rabies was caused by a microorganism, the best efforts of the leading experts failed to identify it. For several years Pasteur searched for rabies microbes – 'On two occasions he suspected he had seen them – in 1881 in the form of encapsulated bacteria and in 1883 as fine particles in the brain tissue of rabid animals' (Hughes, 1977, p. 32). From a modern point of view, the failures were due, in part, to the fact that the causal agent is a virus and, therefore, too small to be detected given the equipment and methods then in use. However, Pasteur was not deterred by his inability to identify a causal organism.

Pasteur tried injecting saliva from rabid dogs directly into the brains of live rabbits. He found that brain fluids taken from these rabbits were maximally virulent. Inoculating these fluids into healthy dogs usually produced rabies within days. Although he could not identify a causal organism, Pasteur may have wondered if the virulence of the supposed organism could be reduced in the same manner he had attenuated the bacteria of anthrax and chicken cholera. Developing results that had been announced by other researchers, Pasteur confirmed that the virulence of the rabies virus for animals of one species could be affected (in some cases increased, in others decreased) by passage through series of animals of a different species. Early on, Pasteur also concluded that the elusive virus was most likely to be found in brain tissue rather than in blood or saliva. These insights led to experiments involving spinal cords from rabbits that had been dried in sterile air. He found that the longer the spinal cords were allowed to dry, the longer the incubation period for inoculations using matter taken from those cords. Pasteur inferred that the causal agents contained in the dried cords had become less virulent (Pasteur, 1884, pp. 593f.). Beginning with injections of tissues that had dried for two weeks and were nearly inert, he injected dogs with matter that was progressively more virulent. He hypothesized that at some stage test animals would be immune. This, he believed, could be shown if injecting full-strength brain tissue into immunized dogs had no ill effects (Pasteur, 1885, p. 603).[14]

While still engaged in this research and before he had conclusive evidence his methods would work, Pasteur was urged to try his procedure on a human being. On 4 July 1885, a nine-year-old Alsatian boy, Joseph Meister, had been badly bitten by a rabid dog, and the boy had been brought to Pasteur.[15] Pasteur knew that only a small percentage of similarly bitten humans would contract rabies. He also acknowledged that his experiments were incomplete and that he had never tried inoculations on test animals *after* they had already been bitten (Pasteur, 1885, p. 606). Yet Pasteur took a chance that could be described as irresponsible: on 6 July he began inoculating Meister with tissues from the dried spinal cords of diseased rabbits. On 16 July 1885, having given Meister 13 shots in 10 days, Pasteur used fluids containing fresh and fully virulent rabies material. When this produced no evidence of the disease, Pasteur pronounced the boy cured. Given that inoculations did not always produce rabies and that the disease had an uncertain incubation period, the announcement was premature. However, Joseph Meister remained healthy, and Pasteur's work was proclaimed around the world as a brilliant success.

Within months thousands of exposed persons began flocking to Pasteur's laboratory from all over the world. Between 1886 and 1934, 34,111 persons who had been bitten by confirmed rabid animals were treated at the Pasteur Institute. Of these thousands, only three persons died; among untreated victims, the average mortality was 16 per cent (Malkin, 1986, p. 45). Thus, even though the cause of rabies had not been identified (and even though it turned out, ultimately, not to be bacterial), since the inoculations clearly emerged from what Pasteur called the theory of germs, the success of the inoculations was taken as further support for that theory.

In their work on anthrax, both Koch and Pasteur accumulated empirical evidence of causality and their evidence was of different kinds.
However, it is impossible to prove causation by empirical evidence
alone. This is reflected in the standard objection – which continued to
be raised throughout the century – that, no matter how carefully organisms were isolated, it was always possible that an unknown virus or
some totally different entity in the blood was the true cause of the
disease. Proving bacteria cause a particular disease, such as anthrax,
was impossible in the absence of a theory within which bacteria were
recognized as possible causes – one needed an assumption like the
Bacterial Hypothesis.

However, it would have been at least as difficult to adopt the bacterial theory as to accept *Beauvaria bassiana* as the cause of muscardine
or decaying organic matter as the cause of childbed fever. It was not just
a matter of accepting a new kind of cause for a particular disease; the
bacterial theory was a whole new way of thinking about diseases in
general – it meant exchanging what were the norms and what were the
anomalies that required explanations. There is inevitable resistance to
such a revolution. As in all such cases, innovators were confronted by a
vicious circle: observations (such as those made by Davaine, Pasteur,
and Koch) could count as evidence that bacteridia cause anthrax and,
therefore, as evidence for the bacterial theory in general, but only if one
accepted something like the Bacterial Hypothesis in the first place, and
this, of course, was itself a central part of the bacterial theory. Thus,
any attempt to accumulate *direct* evidence for the bacterial theory
depended on accepting the theory to begin with – a circular argument.
In the absence of direct evidence, researchers fell back on analogical
reasoning involving diseases known to be caused by minute but visible
parasites like acari and trichinae. Yet, although these analogies had
some heuristic value, they were never entirely persuasive. So how were
skeptics to be won over?

Where rational persuasion fails, the only alternative is *conversion*,
and converting opponents to the bacterial theory required successes
that were 'supernatural' in the sense of being outside what could
reasonably have been expected within the framework of traditional
medicine. To achieve conversion, bacteriologists required, not mere
evidence, but something akin to *miracles*.[16]

According to Pasteur, the theory of germs became generally accepted
in the early 1880s, at about the time of the London International
Medical Congress (Pasteur, 1881c, p. 370). What miraculous successes
at about that time would have made the theory of germs dramatically
more plausible than it had previously been? Among the sensational
accomplishments of this period were Pasteur's anthrax and rabies in-

oculations and Koch's discovery of tuberculosis and cholera bacilli. The cumulative effect of such developments was a sea change in medicine – a fundamental reorientation in how physicians thought about disease. Given the new standpoint, which encompassed the Bacterial Hypothesis, *empirical* evidence about the presence or absence of bacteria in disease processes became evidence for the *theoretical* relation of disease causation.

In respect of winning support for the bacterial theory, however different and even opposed their work may appear, Koch and Pasteur were mutually supportive. Since proving that bacteridia caused anthrax was possible only within the bacterial theory, if one asks which of Koch or Pasteur ultimately proved that the anthrax bacillus causes anthrax, the best answer may be: both together.

Notes

1. This was the paper we considered in Chapter 5 in which Leplat and Jaillard attacked Davaine.
2. Pasteur himself pointed this out in the preface to *Études sur la bière* (Pasteur, 1876a, p. 5; cp. the diary entry reprinted in Pasteur, 1922–35, vol. 6, pp. vf.).
3. In the next year Pasteur strengthened his claim: 'It has been impossible for me to discover a worm struck by *flacherie*, advanced or beginning, without establishing immediately under my own eyes or those of my collaborators, that the intestinal matter contained one or several of the microscopic organisms that one finds in fermenting mulberry leaves' (Pasteur, 1878e, p. 702).
4. Pasteur cited his *Études sur la maladie des vers à soie* (Pasteur, 1870, pp. 231f.).
5. Pasteur frequently referred to his argument for this principle which first appeared in 1863 (Pasteur, 1863b).
6. For example, Paul Bert, who had rejected Koch's argument, was persuaded by Pasteur's (Bert, 1877).
7. Koch's collected works also contains a letter on anthrax written to the Secretary of the Interior (Schwalbe, 1912, vol. 2, pp. 831f.).
8. Geison's account of events surrounding this development is essential reading for anyone seeking to understand this crucial chapter in the rise of the bacterial theory of disease (Geison, 1995, pp. 146–76).
9. Through this paragraph, page numbers in parentheses are references to Koch (1881b).
10. This will be discussed in more detail in the next chapter.
11. This may also be an attempt to discredit Pasteur since Koch, having been trained in pathology, was qualified to undertake such a study whereas Pasteur, a chemist, was not.
12. Bruno Latour has shown that, in France, Pasteur's theories were accepted in some groups far more readily than his evidence would warrant (1984). In part, this resulted from a kind of bilateral leveraging made possible by

the intersecting interests of Pasteur and the Hygienists. However, as Latour admits, Pasteur's 'opponents were numerous enough in the Académie de Médecine' (p. 29). In my discussion, 'the critics' who required conversion were these members of the Académie – physicians, pathologists, physiologists, researchers and scientists. It was they who raised rational arguments against Pasteur; and it was they against whom Pasteur's rational arguments were directed. I will have more to say about Latour in the concluding chapter entitled 'Some Final Thoughts'.

13. The first four paragraphs of this section are based on an earlier publication (Carter, 1982b); documentation for all the treatments mentioned here and below can be found in that source.

14. The story of Pasteur's rabies research is more complex than this superficial account suggests. For what is, as yet, the most complete and enlightening discussion see Geison (1995).

15. As Geison has revealed, before Joseph Meister, Pasteur had treated two other persons with only equivocal results (Geison, 1995, pp. 195–203).

16. After writing this, I discovered that Latour uses a similar metaphor (1984, pp. 87f.).

CHAPTER EIGHT

The Etiological Standpoint

With a bacterial theory in place, it is possible to identify causes of certain pathological processes, to define diseases in terms of those causes, and to secure the practical and theoretical benefits of a system of universal and necessary causes. However, the etiological standpoint – the research programme we are investigating – was never limited to the bacterial theory. It began with diseases caused by fungi, by minute but visible parasites, and by decaying organic matter. And while the bacterial theory eclipsed (and in one case assimilated) these earlier accomplishments, it seems always to have been clear that the research programme was not limited to bacterial diseases. Koch spent most of his professional life investigating diseases he knew to be non-bacterial and he clearly regarded all this work as falling within what he called the etiological standpoint. More revealing yet was a comment by Adolf von Strümpell, a physician writing in the 1880s about psychological disorders: 'one can justly claim that the scientific treatment of the etiology of diseases constitutes the most characteristic thrust of modern pathology, and ... the secure establishment of the doctrine of organized, externally invading disease agents is until now the most beautiful and important achievement of this effort' (Strümpell, 1884a, p. 2). Implicit in this comment is the recognition that the 'scientific treatment of the etiology of diseases' is not limited to 'externally invading disease agents'. Indeed, Strümpell's article discusses the etiology of non-bacterial psychological disorders. So, as he conceived it, the etiological reorganization of medicine was not just about bacteria.

Koch's causal criteria (his so-called Postulates) can be seen as the culmination of one aspect of the bacterial theory: The Postulates include a thoughtful and explicit formulation of causal criteria within that theory. However, the Postulates also point beyond the bacterial theory to the possibility of establishing alternative theories in which factors other than bacteria are recognized as causes. Seen in this light, the Postulates begin to hint at the full breadth of the etiological standpoint.

The origin of Koch's postulates

Koch used explicit causal criteria in fewer than ten of his more than 100 published papers, and, with the exception of one 1890 lecture, all of these papers appeared between 1878 and 1884. There are important differences in the causal criteria that Koch stated: later versions included conditions absent from the earlier ones, and some of the conditions were given in several non-equivalent versions. We will examine Koch's discussions of causation in his first anthrax paper, in two 1878 papers on wound infections, and in several papers published between 1882 and 1884. However, his later accounts are most interesting, and discussion of individual criteria will be postponed until we have reviewed all the publications.

We have already considered Koch's 1876 anthrax paper; in this context, a few additional comments are necessary. In this first paper, Koch neither discussed nor even mentioned causal criteria; he gave little explicit attention to proving that anthrax bacilli cause anthrax, and the few arguments he put forward focused on necessity. By the time Koch wrote this paper, he knew that the mere presence of anthrax bacilli in a susceptible host was not sufficient to insure onset of anthrax: ingesting bacilli did not usually provoke the disease (Koch, 1876, p. 11), some inoculation procedures were unreliable (Koch, 1876, p. 2), and among exposed susceptible animals, vulnerability varied (Koch, 1882b, pp. 101f.). Koch never claimed the bacilli were sufficient to cause anthrax. After some early failures, he developed a reliable inoculation procedure; thus, this procedure (as opposed to the organisms alone) was sufficient for the disease. However, in describing the procedure, he wrote only that it provided a useful test for the viability of his cultures (Koch, 1876, p. 2). Nowhere did he suggest that the inoculations constituted direct or conclusive evidence that bacilli caused anthrax. Instead, here is his only argument for causation: 'anthrax substances, whether they are fresh, decayed, or dried, can only cause anthrax if they contain *Bacillus anthracis* or its viable spores. This fact removes all doubt that *Bacillus anthracis* is the actual cause and contagium of anthrax' (Koch, 1876, p. 13). Thus, as he himself presented his argument, he seems to have been most influenced by his unsuccessful inoculations with substances lacking bacilli and spores. Of course, such experiments provided evidence of necessity.

In 1878, Koch published two papers on wound infections. The first was a summary lecture; the second was a long account of his research. Koch began the summary by observing that the regular identification of microorganisms in infected wounds did not prove that these diseases

> come about only when organisms enter the body and proliferate there, in other words, that the diseases are parasitic. This is because in many cases of unquestionably infectious diseases, either no organisms are found or too few are found to explain the symptoms or the fatal termination of the disease.
>
> (Koch, 1878b, p. 58)

According to this passage, regularly finding parasites in infected wounds does not prove that wound infections are parasitic because, in other cases, no parasites or too few parasites are found. Thus, presumably, to support the parasitic concept, one must show that a sufficient number of parasites are always present in infection. As he here explains it, his goal was, therefore, to show that infections do not occur without parasites – in other words, that the parasites are necessary for disease. By using accepted methods, Koch was able to identify organisms in only a few test animals, so his results were inconclusive. However, he reported that by using new staining and illumination techniques, which he had developed, he could invariably locate microorganisms (Koch, 1878b, pp. 58f). This effectively removed objections to the parasitic account. Koch also conducted inoculation experiments, but, as in the first anthrax paper, seems not to have regarded them as central to the causal argument; he reported only that inoculations were useful for insuring the availability of diseased animals in which organisms could be identified. He also wrote that inoculations proved wound diseases were indeed infectious. He did not cite these experiments in his arguments for causality – therefore, in the short paper on wound infections, Koch's concept of causation seems to have been the same as in his first anthrax paper.

In his long paper on wound infections, Koch first explicitly stated causal criteria, although they are quite different from those now attributed to him. He wrote that a conclusive proof of the parasitic origin of some disease 'would require that we find parasitic microorganisms in all cases of the disease, that their presence is in such numbers and distribution that all the symptoms of the disease can be explained, and finally that for every individual traumatic infective disease, a morphologically distinguishable microorganism is identified' (Koch, 1878a, p. 29). We can summarize these conditions as follows:

Rw1. The organism must be exhibited in every examined case of the disease.

Rw2. The distribution of the organism must correlate with and explain disease phenomena.

Rw3. For each different disease, a morphologically distinguishable organism must be identified. (This is a strong version of the Distinguishability Hypothesis.)

Koch stated the same criteria in another passage, and he mentioned Rw1 and Rw2 in a third passage as well (Koch, 1878a, pp. 48, 27). These criteria do not include isolation and inoculation – procedures central to his later attempts to prove causation.

Koch's discussions of particular wound infections were loosely organized around these criteria. For each disease, Koch identified a particular organism and showed that its distribution in diseased animals could explain the pathological changes, some of the symptoms, and the eventual death of the animal: to some extent, this confirmed Rw2 and Rw3. As in the summary paper, Koch attributed earlier failures in finding organisms to technical problems and suggested that his improved methods showed organisms were always present (Koch, 1878a, p. 48). Exactly as in the anthrax paper, these observations provided evidence of necessity and also supported necessity indirectly by explaining apparent counter evidence. However, Koch's evidence for Rw1 and Rw3 was relatively weak. Here, as in his anthrax paper, Koch's discussion rested almost entirely on artificial cases of disease: he did not locate parasitic organisms in natural infections, and he applied his results to human infections only by an analogical argument (Koch, 1878a, pp. 19, 48). This may help explain why Koch never claimed his work on infected wounds conclusively established causality.

In his early research, Koch introduced several important technical innovations. Recognizing that the identification of microorganisms was too subjective, he developed new methods for staining and illuminating slides and for photographing microorganisms. His photographs were so well done that, according to one modern microbiologist, they 'are as good as many that are published in scientific journals today' (Collard, 1976, p. 20). At the time, bacteriologists relied almost exclusively on liquid media for cultures. Solid media such as cooked potatoes were known, but their significance was not widely recognized. With liquid media it was impossible to separate various strains of organisms that happened to invade a given culture and this made pure cultivation difficult. To overcome this problem, Koch pioneered the so-called 'poured plate method' of cultivation. In using this method, one inoculates a liquid medium with the organisms one wishes to cultivate and then pours the mixture onto plates where the medium solidifies. Individual bacteria grow into discrete colonies that can be protected from contamination.

In the decades preceding the end of the nineteenth century, what we now call tuberculosis consisted of various anatomically and symptomatically distinct disorders the most prominent of which were called scrofula and consumption or phthisis. In Europe these disorders probably accounted for about one-seventh of all deaths and for about one-third of all adult deaths (Koch, 1882a, p. 83). Consumption, the most prominent disease of the age, became an artistic and literary symbol and significantly influenced contemporary thought about the human condition (Sontag, 1979). There were different opinions about the etiology of the disease. Some believed consumption was due to general social causes and could only be controlled through social reforms; others believed consumption, scrofula, and diseases like syphilis and hysteria were inevitable consequences of the degeneration of the human race. Virchow, like many other pathologists, believed the morbid changes in terms of which consumption was defined were non-specific tissue reactions that could not have a unique causal explanation.

Some physicians suspected that consumption may be contagious, but the evidence was inconclusive. In the 1860s Jean Antoine Villemin published a series of studies supporting the contagious concept by showing the disease could be conveyed between susceptible animal species (Villemin, 1868). Villemin believed consumption was due to a living contagium, but he could not identify it. One problem obstructing early research was the difficulty of distinguishing reliably between natural and artificial cases of the disease. There was always the possibility that animals used in inoculation tests had simply contracted natural tuberculosis that was not due to experimental inoculations. Julius Cohnheim and Carl Julius Salomonsen solved this problem by selecting the anterior ocular chamber of rabbits as the inoculation site (Cohnheim and Salomonsen, 1877). Since rabbits did not contract spontaneous tuberculosis of the eye, this seemed to provide conclusive evidence that at least some forms of tuberculosis could be conveyed by inoculation. Cohnheim and Salomonsen believed tuberculosis was parasitic, but they, too, were unable to identify the parasite.

Koch began studying tuberculosis in August 1881 (Brock, 1988, pp. 117–39). His work was carried out in great secrecy – apparently not even Ferdinand Cohn, who had been his friend and mentor since his first work on anthrax, was informed of the study. Koch and his associates conducted their work at a frantic pace and after only a few months, on 24 March 1882, they announced their initial results. The announcement was made at an evening medical meeting in Berlin; it was held in a small reading room, 30 by 45 feet in size.

> A total of seventy-two chairs were available, and table space for 200 preparations was also required. ... The room was filled to the last available seat. Virchow was conspicuously absent. He had recently taken a strong stand against the 'juvenile work' of the 'youngsters' of the Imperial Health Office.
>
> (Lechevalier and Solotorovsky, 1965, p. 84)

Koch's paper was marvelously clear – the most compelling and persuasive essay he ever wrote.

As usual, technical innovations were central to his argument. Koch found that adding potassium to the standard methylene-blue stain intensified the effect and revealed a new kind of bacillus in tuberculous materials. He then grew cultures of these bacilli in coagulated serum.

> His genius was revealed by his patience in waiting several weeks for growth to occur. All known bacteria, at the time, appeared in culture media within a few days; if nothing was visible, the cultures were usually discarded. Just what went on in Koch's mind to make him preserve his cultures of tuberculous material and patiently wait for several weeks he does not say. Perhaps he forgot to discard them, or perhaps he did not know himself; therein lay his genius.
> (Bloomfield, 1958, p. 212)

Extensive inoculation tests supported the conclusion that the bacillus in question was the causal agent for tuberculosis.

Koch's presentation was stunning; 'the audience was left spellbound, and for a time after he had ended the presentation not a word was uttered' (Lechevalier and Solotorovsky, 1965, p. 84). In later years, Paul Ehrlich wrote of the meeting: 'all who were present were deeply moved and that evening has remained my greatest experience in science' (Lechevalier and Solotorovsky, 1965, p. 84). Koch's paper created an immediate sensation and probably did as much as any single accomplishment to establish the bacterial theory of disease. Later in 1882, Koch published a second paper on tuberculosis. Other papers appeared over the next two years culminating in his 1884 paper on the etiology of the disease. In these papers, Koch meticulously followed specific criteria for establishing disease causality – criteria we now know as Koch's Postulates. The centrality of the Postulates in Koch's famous and eminently influential tuberculosis papers ensured that they would profoundly influence subsequent etiological research.

In the first tuberculosis paper, Koch observed that 'the first goal of the investigation was to exhibit certain parasitic forms foreign to the body and that could cause the disease' (Koch, 1882a, p. 84). He reported finding tuberculosis bacilli in materials from dozens of natural cases of human and animal tuberculosis and in approximately 200 animals that had been inoculated with tuberculous materials. He concluded that 'tubercle bacilli occur in all tuberculosis disorders and ... are distinguishable from all other microorganisms' (Koch, 1882a, 87). Up to this point, Koch had presented evidence that the bacilli are necessary for the disease. Next he observed that the bacilli 'are distinguishable from all other microorganisms'. In both 1882 tuberculosis papers, Koch observed that establishing a regular coincidence between a disease and a specific organism did not prove causality; he wrote that even identifying the parasite in the organs where the disease is known to originate is not conclusive (Koch, 1882c, p. 446). The next step was to isolate the suspected disease agent in pure culture and to confirm it was alive. Even after all of this,

> it remains to prove the isolated parasite is really the cause of the disease. To accomplish this, one must show that animals inoculated with pure culture contract the original disease. The inoculation must succeed not only sometimes, but in every attempt as is achieved in such infectious diseases as anthrax.
>
> (Koch, 1882c, pp. 446f.)

In substantial sections of both 1882 papers, Koch reported attempts to inoculate materials from pure cultures. The effort devoted to this part of the argument, together with his own explicit assertions, show clearly that he regarded this as the decisive step in proving causation. After reporting his inoculation experiments, he concluded, 'All these facts, taken together, show that the bacilli in tuberculous substances are not merely coincidental with tuberculosis, but cause it. These bacilli are the real tuberculosis virus' (Koch, 1882a, p. 93). Koch reclassified, as one disease, all the symptomatically and pathologically distinct cases in which the organism could be identified and excluded all other cases as not true tuberculosis (Koch, 1882a, pp. 93f.) thereby, in effect, giving a new definition to 'tuberculosis' (Taylor, 1979, pp. 18f.).

In 1882 Koch also published a paper criticizing Pasteur's attempts to immunize animals against anthrax (Koch, 1882b). In this paper, he described what he called his own method of studying infectious disease, and he contrasted this method with what was supposedly Pasteur's method. Koch claimed to begin by examining 'all the body parts that are altered by the disease. In this way, one can establish the presence of the parasites, their distribution in the diseased organs, and their relation to body tissues' (Koch, 1882b, p. 98). However, this study provides only 'a complete orientation' to the disease – it still remains to prove causation. For this purpose, the organisms 'must be cultured in pure form. Then, after they have been freed from all the parts of the diseased body with which they were originally associated, they must be inoculated back into animals of the same species as those in which the disease was originally observed' (Koch, 1882b, p. 98). Koch mentioned tuberculosis as a disease for which these criteria had been fully satisfied. Thus, in this 1882 anthrax paper, Koch endorsed the same steps for proving causality as in the tuberculosis papers appearing in the same year. As we have seen, these were not the steps he himself followed in his original work on anthrax; in fact, Pasteur's study of anthrax came closer to following these steps than did Koch's.

Koch's monumental 1884 paper on the etiology of tuberculosis contains his most complete discussion of causation. He wrote:

First, it was necessary to determine whether the diseased organs contained elements that were not constituents of the body or composed of such constituents. If such alien structures could be demonstrated, it was necessary to determine whether they were organized and showed any sign of independent life. Such signs include motility – which is often confused with molecular motion – growth, propagation, and fructification. Moreover, it was necessary to consider the relation of such structures to their surroundings and to nearby tissues, their distribution in the body, their occurrence in various states of the disease, and similar other conditions. Such considerations enable one to conclude, with more or less probability, that there is a causal connection between these structures and the disease itself. Facts gained in these ways can provide so much evidence that only the most extreme skeptic would still object that the microorganisms may not be the cause, but only a concomitant of the disease. Often this objection has a certain justice, and, therefore, establishing the coincidence of the disease and the parasite is not a complete proof. One requires, in addition, a direct proof that the parasite is the actual cause. This can only be achieved by completely separating the parasites from the diseased organism and from all products of the disease to which one could ascribe a causal significance. The isolated parasites, if introduced into healthy animals, must then cause the disease with all its characteristics.

(Koch, 1884b, p. 131)

Here, and in his 1882 papers, Koch outlines a series of steps for proving causation. These steps can be summarized as follows:

Rt1. An alien structure must be exhibited in every case of the disease.

Rt2. The structure must be shown to be a living organism and must be distinguishable from all other organisms.

Rt3. The distribution of organisms must correlate with and explain disease phenomena.

Rt4. The organism must be cultivated outside diseased animals and isolated from all disease products that could be causally significant.

Rt5. The pure isolated organisms must be inoculated into test animals and these animals must then display the same symptoms as the original diseased animal.

Several of these steps require comment:

1. Rt1 corresponds approximately to Koch's earlier Rw1. In Rt1 Koch refers to the structures as 'alien' by which he presumably meant that they are not normally found in healthy bodies. If so Rt1 (in contrast to Rw1) implies that structures are found in all *and only* cases of the disease. Thus Rt1 requires observational evidence both

of necessity (structures present in all cases of pathology) and of sufficiency (structures present only in cases of pathology).

2. Rt2 corresponds approximately to Rw3. Rw3 requires that the organism is *morphologically* distinguishable from all other organisms. However, by the time he wrote the tuberculosis papers, Koch realized that this requirement was too strong. In 1884 he wrote that 'morphological characteristics are not normally sufficient to distinguish bacteria' (Koch, 1884c, p. 171), and later, in 1890, he urged that every possible characteristic of different strains of organisms be considered before identifying them (Koch, 1890, pp. 180f.). As finally stated in the 1884 tuberculosis paper, Rt2 is the Distinguishability Hypothesis.

3. Rt3 is the same as Rw2. As we have stated this condition, it requires that the purported cause both correlate with *and explain* the observed disease phenomena, and this is how Koch usually (but not always) phrased it. Occasionally, Koch followed Klebs who (in E1) required correlation but did not mention explanatory adequacy. Explanatory adequacy is essential in proving causation, so Koch's way of putting this condition is superior to Klebs' formulation.

4. As we have seen, Rt4 and Rt5 have no counterpart in the 1878 papers on infected wounds or in Koch's first anthrax paper. However in a later paper on anthrax, Koch spoke of Rt4 and Rt5 as providing the real proof of causality – he regarded the earlier steps, Rt1 through Rt3, as providing only an orientation preliminary to the actual proof (Koch, 1882b, p. 98). Rt4 and Rt5 provide strong evidence of sufficiency. Together they correspond approximately to Klebs' E2 (p. 96); later we will review evidence that Klebs was the source of Koch's isolation and inoculation criteria.

Through the 1880s, Koch and his fellow workers discovered the causal agents for a range of bacterial diseases. They also published important papers on applying bacteriology to public health, they announced techniques for measuring the bacterial content of air, soil, and drinking water, they tested new methods for disinfection, and they developed a procedure for steam disinfection. Later, Koch discussed the methods that produced these results:

> These new methods proved so helpful and useful in dealing with various problems that one could regard them as the keys for the further investigation of microorganisms, at least insofar as they relate to medicine. Once I had developed them and gained some experience in their use, I utilized them in the study of the pathogenic microorganisms. In a rapid sequence, my colleagues and I were successful in discovering the cause, and thereby the etiology, of a number of infectious diseases. These included the wound

infections, tuberculosis, cholera, typhoid, and diphtheria. Once the appropriate methods had been found, these discoveries fell into our laps like ripe fruit, and they were then used for practical purposes such as the control of such plagues as cholera, typhoid and malaria (Koch, 1909, p. 4).

Two further matters require attention before we turn to a broader interpretation of Koch's Postulates. First, we will give more attention to the sufficiency criteria, Rt1, Rt4 and Rt5. Second, we will review the evidence that Koch derived the Postulates – in particular Rt4 and Rt5 – from Edwin Klebs.

Can we be sure that any organism that satisfies Rt4 and Rt5 is *always* followed by a particular disease? Of course, one could insure sufficiency in the same way one insures necessity, namely, by defining the disease so that the organism is sufficient as well as necessary. This would mean stipulating that a person has a disease, say, tuberculosis, if, and only if, that person harbors the causal bacterium. There are diseases for which this approach seems appropriate: embedded fertilized female acari mites are both sufficient and necessary for scabies; embedded live trichinae are sufficient and necessary for trichinosis. We define both diseases so that hosting these parasites is having the diseases. Henle proposed that causal agents should be sufficient and necessary, and Pasteur sometimes claimed that causal organisms were sufficient and necessary (Pasteur, 1881e, p. 554).

However, in many cases, practical considerations count against taking the mere presence of an organism as sufficient for having a disease, and some of these considerations were apparent in early research. Semmelweis reported a case in which decaying organic matter from a patient with a discharging medullary carcinoma spread fatal childbed fever throughout her ward while she herself remained healthy (Semmelweis, 1861b, pp. 43f). Davaine, Pasteur, and Koch all knew that sheep could consume anthrax bacilli without becoming diseased and that inoculations with virulent anthrax blood sometimes had no effect. Koch admitted that tubercle bacilli could exist in a suitable host without causing symptoms (Koch, 1882a, pp. 94f.). If, as a matter of definition, the presence of causal organisms is made sufficient for these diseases, the preceding examples all become asymptomatic cases of the respective diseases. However, in practice it is more useful to label as diseased only persons who require medical intervention, rather than everyone infected with the causal agent, so there are practical advantages to restricting 'tuberculosis' to conditions involving more than the simple presence of the cause. While we do recognize clinically inapparent cases of many diseases, most disease names are so used that, in order to have the disease, victims must

both harbor the causal agent and manifest symptoms of a certain intensity or otherwise require medical intervention. Thus, for practical reasons,
we often decide *against* making causes definitionally sufficient for their
diseases.

Exactly what evidence is furnished by Rt1, Rt4 and Rt5? One can
think of Rt1 as providing observational evidence of sufficiency; alternatively, Koch suggested that one could also regard this criterion as
providing motivation (what he called an orientation (Koch, 1882b, p.
98)) for investigating causality rather than as part of the actual proof.
What about Rt4 and Rt5 – the isolation and inoculation test? In a
tuberculosis paper, Koch insisted that 'inoculation must succeed not
only sometimes, but in every attempt as is attained in such infectious
diseases as anthrax' (Koch, 1882c, pp. 446f.). Even if this is achieved, it
does not mean the organism is sufficient for the onset of symptoms. As
we have seen, Koch knew that the mere presence of anthrax bacilli was
not sufficient for anthrax: ingesting them did not usually provoke symptoms (Koch, 1876, p. 11), even some inoculation procedures were
unreliable (Koch, 1876, p. 2), and vulnerability varied among susceptible animals (Koch, 1882b, p. 101). Koch never claimed bacilli alone
were sufficient for anthrax, and current definitions of 'anthrax' allow
organisms to occur in test animals in the absence of the disease. Thus,
even the invariable success of inoculations does not – and, given most
definitions, can not – demonstrate that the organism alone is strictly
sufficient: universal success shows only that the organism can be used in
an inoculation procedure that is sufficient. This claim is obviously
weaker than the claim that the factor itself is sufficient. Because criteria
like Rt4 and Rt5 support only this weaker claim, they have been called
weak sufficiency criteria (Carter, 1985b, pp. 358f.). As here defined, a
weak sufficiency condition requires that there is some means by which
the organism can be introduced into a host in such a way that the host
will invariably become diseased.

Are weak sufficiency criteria essential to proving causation? As we
have seen, both Koch and Pasteur started out arguing for causation
using only evidence of necessity. However, after criticism by contemporary physicians who expected causal arguments to establish sufficiency,
both adopted weak sufficiency criteria. Indeed, both insisted that isolation and inoculation was the only way of proving causation. Yet within
months of making this claim, Koch admitted he was unable to find an
animal vulnerable to experimental cholera; he also acknowledged that
no susceptible animals had been found for leprosy or for abdominal
typhus. He concluded: 'we must therefore be content that we have
established the constant occurrence of a specific species of bacteria in
some disease, and that these bacteria do not occur in other diseases. ...

This is acceptable because we already know of other infectious diseases that are caused by pathogenic organisms and that resemble these in every respect' (Koch, 1884d, p. 161). Thus, unable to satisfy his own weak sufficiency criterion, Koch fell back on observational evidence of necessity and an analogical argument based on what was known of other diseases.

Even when inoculations are successful, they may not meet Koch's conservative standard – namely, of succeeding 'not only sometimes, but in every attempt' (Koch, 1882c, pp. 446f.). One may be able to show only that exposure increases the likelihood of the disease. In fact, while he never made this explicit, this is all Koch achieved in his first anthrax inoculations. If this is the most that can be shown, the organisms could be thought of only as a risk factor – like smoking or malnutrition. Alternatively, the success of inoculations may depend on meeting special ancillary conditions. Pasteur found that chickens could contract experimental anthrax, but only if one lowered their body temperatures so bacteridia could flourish in their blood. If such special conditions are essential for success, a causal agent may be thought of only as a cofactor in the disease. Risk factors and cofactors both fall short of strict causality, but they do involve causation in a broad sense, and causal criteria have been proposed that accommodate them. For example, rather than Koch's conservative Rt4 and Rt5, a more liberal criterion may require only that 'incidence of the disease is significantly higher among those exposed to the putative cause than among those not so exposed' (Evans, 1976, p. 192). We now accept, as evidence of kinds of causation, weak sufficiency conditions that are considerably more liberal than the conservative criterion Koch himself claimed to follow. Indeed for some disorders, we recognize causation even when there is no possibility of ever satisfying *any* weak sufficiency criterion whatsoever; we sometimes identify specific causes in the absence of all experimental evidence of sufficiency. At present, this is true for all human genetic disorders; for example, trisomy 21 is the most common cause of Down's Syndrome but there are no experimental tests for sufficiency. This suggests that weak sufficiency criteria, whether liberal or conservative, may not actually be essential even in proving causation. Nevertheless, for at least some kinds of diseases, especially for bacterial diseases, since the middle of the nineteenth century, evidence of weak sufficiency has been part of what one normally expects in causal arguments.

Henle's ideal was that rational medicine should accept only causes that are necessary and sufficient. However, the causes we now identify are not usually sufficient, and there is seldom any point in defining diseases so that their causes will be. Moreover, while (for at least some kinds of diseases) we expect demonstrations of causation to include the satisfaction of weak sufficiency criteria, even sufficiency in this sense may not be absolutely essential to the concept of a specific cause.

In 1840 Jacob Henle speculated about proving causation by separating living organisms from the fluids in which they are located and by observing the powers of each separately (Henle, 1840, p. 948). Since Henle was Koch's teacher at the University of Göttingen, Koch is often thought to have adopted the Postulates, or at least Rt4 and Rt5, from Henle (Evans, 1976, p. 175; Richmond, 1978, p. 85). There are reasons for doubting this view. First, while admitting that he owed Henle a great debt of gratitude (Koch, 1909, p. 3), Koch never suggested Henle had influenced his thinking about disease causation or even his interest in bacteriology. Indeed Koch wrote that he received no encouragement to study bacteriology while he was a student at Göttingen since 'bacteriology did not exist at that time' (Koch, 1909, p. 3). The recollections of Elie Metchnikoff, who worked with Henle in Göttingen just at the time Koch was graduating, confirm Koch's remark. 'When, in 1866, I worked under Henle, in Göttingen, at a time when there were serious investigations on the microscopic agents of infectious disease he remained indifferent and ... at no time did the question of contagious diseases come up in his laboratory' (Lechevalier and Solotorovsky, 1974, p. 65).

Second, in his early work on anthrax, Koch isolated relatively pure cultures of anthrax bacilli and inoculated them into test animals. However, at that time, he seems not to have regarded this procedure as particularly significant in establishing causality. The causal arguments in his early anthrax papers stressed necessity rather than sufficiency. The first weak sufficiency criterion appeared in his long 1878 paper on infected wounds, and Koch first used isolation and inoculation as a way of proving causality in his 1882 tuberculosis papers. If, as a student, Koch had adopted Rt4 and Rt5 from Henle, one would have expected these criteria to figure in his early causal arguments.

When Koch began studying anthrax as a district physician in Wollstein, he was isolated from everyone else who was studying microorganisms. In his first anthrax paper, he admitted he did not have access to several important publications (Koch, 1876, p. 7) and he relied on reviews and abstracts rather than original papers. His first anthrax papers and his summary version of the 1878 paper on infected wounds, delivered before the Society for German Natural Scientists and Physicians, contain no explicit causal criteria. The Society was the same organization before which Klebs had presented his famous 1877 lecture on the revolution in medical thought, and, in the 1878 meetings, again criticized Virchow's research programme (Klebs, 1878b). In 1878 Koch was engaged in his priority dispute with Pasteur regarding the role of bacteridia in anthrax. Klebs and Koch were often together at the 1878 meetings (Heymann, 1932, p. 236), and, in light of the priority dispute and Klebs' own earlier attempt to prove causation for anthrax by isolation and inoculation, they certainly could have discussed methods for proving causation. Shortly thereafter Koch published his long paper on wound infections – the paper containing his first explicit use of causal criteria. In this paper Koch cited several of Klebs' essays (Koch, 1878a, pp. 22, 26) and he mentioned Klebs' method of fractional cultivation (Koch, 1878a, p. 26). Koch credited Klebs with having been the first to attempt to prove that microorganisms cause wound infections (Koch, 1878a, p. 22). In his paper on infected wounds, Koch also frequently cited Felix Victor Birch-Hirschfeld's textbook on pathology. In this text, Birch-Hirschfeld credited Klebs with developing the two main strategies for proving disease causation and he referred to Klebs' work as 'epoch making' (Birch-Hirschfeld, 1872, p. 98).

Koch cited Klebs in several papers that he published in the early 1880s (Schwalbe, 1912, vol. 1, pp. 133, 158f., 183). In his famous tuberculosis papers of 1882 and 1884, he cited Klebs but did not associate Rt4 and Rt5 with him (Schwalbe, 1912, vol. 1, pp. 433, 437, 468, 525, 529). However, in his less famous and less commonly read *second* 1882 paper on tuberculosis, Koch explicitly attributed the strategy to Klebs. He mentioned that, while various methods had been used to prove causality, 'the best method, the method used by everyone who has been seriously occupied with these investigations, was introduced and refined by Klebs' (Koch, 1882c, p. 446). He then described this method as, first, producing successive pure cultures to separate the parasite from all disease products and, second, inoculating isolated parasites into test animals. Koch wrote that his own study of tuberculosis followed this procedure.

Thus, it seems likely that Klebs was the immediate source for Koch's Rt4 and Rt5. Koch first invoked isolation and inoculation at about the time of the 1878 meetings. Perhaps, at that time, he was concerned with causal arguments because of his dispute with Pasteur, and perhaps discussions with Klebs helped him see the necessity of this approach.

The etiological standpoint

By the second half of the nineteenth century, medicine was beginning to prize causes of a particular kind: universal necessary causes that met recognized criteria, that explained disease phenomena and held out the promise of control. One contemporary described the quest for such causes as 'the chief science of medicine' (Stamm, 1865, p. 477). Of course the greatest success of this effort was the bacterial theory of disease.

However, through the 1890s it began to appear that many common disorders were not bacterial. Careful study failed to reveal bacterial causes for hysteria, rabies, smallpox, measles, beriberi, and other disorders. At this point, one could simply have concluded that only certain pathologies – bacterial diseases plus the few diseases attributed to non-microscopic parasites – could be associated with specific causes. This would have allowed for the possibility that other disorders could only be traced to the familiar varieties of causes (miasms, anxiety, gluttony, dissipation, self-abuse) that had been acknowledged for centuries. Indeed, some fifty years earlier, this is exactly how everyone had responded to the realization that acari and *Beauvaria bassiana* caused scabies and muscardine, and to Semmelweis's discovery that decaying organic matter caused childbed fever. Earlier in the century, such diseases were anomalous, and no one inferred, from these anomalies, that other diseases could also be organized in terms of universal and necessary causes. By contrast, in the 1890s, no one seems to have inferred, from the failure to identify causal bacteria for some disorders, that those pathologies must lack specific causes – one searches in vain for any such idea in the medical literature of the period. While traditional causes continued to be mentioned perfunctorily in connection with such illnesses as hysteria,[1] everyone seems to have been open to the possibility that specific causes would be identified for these disorders as well. By this time there had been a reversal in the accepted norms and in what was regarded as anomalous. As it began to appear that a particular disease may not be bacterial, researchers simply turned to other possible specific causes.

Of course, expanding the research programme to include non-bacterial diseases encountered obstacles: new domains of causes had to be identified, new experimental techniques had to be developed, and new theories of disease – including new causal criteria – had to be constructed. But *conceptually* there was no significant hesitation, and researchers moving in new directions encountered nothing like the resistance that Bassi, Semmelweis, Davaine, Mayrhofer, and even Pasteur had encountered through the middle decades of the century. While the medical profession accepted new discoveries only as evidence was forthcoming, everyone was open to the idea that universal necessary causes could be found even for non-bacterial diseases. The reason for the difference is clear: by the 1890s, medical researchers had been converted, not just to the bacterial theory, but to the research programme from which the bacterial theory had emerged – to the etiological stand-point. Even in the face of substantial obstacles, no one seems to have questioned that all pathological processes could be so organized that each disease would have a specific cause. By the 1890s the quest for such causes drove virtually all medical research.

How do Koch's Postulates relate to identifying causes for non-bacterial diseases? While there is little textual evidence that Koch envisioned using the Postulates beyond bacterial diseases, he would likely have been open to the possibility. He consistently resisted the idea that all diseases were bacterial, and his concept of an etiological standpoint surely encompassed more than bacterial diseases. But, whatever Koch himself may have thought, in fact, one can easily interpret Rt1 through Rt5 as a heuristic for finding causes generally rather than merely as causal criteria within the bacterial theory. Indeed given that the whole point of the etiological research programme – Koch's etiological standpoint – is understanding and controlling diseases by means of causes, it would be surprising if the Postulates could not be generalized in this way.

By reorganizing the order slightly, by supplementing the Postulates with other considerations we have found to be necessary, and by abstracting from bacteria (the particular causes in terms of which Rt1 through Rt5 were originally stated), we can recast the Postulates as a series of steps that constitute a general strategy for finding causes:

1. One or more theories of disease must be in place. Each theory will include at least
    a. some basic assumptions such as:
        - a hypothesis (for example, the Bacterial Hypothesis) specifying a domain of potential causes,
        - the Distinguishability Hypothesis (Koch's Rt2) to insure there are differences in the potential causes to account for differences in the pathological processes to which the theory is applied, and
        - such other assumptions as dictated by the nature of the causes in the domain (for example, theories dealing with living organisms will require the Dissemination Hypothesis); and
    b. criteria that a particular factor must satisfy to qualify as the cause of a specific pathological process. Which possible criteria are included will be determined by the nature of the causal factors in the domain; normally the criteria will include one or more weak sufficiency conditions (for example, for bacterial theories, Klebs' E1 or Koch's Rt4 and Rt5).
2. Given some unexplained pathological process, one determines which

available theory (if any) to invoke. One makes this judgment by considering analogies between the morbidity in question and other pathological processes previously assimilated to the different available theories. Of course, some pathologies may defy assimilation and call for the creation of altogether new theories.

3. From among the potential causes in the domain, one seeks a possible cause that is present in most cases of the pathological process and absent otherwise (Koch's Rt1).

4. One establishes that the presence of the potential cause can explain the observed pathological phenomena (Koch's Rt3).

5. One demonstrates that the potential cause satisfies the criteria encompassed by the theory. Together, steps (4) and (5) show that the factor in question is the cause of the pathological process under investigation.

6. Following Semmelweis's tactic, one characterizes a new disease in terms of the cause. This new characterization makes the cause necessary and universal, and, if practical considerations warrant such a definition, sufficient as well.

7. Since every case of the newly characterized disease shares a common necessary cause, one now seeks ways of controlling the disease by manipulating the cause and explanations of disease phenomena in terms of that cause. Success in these efforts confirms the causal claim, supports the specific theory within which the claim is advanced, and even reinforces the entire etiological research programme of which the theory is a part.

It is important to distinguish *in principle* between theories of disease (with their associated assumptions and sets of causal criteria) and the strategy for finding causes that we have here outlined. Each theory, along with its causal criteria, will be constructed to address a particular domain of potential causes (one domain being bacteria), and each domain of potential causes will require its own theory. This is true even though theories of disease often include assumptions analogous to the assumptions in other theories. For example, each theory will include the Distinguishability Hypothesis and some assumption (such as the Bacterial Hypothesis) that identifies a domain of possible causes. By contrast, the strategy for finding causes is central to the heuristic of the research programme as a whole. Thus it is not restricted to any one domain of potential causes, and it encompasses the bacterial theory and every other theory aimed at understanding and controlling disease through the identification of causes.

Described in these terms, the research programme virtually calls out for theories of disease beyond the bacterial theory (in Lakatos's words, such applications were 'adumbrated at the start' (Lakatos, 1968, p. 132)). In the remaining chapters, we will now see how new domains of causes and new theories of disease were assimilated by the programme.

Note

1. And, to repeat a point made in Chapter 1, insofar as one is seeking a sufficient cause for the onset of a particular case of illness, such factors were and still are today potentially relevant.

CHAPTER NINE

An Ideational Theory of Disease

It is generally acknowledged that late nineteenth-century medical researchers were preoccupied with the bacterial theory of disease. 'With the work of Pasteur and Koch, ... there penetrated rapidly into all fields of medicine the idea that infinitely small beings, endowed with special pathogenic qualities, played a pre-eminent role in producing many diseases. The new concept made such a great impression that for a while it was believed that the cause of all diseases could be ascribed to microbes alone. ... Almost completely dominant, bacteriology at this period became the center and goal of medical investigation' (Castiglioni, 1947, p. 809). However, this account is misleading because the change that swept medicine in the late nineteenth century involved more than just acceptance of a particular theory of disease.

In 1884 (in a passage we encountered earlier), Adolf von Strümpell wrote, 'one can justly claim that the scientific treatment of the etiology of diseases constitutes the most characteristic thrust of modern pathology, and ... the secure establishment of the doctrine of organized, externally invading disease agents is until now the most beautiful and important achievement of this effort' (Strümpell, 1884a, p. 2). Strümpell distinguished clearly between scientific etiology and the bacterial theory, which he described as 'until now [scientific etiology's] most beautiful and important achievement'. Implicit in this description is the recognition that non-bacterial etiologies could also be studied scientifically and that such studies could yield achievements as impressive as the bacterial theory itself. Strümpell was clear – clearer perhaps than some modern historians – that the etiological standpoint was not exhausted by the bacterial theory. It was inevitable that the methods of the research programme, having successfully accounted for many bacterial diseases, would be brought to bear on other diseases as well.

Sigmund Freud's early work in psychopathology was among the earliest attempts to assimilate a class of non-bacterial diseases to the etiological standpoint. Yet this aspect of Freud's early work has been entirely ignored. To take one prominent example, a great part of Ellenberger's *The Discovery of the Unconscious* is 'devoted to authors and systems of thought, which ... could be called sources or precursors of Freud'. In a 12-page summary, he gives 'a succinct list of these sources, insofar as they are known today'. The list includes more than two dozen persons and movements, but neither the etiological standpoint nor even its first outstanding success – the bacterial theory of disease – is mentioned (Ellenberger, 1970, pp. 34–46).[1] By ignoring the connection between Freud's investigations and the great research programme of late nineteenth-century medicine, one overlooks aspects of Freud's work that are *both* different from the research of many of his contemporaries who wrote on psychopathology *and* fundamentally allied to work that was being carried out at the same time in other areas of medicine.

In the late nineteenth century, hysteria was among the most widely discussed diseases. Partly because Freud's early work focused on hysteria, nineteenth-century discussions of that disorder have been the subject of continuing interest. Unfortunately, certain misconceptions, partly initiated by Freud himself, have been perpetuated in contemporary accounts. Because of these misconceptions, Freud's own contribution to the discussion has been misunderstood. We begin by reviewing standard medical opinions about hysteria in the 1880s, the decade in which Freud began his work.

Medical opinions about hysteria in the 1880s

In the 1880s, hysteria was generally regarded as a functional nervous disorder where 'functional' meant a disturbance of function without an identifiable organic foundation. It was usually classified as a psychosis or a neurosis. In 1883 Martin Cohn classified hysteria as a functional psychosis, that is, a disease 'such that, given the current state of knowledge, no organic alteration of the central organs can be exhibited' (Cohn, 1883, p. 44). Cohn noted that Emanuel Mendel, a medical professor at Berlin, distinguished hysteria from other psychoses as a neurotic condition from which psychotic states follow. In 1884, the publications by Cohn and Mendel were reviewed in a comprehensive survey by a Dr Schäfer of Berlin (Schäfer, 1884). Schäfer adopted the same definition of 'hysteria'. The first edition of Adolf von Strümpell's influential text, *Diseases of the Nervous System*, appeared in the same year; Strümpell defined 'hysteria' as a functional disturbance without gross changes in the anatomy of the nervous system (Strümpell, 1884b, vol. 2, p. 417). Also in 1884, J. Weiss, docent for psychiatry in Vienna, wrote that hysteria has symptoms and a course of development that could only belong to a psychosis and could only be treated by psychiatric methods (Weiss, 1884, pp. 457f.). He wrote that the disease is functional and that attributing the disease 'to a palpable disorder of the central nervous system is entirely unthinkable'. Schäfer's survey, together with the independent article by Weiss, provided the basis for an 1885 essay by Maximilian Herz, docent for childhood diseases in Vienna (Herz, 1885). Herz adopted the definition of 'functional psychosis' from Schäfer and Cohn, and agreed that hysteria should be so classified. Herz added that numerous attempts to trace hysteria to anatomical lesions – he mentioned Theodor Meynert, Hermann Nothnagel, and others – had produced no significant results (Herz, 1885, col. 1371). By 1886, even pathological anatomists described hysteria as a functional disorder.

In this respect there were no significant differences between the Viennese and Jean Martin Charcot in Paris. Charcot observed that there are 'a great number of morbid states, evidently having their seat in the nervous system, which leave in the dead body no material trace that can be discovered. Epilepsy, hysteria, even the most inveterate cases, [and] chorea ... deny the most penetrating anatomical investigations' (Charcot, 1892–95, vol. 3, pp. 14f.). Charcot identified such disorders as neuroses – a term defined by his English translator as 'diseases of the nervous system apparently due to functional or dynamic causes; which are not, so far as we know, attended by any organic lesion' (Charcot, 1889, vol. 3, p. 13). This, of course, is essentially the same definition that appears so frequently in the German and Austrian medical literature of the period.

Hysteria was generally regarded as irregular, both because symptoms could change dramatically in a given patient and because symptoms could vary fundamentally from patient to patient. Emanuel Mendel cited Sydenham as having referred to the disease as a veritable Proteus displaying as many colors as the chameleon (Mendel, 1884, p. 241). In 1883, Heinrich von Bamberger described hysteria as a collection of 'disturbances in different parts of the body, often contradictory in nature and highly variable, without any anatomical foundation being discovered in necropsy' (Bamberger, 1883). Weiss noted that one is justified in thinking of a hysterical condition whenever one encounters a group of symptoms that resembles some definite organic illness, but that departs in some respects from the nature or course of development of that disease. 'There is hardly a symptom, whether or not we are in a position to ascribe it to a particular anatomical foundation, that cannot, either alone or with other symptoms, belong to the picture of hysteria' (Weiss, 1884, p. 452). But, in spite of these irregularities, physicians tried to detect patterns.

Charcot characterized hysteria by the use of five 'stigmata' which he felt were always present in a greater or lesser degree: (1) sensorial hemianesthesia, 'that stigma which almost surely characterizes the hysterical condition'; (2) the ovarian phenomenon, that is, the fact that in many female hysterics an attack could be provoked or arrested by direct pressure on an ovary; (3) the existence of hysterogenic points that function like the ovary in provoking and arresting attacks but whose location varies from patient to patient; (4) the manifestation of a definite series of stages in hysteric attacks; and (5) paraplegic or hemiplegic paralysis (Charcot, 1892–95, vol. 3, pp. 115f.). Charcot first presented this scheme in 1883 (Charcot, 1883, p. 39) and the first German translation (Freud's) appeared in 1886. Charcot's work was known and followed in Austria and Germany. In 1882, Moriz Rosenthal, who maintained personal contact with Charcot, characterized hysteria in terms of Charcot's stigmata, and distinguished three major classes of hysterics depending on which symptoms were most pronounced (Rosenthal, 1879). Eduard Heinrich Henoch's text on childhood diseases, which went through 11 editions beginning in 1881, contained a discussion of hysteria based on Charcot. Henoch, like Rosenthal, distinguished classes of hysterics depending on which symptoms were most apparent: psychotic hallucinations; convulsions; motor disturbances including paralysis; and sensory disturbances including hemianesthesia (Henoch, 1881). Henoch's system was adopted by both Herz and Cohn in works cited above. Strümpell's account of hysteria in his text on diseases of the nervous system was heavily dependent on Charcot. In the second edition of his text, published in 1885, Strümpell cited Charcot ten times in a 22-page account (Strümpell, 1885, vol. 2, pp. 450–71). He discussed and adopted Charcot's five stigmata and the stages that Charcot identified as characteristic of hysteric attacks. Strümpell's discussion reflects a thorough grasp of Charcot's main ideas; the text was among the most widely used in the field, and would certainly have been well known in Vienna.

Standard characterizations of hysteria were symptomatic: 'hysteria, like neurasthenia, is only a symptom or a complex of symptoms' (Herz, 1885, col. 1305); 'we seek the constituent elements of hysteria, the hysterical symptoms' (Tuczek, 1886, p. 511); and 'hysteria designates a series of the most variable symptom-complexes' (Cohn, 1883, p. 51). In each of these passages, hysteria was identified with certain combinations of symptoms. This seemed particularly appropriate (indeed necessary) given that no organic lesions could be conclusively demonstrated in autopsies of hysterics – what could hysteria be besides symptoms? Charcot's stigmata were obviously of this nature. Weiss, Henoch, Herz, Cohn, and Oppenheim (Oppenheim, 1890, p. 554) all adopted symptomatic characterizations. Ludwig Seeligmuller argued that chorea should be regarded as a form of hysteria since choreatics invariably display hysterical symptoms (Seeligmuller, 1881, p. 584); later F. Tuczek argued that hysteria could only be defined symptomatically (Tuczek, 1886, p. 511). Given that other nervous disorders were also characterized symptomatically and that, in some cases, it was difficult or impossible to make differential diagnoses, these disorders seemed to blend together. Physicians regularly suggested that the nervous disorders were ultimately all one or that they differed only in degree.

As early as the 1850s, cases of male hysteria were regularly described in European medical literature; 30 years later, in the period we are considering, it was common knowledge in Vienna and throughout Europe that either sex was vulnerable (Carter, 1980). In this period there was great interest in infantile hysteria; this interest, together with the long recognition of male hysteria, completely exploded the old idea that hysteria was connected with movements or irritation of the uterus. Writers in the 1880s occasionally began essays on hysteria by noting that this connection had been totally abandoned. Tuczek asserted that 'associating hysteria with the uterus is like associating melancholy with black bile' (Tuczek, 1886, p. 511).

Hysteria was generally regarded as caused by the usual combination of predisposing and exciting factors. Heredity and such conditions as chronic illness, malnutrition, emotional instability, ethnic origin, adverse climate or meteorological conditions, sexual abnormality, and persistent irritations (either physical or emotional) were mentioned as predisposing factors. Even more exciting causes were mentioned; these included (but were by no means limited to) sexual trauma, illness, various infections, emotional shocks, inadequate or excessive exercise, intellectual exertion, and fear. In this respect Charcot was entirely typical. He distinguished predisposing and provocative causes (Charcot, 1892–95, 2:31[2]); the former included heredity in a broad sense as well as other factors;[3] provocative causes included dog bites, lightning bolts, unrequited love, and alcoholic and lead poisoning. Charcot explicitly insisted both that different cases of a single nervous disease such as hysteria could have a variety of different causes and also that different diseases – for example, hysteria and epilepsy – could have exactly the same exciting cause (1:371f., 2:32f.). He also discussed cases of hysteria that 'could be assigned to no cause' (Charcot, 1892–95, vol. 1, p. 366). Charcot explained that, while he could not ignore causes, as a clinician his task was to portray and to treat the disease as he presently saw it (2:360).

There were obvious similarities between the concept of hysteria in the 1880s and the concepts of most diseases at the beginning of the nineteenth century. Hysteria was defined and classified symptomatically; etiological accounts were vague and inconsistent, and included the usual range of possible factors contributory to sufficient causes of particular cases. The causes of hysteria were not used to explain other aspects of the disease. As the contrast between this confusion and the orderly scientific explanations of the infectious diseases became progressively more apparent, it was inevitable that neurologists and psychiatrists would look to the bacterial theory for a model.

In 1884 Adolf von Strümpell advocated a new approach to hysteria and to the other nervous disorders (Strümpell, 1884a). Strümpell observed that symptomatology and pathological anatomy could not significantly advance the comprehension of any disease. Even a complete microscopical description of a diseased organ could not satisfy the standards for comprehension that had been established for the bacterial diseases. Such comprehension, Strümpell observed, could be achieved only when the symptoms and the anatomical lesions could themselves be explained as necessary developments from the original cause of the disease and this required following the model of the bacterial theory (Strümpell, 1884a, p. 3).

In 1888, P. J. Möbius offered an etiological characterization of hysteria and attempted to give causal explanations for its symptoms. 'All those diseased modifications of the body are hysterical that are caused by ideas' (Möbius, 1888, p. 66).[4] Möbius admitted he was unable to trace all hysterical symptoms to ideas – indeed, even patients may not be able to give an account of all their mental processes. It is, however, a common experience that hysterical symptoms often come and go because of ideas. In what he called an argument by analogy, Möbius alluded to Charcot's findings that all hysterical symptoms could be induced by hypnotic suggestion and concluded that all these symptoms were caused by ideas. He observed that this definition was confirmed by clinical experience, but he also mentioned the definition's theoretical and practical advantages: it provided conceptual clarity and unity by realigning the boundaries between hysteria and other nervous disorders, and a conceptual basis for existing psychiatric therapies; and suggested new therapies as well (Möbius, 1888, p. 67).

Möbius's definition was mildly influential; it was given serious critical attention in European medical literature and was adopted by some writers. In a later essay (Möbius, 1892), Möbius made it clear that the definition was intended to bring unity and coherence into discussions of hysteria by using the same strategy employed in defining the infectious diseases. He also gave interesting arguments that pathological anatomy could not provide an adequate basis for understanding or for classifying diseases, that the nervous disorders must be treated along exactly the lines exemplified by contemporary work in infectious diseases, and that this approach, which he regarded as essentially new, would totally alter the concept of psychological medicine (Möbius, 1892, p. 299). Later, in their publications on hysteria, Freud and Josef Breuer gave more critical attention to Möbius than to anyone else (Strachey, 1955–74, vol. 2, pp. 8n., 186–91, 215, 243, 248n.). In 1894 several of Möbius's essays were reprinted in a volume entitled *Contributions to Neurology*. Freud wrote to his friend, Wilhelm Fliess, that Möbius's essays were 'very well done; they are important on the subject of hysteria. His mind is the best among the neurologists; fortunately,' Freud continued, 'he is not on the track of sexuality' (Freud, 1954, p. 101).

In 1892, Strümpell delivered a lecture entitled 'On the Origin and Healing of Diseases through Ideas' (Strümpell, 1893), which carried one step further the project of explaining the nervous diseases by appealing to their causes. After some introductory comments, Strümpell noted that the most characteristic thrust of contemporary medicine was the quest for causes of diseases. 'The empty generalities of the past only appeared, superficially, to satisfy the need for causes; this need can only be met through the discovery of causes that operate in every single case, only through a knowledge of their nature, of the manner of their operation, of the site of their influence, and of the necessity of their consequence' (Strümpell, 1893, pp. 22f.). Everyone knows, he continued, how much our opinions have been enriched and deepened in these respects in the last 20 years, particularly through work in the area of the infectious diseases (Strümpell, 1893, p. 23). Strümpell then considered the influence of psychiatric processes in the generation and healing of disease. Also in this area the quest for insight into causes has achieved a level from which the physician, freed from earlier prejudices, can obtain a clear and realistic perception of the actual situation. Strümpell considered some of the specific neuroses and showed how regarding them as diseases of ideas could explain them and the therapeutic measures employed in treatment.

Between 1884 and 1892, both Möbius and Strümpell took steps toward etiological accounts of hysteria; however, neither had the persistence or the imagination to generate a theory with lasting impact. By the following year, 1893, Freud was beginning to develop just such a theory.

Freud on hysteria

Freud's earliest medical studies emphasized neurology and anatomy. We know that Josef Breuer called Freud's attention to one remarkable hysteric, the woman referred to as Anna O., before Freud went to Paris in the autumn of 1885. Freud reported this case to Charcot, but, he wrote, 'the great man showed no interest in my first outline of the subject, so that I never returned to it and allowed it to pass from my

mind' (Freud, 1925, pp. 19f.). Apparently Freud began studying hysteria when he was unable to obtain adequate laboratory facilities for the
neurological research that had been his first interest (Freud, 1886, pp.
8f.). James Strachey estimates that this momentous shift occurred in
early December 1885 (Strachey, 1955–74, vol. 1, p. 4).

After Freud returned to Vienna, he presented a paper on male hysteria before the Viennese Society of Physicians. This paper has not survived.
The contents of his presentation and the events of the meeting are
known only from reports published in Viennese and German medical
journals and through a preliminary report that Freud presented to the
Viennese Medical Faculty (Freud, 1886). In this preliminary report,
Freud discussed 'what was completely novel' in the studies of Charcot:
he claimed that, prior to Charcot, hysteria had not been well defined,
and that no definitive symptomatology had been assigned to it (Freud,
1886, pp. 10f.). Freud objected to the 'widespread prejudices' that
hysteria was attributable to genital irritation, and he credited Charcot
with having refuted this prejudice by demonstrating the unsuspected
frequency of male hysterics. He further attributed to Charcot the discovery of special somatic signs by which hysteria could be conclusively
diagnosed. 'Thus,' Freud concluded, by Charcot's efforts, 'hysteria was
lifted out of the chaos of the neuroses, was differentiated from other
conditions with a similar appearance, and was provided with a symptomatology which makes it impossible any longer to doubt the rule of
law and order' (Freud, 1886, p. 12). These claims were certainly not
impressive to Freud's audience: Charcot's attempts to systematize the
symptomatology of hysteria were neither unique nor unknown. The
'widespread prejudices' to which Freud objected had, in fact, been
abandoned years earlier, and Briquet's estimation of the frequency of
male hysteria, which formed the basis of Charcot's opinions, had been
accepted by the Viennese and Germans for years (Carter, 1980, p.
265n.). Freud, who first became seriously interested in hysteria while in
Paris, may simply not have been familiar with existing literature on the
disease. In any case, Freud's misconceptions, together with his un-
restrained admiration for Charcot, no doubt contributed to the
disappointing reception his paper received (Freud, 1925, p. 15).

Between 1886 and 1893 Freud published little about hysteria. Apart
from an unsigned article in one medical encyclopedia, which Freud
almost certainly wrote (Freud, 1888), there are only items of minor
interest. Assuming that the article is Freud's, it shows that as late as
1888 Freud had not departed significantly from the position taken in
his report: hysteria is still described as an orderly disease accurately
characterized by Charcot's stigmata; there is no indication that Freud
had become interested in an etiological account of hysteria; the causes

of the disease are still the familiar predisposing and exciting factors (Freud, 1888, pp. 50f.). Perhaps the most significant difference between Freud's preliminary report and the 1888 article is that the article reveals a greater familiarity with the literature on hysteria.

Freud's publications in 1893 – the year following the publications by Möbius and Strümpell considered above – depart, for the first time, from Charcot's symptomatic characterization of hysteria. Freud's translation of Charcot's lectures, which was published in that year, contains a series of footnotes clearly indicating the new direction of his thought.[5] In one note, he objects that Charcot's etiology did not separate the disposition to neuroses from the disposition to organic nervous disorders (Charcot, 1892–95, 1:237n.[6]). Given a purely symptomatic concept of the neuroses there would be no reason to expect etiology to make this separation. Indeed such a distinction would be impossible if, as most people assumed, symptomatically-defined functional disorders could be caused by the same factors that, on other occasions, caused related organic diseases. After adopting symptomatic definitions of hysteria, various writers explicitly denied that hysteria could be causally distinguished from other organic or functional disorders. One would expect etiology to reflect this distinction only if one assumed that distinguishable diseases must have distinguishable causes – that is, only if one assumed the Distinguishability Hypothesis which we encountered in the bacterial theory. In fact, in an 1892 publication, Möbius rejected as nonsense the idea that different diseases could have the same cause (Möbius, 1892, p. 290). But this would be nonsense only to those who viewed diseases from the etiological standpoint. At the time he was translating Charcot's lectures, Freud knew Möbius's publication and, in a footnote, recommended it to Charcot's readers (1:149n). In the same publication, Möbius observed (as Strümpell had before him) that redefining the nervous diseases in causal terms would entail reclassifying them. Several of Freud's footnotes express objections to Charcot's scheme for classifying the nervous disorders, the so-called *famille neuropathique*. In one note Freud explained that his objections to Charcot's scheme were at least partially the result of his work on the etiology of tabes (1:8n). In another note, he observed that his own theory of 'hysterical counterwill', connected together various hysterical symptoms and thereby cast light on the mechanism of the hysterical condition (1:137n). At about the same time, in a preliminary draft for a subsequent joint publication, Freud and Josef Breuer objected that Charcot had only described hysteria, and that 'this description throws no light at all on any connection there may be between the different phases, on the significance of attacks in the general picture of hysteria, or on the way in which attacks are modified in individual patients' (Freud, 1893,

p. 151). Strümpell and Möbius had pointed out that the etiological definitions of the bacterial theory had shed light on just these factors in the infectious diseases.

Thus, Freud's writings from 1893 and 1894 show he was moving away from Charcot's symptomatic treatment of hysteria and toward an etiological approach. It has been universally recognized that Freud began criticizing Charcot in 1893, but the significance of the criticism has been generally overlooked. Ernst Jones wrote: 'What Freud maintained as the result of his observations was that, whenever a thorough investigation of the patient could be carried out, sexual etiological factors would be found which were different in [hysteria and the anxiety neuroses]; this was his justification for separating them' (Jones, 1953, vol. 1, p. 256). Jones mentions Möbius only as one 'from whom ... Freud could have derived but very little' (Jones, 1953, vol. 1, p. 370). There is no indication that Jones sees any novelty or special importance in this new strategy, and Freud's other commentators generally overlook the change altogether.[7] Yet these steps, which Möbius and Strümpell had advocated, fundamentally severed Freud's work from the ideas of most of his other predecessors; he thereby adopted an orientation, never to be abandoned, that brought his work on psychopathology into harmony with the prevailing orientation of medical research in his time. These facts can be ignored only at the cost of failing to understand the true nature of Freud's contribution.

We must now consider Freud's work in the few years following 1893. It is unnecessary to follow the evolution of Freud's thought or to summarize his ultimate views. Our goal is only to trace Freud's quest for etiological characterizations of the nervous disorders, especially hysteria, and his use of those characterizations to provide explanations that were exactly analogous to the explanations that were, at the same time, being derived from the etiological definitions of the infectious diseases. To accomplish this it will be necessary only to review certain prominent themes in Freud's writings through 1896, the year in which Freud published both 'Heredity and the Etiology of the Neuroses' and 'The Etiology of Hysteria'.

In 'Heredity and the Etiology of the Neuroses' Freud asks: 'Is it possible to establish a constant etiological relation between a particular cause and a particular neurotic effect, in such a way that each of the major neuroses can be attributed to a specific etiology?' (Freud, 1896a, p. 149). His answer is that each neurosis 'has as its immediate cause one particular disturbance of the economics of the nervous system' and, in particular, disturbances of 'the subject's sexual life, whether they lie in a disorder of his contemporary sexual life or in important events in his past life'. After considering the specific causes of some of the other neuroses, he writes: '*A passive sexual experience before puberty*: this, then, is the specific etiology of hysteria' (Freud, 1896a, p. 152). In 'Further Remarks on the Neuro-Psychoses of Defence' he writes:

> In order to cause hysteria, it is not enough that there should occur … an event that touches [the subject's] sexual existence and becomes pathogenic through the release and suppression of a distressing affect. On the contrary, *these sexual traumas must have occurred in early childhood (before puberty), and their content must consist of an actual irritation of the genitals* (of processes resembling copulation).
>
> (Freud, 1896b, p. 163)

And finally, in 'The Etiology of Hysteria':

> I therefore put forward the thesis that at the bottom of every case of hysteria there are *one or more occurrences of premature sexual experience*, occurrences which belong to the earliest years of childhood but which can be reproduced through the work of psychoanalysis in spite of the intervening decades. I believe that this is an important finding, the discovery of a *caput Nili* in neuropathology.
>
> (Freud, 1896c, p. 203)

How are such passages to be understood? Freud sometimes suggests that these claims are simply empirical discoveries from clinical observation (Strachey, 1955–74, vol. 3, pp. 52, 99). Indeed, it is possible that the theses originated in just that way. However, their logical role in Freud's thought is not that of simple empirical generalizations.

Freud started out believing that Charcot's symptomatic characterization of hysteria was essentially correct. Perhaps for this reason Freud presented his etiological account as a discovery based on Charcot's symptomatic definition. However, there are indications that, at an early stage, Freud regarded the etiological discovery as more fundamental than a simple empirical generalization: In his *An Autobiographical Study*, he explained that Breuer's discoveries in the treatment of Anna O. 'seemed to me to be of so fundamental a nature that I could not believe it could fail to be present in any case of hysteria if it had been proved to occur in a single one' (Freud, 1925, p. 21). In letters to Fliess written in 1892 and 1893 – the first years in which he departed from Charcot's symptomatic characterization and only four years after the entirely orthodox article in the encyclopedia – Freud insisted that 'no neurasthenia or analogous neurosis can exist without a disturbance of the sexual function', and 'the contention which I am putting forward and desire to test by observations is that neurasthenia is always *only* a sexual neurosis' (Freud, 1954, pp. 65f.).

In 'The Neuro-psychoses of Defence', Freud identified two 'extreme forms of hysteria' that did not conform to a characterization of hysteria given by one famous French researcher, Pierre Janet. Both forms are defined etiologically (Freud, 1894, pp. 46f.). Similarly, in a long paper on anxiety neuroses, Freud distinguished six forms of neuroses in women, four in men, and two found in both sexes; all 12 forms were defined etiologically (Freud, 1895). It is clear that Freud used his etiological account of the nervous disorders to generate a nosology more coherent, rational, and precise than had been possible before.

By 1896, the sexual etiology of hysteria had become definitional. Freud repeatedly exploited the tactic of redefining diseases in terms of causes. In 'Heredity and the Etiology of the Neuroses', he set forth a 'nosographic innovation' resulting from his researches into the etiology of the major neuroses (Freud, 1896a, p. 146). His innovation was a fourfold scheme in which each specific neurosis was attributed to a particular abnormality in the subject's sexual behavior. 'What gives its distinctive character to my line of approach,' he wrote, 'is that I elevate these sexual influences to the rank of specific causes, that I recognize their action in every case of neurosis, and finally that I trace a regular parallelism, a proof of a special etiological relation between the nature of the sexual influence and the pathological species of the neurosis' (Freud, 1896a, p. 149). In the next few pages, Freud discussed neurasthenia, other anxiety neuroses, hysteria, and obsessional neuroses; each of these was differentiated from the others by the specific etiology of the symptoms.

However, as Freud saw, the etiological definitions and nosological innovations were not an end in themselves. In an early draft of their book on hysteria, Freud and Breuer objected that Charcot's account explained virtually nothing about the disease (Freud, 1893, p. 151). By contrast, in his own writings, Freud used the etiological account of the nervous disorders to explain an impressive variety of phenomena including certain hysterical symptoms (Strachey, 1955–74, vol. 3, p. 34[8]), the incidence of hysteria (p. 153) and the hysterogenic zones (p. 163), the response of hysterics to hypnosis (p. 59), certain similarities among the neuroses (p. 99), patterns of incidence of anxiety neuroses among married couples (p. 101), neurasthenia occurring in some cases of sexual abuse (p. 113), the suppression of those events that cause specific cases of hysteria (p. 154), the predominance of hysteria among women and of obsessional neurosis among men (p. 169), the apparent familial neurotic disposition and various pathological symptoms (p. 209), habits (p. 169), and phobias (pp. 130f.), the course of development of obsessional neuroses (p. 146), the success and failure of various therapeutic measures (p. 195), the rare occurrence of hysteria in the lower social orders (p. 211) and much much more. Moreover, Freud considered observed facts that could not be explained as possible weaknesses in his theory (Charcot, 1892–95, vol. 1, p. 314n.). In one discussion of organic lesions, Freud commented that the physician's representation of the causes and alterations of these lesions must be right 'since they allowed him to understand the details of the illness' (Freud, 1909, pp. 11f.). By 1896 he wrote that 'the symptoms of hysteria can only be understood if they are traced back' to etiological factors (Freud, 1896b, p. 163). In a lecture of the same year he asserted, 'In the sole attempt to explain the physiological and psychical mechanism of hysteria which I have been able to make in order to correlate my observations, I have come to regard the participation of sexual motive forces as an indispensable premise' (Freud, 1896c, p. 200). Thus, at least by 1896, Freud found the explanatory force of his etiological account most compelling.

Because the theoretical advantages of his new approach were so apparent, Freud persisted even in the face of apparently incompatible clinical evidence. So far as Freud knew at this time, the case of Anna O. was an exception to his theory (Freud, 1925, p. 26), and there were other likely exceptions as well (Breuer and Freud, 1893, p. 14). In an 1893 letter to Fliess, Freud admitted that it required courage to insist on his etiological theories in the face of intractable clinical evidence, and, in another letter, he confessed that 'the connection between obsessional neurosis and sexuality does not always lie so near the surface ... if it had been sought for by anyone less obstinately wedded to the idea, it would have been overlooked' (Freud, 1954, pp. 78, 81).

We now see striking parallels between Freud's post-1893 approach to psychopathology and work that was being done at about the same time on the infectious diseases. At least initially, Freud and Breuer saw their work as closely associated with the positions of Möbius and Strümpell (Strachey, 1955–74, vol. 2, pp. 7f., 187, 215; vol. 3, p. 51), and both Möbius and Strümpell, in turn, saw their own work as modelled on the bacterial theory. Indeed, Möbius and Strümpell explicitly set out to do for the nervous disorders what had been accomplished in the infectious diseases by using an etiological approach. Freud was less candid about the ultimate source of the strategy he followed, but he used the contemporary infectious account of tuberculosis as an analogy in explaining and justifying some aspects of his views about the causes of anxiety neuroses (Strachey, 1955–74, vol. 2, p. 187; vol. 3, pp. 137, 209) and certain of the metaphors chosen by Freud and Breuer also suggest that they were aware of the connection between their work and the bacterial theory (Carter, 1980, p. 273n.). In any event, whether intentionally or not, Freud's work on psychopathology ended up exactly in harmony with the main orientation of the medical research of his time. At the very least, given the successes of bacterial theory, this fact must have made his account more appealing than other simultaneous accounts that were not etiological and did not have the same explanatory force.

Why have Freud's commentators ignored the parallels between his early work and simultaneous research on the bacterial diseases? In part, this may reflect a simple lack of historical perspective. We have become so accustomed to etiological characterizations and classifications that Freud's etiological approach may appear to require no special consideration. In his time, however, the situation was different: this approach was still relatively new, even in accounting for the infectious diseases. Until 1884 no one seems to have envisioned characterizing the nervous disorders etiologically, and until the end of the 1880s no one actually tried to do so. Freud was certainly the first to use this approach to provide coherent explanations for the nervous diseases.

In recent years, Freud's work has been eulogized as revolutionary – as the introduction of a new paradigm in science (Mujeeb-ur-Rahman, 1977). Freud's admirers (beginning with Freud himself) have compared him with Darwin and Copernicus.[9] Viewed in relation to any of his recognized sources, his work does seem revolutionary and without precedent. Charcot – like most other late nineteenth-century physicians who dealt with nervous disorders – started with symptoms and ended up with total chaos in the discussion of causes. As a result there were no coherent explanations of anything. By starting with causes, Freud was able to explain the symptoms as well as many other facets of the nervous diseases – and, ultimately, everything from jokes and dreams to spelling errors. In the context of his recognized sources, this was indeed a revolution. However, if we inquire into the nature of this revolution, and if we view Freud against the background of nineteenth-century medicine, from which his thinking emerged, his work takes on the appearance of an ingenious application of a strategy that was already being employed with enormous success in other areas – a strategy Freud applied with considerable ingenuity but did not create. From this point of view, therefore, we must be more cautious about describing Freud as a paradigm initiator or scientific revolutionary. These facts, too, may relate to his commentators' inability to see what must be among the crucial factors that guided his work and helped to secure its acceptance.

It now appears that the model of comprehension exemplified by the bacterial theory underlies our way of thinking about other classes of diseases that have nothing to do with bacteria. The current pervasiveness of this way of thinking is illustrated by the fact that none of Freud's commentators sees any change at all when Freud completely reversed himself and adopted it. Thus, while taking account of the relation between Freud's work and the etiological standpoint may challenge his role as a paradigm initiator, by so much the more does it confirm, in that role, those who first adopted the basic principles of the etiological standpoint.

Notes

1. Hannah S. Decker (Decker, 1977), Ernest Jones (Jones, 1953) and Ola Andersson (Andersson, 1962) also ignore the bacterial theory in their discussions of the origins of Freud's doctrines.
2. Through this paragraph, references such as this one are volume and pages references to Charcot (1892–95).
3. Under heredity Charcot included such factors as a father abandoning his family (2:6), alcoholic aunts (2:227), and a suicidal father (2:319) in addition to hysteric, epileptic, or nervous relatives. Even Freud objected when Charcot called an arthritic tendency in relatives a hereditary neuropathic disposition (1:237).
4. This definition presupposes what we could call an Ideational Hypothesis. It implicitly identifies a domain of causes for a new theory of disease, and in this respect it is parallel to the Bacterial Hypothesis discussed in earlier chapters.
5. For an enlightening study of 'Freud's rebellion' from Charcot's point of view, see Gelfand (1989).
6. Through this paragraph, references such as this one are volume and page references to Charcot (1892–95).
7. Ola Andersson writes 'In the late 1880s and 1890s P. J. Möbius and A. v. Strümpell had published papers on the traumatic neuroses and on hysteria in which they espoused views very similar to those of Charcot [!]' (Andersson, 1962, p. 115).
8. Through this paragraph, page numbers in parentheses are references to volume 3 of Strachey (1955–74).
9. For a review and references see, Nigel D. Walker, 'A New Copernicus?' and especially David Shakow and David Rapaport, 'Darwin and Freud: a Comparison of Receptions'; both reprinted in Mujeeb-ur-Rahman (1977, pp. 35–42 and 43–63).

CHAPTER TEN

Protozoal and Viral Theories of Disease

A research programme 'consists of methodological rules: some tell us what paths of research to avoid ... , and others what paths to pursue' (Lakatos, 1968, p. 132). The result of following such rules is a sequence of theories, 'T_1, T_2, T_3 ... where each subsequent theory results from adding auxiliary clauses to ... the previous theory in order to accommodate some anomaly' (Lakatos, 1968, p. 118). By technical innovations and dedicated research, nineteenth-century scientists successfully explained an impressive array of bacterial diseases; each success could be regarded as yielding a new member in a Lakatosian sequence of bacterial theories of disease. A set of basic assumptions such as Klebs' *Grundversuche* was common to all such theories.

However, as medical research continued, various obviously contagious diseases became prominent precisely because, while superficially similar to known bacterial diseases, their causal agents eluded every attempt at identification. In 1894, William Henry Welch observed:

> We have a large number of infectious diseases which have thus far resisted all efforts to discover their specific infectious agents. Here belong yellow fever, typhus fever, dengue, mumps, rabies, Oriental pest, whooping cough, smallpox and other exanthematous fevers, syphilis, and some other infectious diseases in human beings. It will be noted that many of these are the most typically contagious diseases, which it might have been supposed would be the first to unlock their secrets.
>
> (Hughes, 1977, p. 25)

One way of explaining these failures is to say that the diseases in question were caused by such entities as protozoa, viruses, or rickettsia that were different from the bacteria studied by classical bacteriologists. However, this explanation suggests that discovering new causes is like finding previously overlooked shells on a beach – it obscures the theoretical innovations required in recognizing new kinds of specific causes.

A theory of disease must specify a domain of entities over which the theory is to be applied and it must include causal criteria that indicate, in part, how the word 'cause' is to be used within the theory. Given such a theory and some new illness, there may simply be nothing within the domain of the theory that satisfies the criteria with respect to that illness. One cannot expect always to find missing causes simply by looking more carefully – as Davaine's work illustrates, in the absence of an appropriate theory, no amount of empirical evidence may be sufficient to establish causal relations. With respect to the diseases mentioned by Welch, part of what was needed was the creation of new theories defined over new domains of possible causes and adoption of new criteria that could be satisfied by those entities.

Driven by a shared commitment to the etiological research programme, late nineteenth-century scientists worked toward meeting these requirements. In Lakatos's terminology, we can think of this work as the creation of new research programmes subordinate to the overriding programme that we have called the etiological standpoint. In this chapter we will consider two such subordinate programmes – one focusing on protozoa and the other on viruses.

A protozoal theory of disease

Malaria, also known as intermittent fever, has been prominent in Europe for millennia, and there were serious attempts to assimilate it to the bacterial theory. In 1879, Edwin Klebs and Corrado Tommasi-Crudeli described a bacterium they had isolated from swamp-ooze and from the urine of malarial patients. When these bacteria were cultured and injected into rabbits, the rabbits died with symptoms resembling malaria. Upon dissection, the rabbits were found to have spleens that were enlarged and contained black pigment similar to that found in the spleens of human victims of malaria (Klebs and Tommasi-Crudeli, 1879b, p. 125). Klebs and Tommasi-Crudeli named the organism *Bacillus malariae*. They seemed to have met all the conditions for proving causation, and other researchers confirmed their results. Their account of the disease was widely accepted – in 1881 Giuseppe Cuboni and Ettore Marchiafava began a paper by observing: 'knowledge of the parasitic nature of malaria has received the most brilliant confirmation in the recent work of Klebs and Tommasi-Crudeli' (Cuboni and Marchiafava, 1881, p. 265).

On 6 November 1880, a French physician named Charles Louis Alphonse Laveran, noticed unusual 'elements' of three kinds in blood drawn from a young soldier suffering from malaria. Laveran regarded the elements as parasitic and suspected they were causally involved in the disease. He communicated his discovery to the Academy of Medicine in Paris (Colin, 1880a). Laveran's report was presented by Léon Colin, but Colin himself was skeptical about Laveran's conclusions. He did not believe the elements were parasites, partly because malaria was not contagious; he recommended a commission be established to appraise the validity of future communications. One month later, Colin presented another paper on Laveran's behalf, and this time Colin was even more skeptical. He suggested that what Laveran took to be parasites were actually only leukocytes that had ingested pigment (Colin, 1880b).

In October 1881, Laveran himself presented a paper before the Academy of Sciences. Laveran reported that

> the blood of malaria patients contains parasitic elements which present themselves under the following aspects: (1) cylindrical elements, tapered at their extremes, almost always curved into a crescent. ... (2) transparent spherical elements containing movable grains of pigment ... on whose boundaries one can often observe very fine filaments, [the spherical elements] are animated, in every sense, with a very rapid movement. ... (3) spherical or irregularly shaped transparent elements that contain pigment [but with properties] that enable one to distinguish them clearly from pigmented leukocytes. (4) spherical transparent pigmented elements smaller than those mentioned above.
>
> (Laveran, 1881, pp. 627f.)

According to Laveran 'the spherical bodies containing mobile grains of pigment and armed with actively mobile peripheral filaments are undoubtedly alive' (Laveran, 1881, p. 629). By the time he presented this paper, Laveran had examined the blood of 192 victims of different forms of malaria and had identified the parasites in blood samples from 148 of them. Most of the patients in whose blood the elements could *not* be found had been treated with quinine, and, as Laveran confirmed, quinine killed the parasites. He noted that parasitic elements were only found in the blood of malaria patients and that the parasites were most likely to be present just before the onset of fever. Laveran believed that, between attacks, the parasites were concealed in such organs as the spleen and liver. He concluded that 'attacks of malaria are caused by the introduction, into the blood, of parasitic elements that present themselves under the aspects described above; sulfate of quinine leads to the termination of malarial attacks because it kills these parasites' (Laveran, 1881, p. 630).

Laveran's conclusions were challenged both by those who still questioned the role of living parasites in any disease and by those who believed malaria was caused by a bacterium. However, M. Richard, a physician who was one of Laveran's friends and who was also stationed in a hospital in Algeria, confirmed Laveran's findings, and suggested that the presence of the parasites could be taken as a diagnostic criterion for malaria. This, in effect, meant recharacterizing the disease in terms of the presence of the parasites. Other researchers also confirmed Laveran's findings.

In 1882, Laveran travelled to the Roman Campagna where malaria was endemic. He confirmed his earlier discoveries and demonstrated his results to the leading experts in Rome, but the Italians remained skeptical. They proposed that the supposed parasites were only degenerating blood cells. Many observers continued to believe that 'algae or "microphytes" present in marshy waters, were the true pathogens and particular attention was given to the claims of Klebs and Tommasi-Crudeli' (Bruce-Chwatt, 1988, p. 24). In 1883, Marchiafava and A. Celli, who had witnessed Laveran's presentations in Rome, published a paper describing bodies similar to those Laveran had exhibited (although without mentioning Laveran or his work). They pointed out that some of the bodies resembled micrococci, and admitted, guardedly, that the bodies could be parasitic (Marchiafava and Celli, 1883, p. 574). However, the authors favored a different hypothesis: in a letter to Laveran, Marchiafava wrote, 'We believe that the pigmented forms which you have described are nothing but degenerated and pigmented red cells' (Bloomfield, 1958, p. 350). In his account of these events, Arthur L. Bloomfield observed

> It would be interesting if one could reconstruct the medical politics of the time. Klebs and Tommasi-Crudeli were big names. The latter was head of the Bacteriologic Institute in Rome; Marchiafava worked in the same institution. There must have been great pressure to take sides in this controversy with a relatively insignificant doctor from Val-De-Grace.
>
> (Bloomfield, 1958, p. 350)

Meanwhile, Laveran found a more sympathetic audience in Paris when he demonstrated the malarial organisms to Pasteur and Roux.

In 1884, C. Gerhardt published the results of experimental inoculations with malarial blood (Gerhardt, 1884). From observations about the spread of the disease, Gerhardt inferred that malaria must be due to a 'poison' that multiplies within the human body and is carried by a lower organism. If so, he reasoned, it should be possible to convey the disease by the inoculation of infected blood. He mentioned that Marchiafava and Cuboni had inoculated dogs with blood from malarial patients and that other researchers had conducted inoculation experiments on human volunteers, yet these experiments had produced only equivocal results. 'The conclusive experiment,' he wrote, 'appeared to be the inoculation of blood from a malarial patient to a healthy person ... using blood drawn during an attack of fever' (Gerhardt, 1884, p. 373). Gerhardt also listed four conditions that, he felt, should be satisfied in performing the test: (1) the experiment must be performed in a region free from malaria, (2) the patient who supplies the blood must have no other infectious diseases, (3) the subjects to be inoculated must volunteer and must not be required, by the experiment, to sacrifice an opportunity for gainful employment, and (4) the subjects' temperature curves must have been recorded since long before the inoculation to insure that they were free from fever (Gerhardt, 1884, pp. 373f.). Gerhardt was able to induce artificial malaria in two volunteers who met these conditions and, subsequently, to control both cases by administering quinine. Gerhardt did not mention Laveran's work, and he did not report any microscopic examinations of the subjects' blood before or after the inoculations.

By 1885, Marchiafava and Celli had been converted to the idea that malaria was parasitic. They cited Laveran, Richard, and Gerhardt and reported further microscopic studies of malarial blood (Marchiafava and Celli, 1885a). They described an attempt to transmit malaria by injecting a volunteer with blood freshly drawn from a malarial patient; the injection produced typical fever symptoms. Marchiafava and Celli identified the characteristic organisms in the blood of the volunteer, and controlled the disease by administering quinine. 'All of these conditions,' they concluded, 'make probable our hypothesis that these forms are living agents' (Marchiafava and Celli, 1885a, p. 353). Marchiafava and Celli also reported attempts to cultivate the parasites in various media. The attempts failed, but they reported finding an organism in mud from swamps that, when cultured, appeared 'morphologically similar to the initial forms' of the supposed malarial parasite, and, they reported, 'the multiplication of these bodies was especially obvious in slide cultures of malarial blood' (Marchiafava and Celli, 1885a, p. 354). According to Bloomfield, this comment reveals 'that Marchiafava and Celli were still unclear about the significance of their findings'; he concludes that they 'did little more than confirm Laveran's findings' (Bloomfield, 1958, pp. 350f.). However, their paper had this heuristic significance: for the first time, it brought together observational reports of the parasite and Gerhardt's reports of successful inoculation experiments on human volunteers.

By the end of the nineteenth century, it was becoming progressively more clear that Laveran's protozoan played a role in malaria. Moreover, the study of malaria had been supplemented by research on other diseases that also appeared to be caused by protozoa. In 1890, Koch summarized the situation as follows:

> In many areas ... indeed precisely where one would least have expected it, bacteriological investigation has been of no avail. This has been the case in the study of several infectious diseases which, because of their pronounced infectiousness, appeared to be easy

objects of investigation. ... I suspect that these diseases involve organized disease agents that are not bacteria but rather belong to completely different groups of microorganisms. This opinion is all the more justified by the recent discovery that the blood of many animals – as for example the blood of malaria victims – contains the unique animal parasites known as protozoa. Of course, as yet one can do no more than demonstrate the presence of these noteworthy and important parasites. Apparently, no further progress will be made until protozoa, like bacteria, can be grown in an artificial medium or under natural conditions outside the body ... Once this is done, and there is no reason to doubt that it will be, the investigation of pathological protozoa and related microorganisms will probably become part of bacteriology. Hopefully this investigation will explain the etiology of these as yet mysterious diseases.

(Koch, 1890, p. 184)

Koch underestimated the changes involved in accepting non-bacterial parasites as causes – there was no reason to think that they could satisfy causal criteria (for example, flourishing in artificial media) that had been developed to accommodate bacteria or that they could be studied by the same techniques used to study bacteria (thereby assimilating their study to *bacteriology*). However, scientists became persuaded that malaria was caused by Laveran's protozoan, and research on malaria attracted so much attention that, for a time, it was believed that all non-bacterial diseases may be caused by protozoa (Joest, 1902, p. 380). Within a few years, it became clear that, while malaria, Texas fever, and a few other diseases were protozoal, many common non-bacterial diseases definitely were not.[1]

A viral theory of disease

In 1879, Adolf Eduard Mayer, a bacteriologist at a Dutch experimental agriculture station, began studying a disorder that affected local tobacco plants. He reported his research in a remarkable paper published seven years later (Mayer, 1886). The tobacco disease was not widely known in Europe, and where it was known, it was called by different names. In the absence of a standard nomenclature, Mayer called it tobacco mosaic disease after the mottled appearance of the leaves of diseased plants. According to Mayer, the many causes to which the disease had been ascribed constitute 'a virtual chaos, likely to induce dizziness, and useful only to confirm the old idea that humans cannot exist without theories' (Mayer, 1886, pp. 453f.[2]). In harmony with earlier beliefs about disease causation generally, various meteorological conditions as well as planting and fertilizing practices had been mentioned as possible causes. Mayer wrote: 'Many regard the disease as entirely inexplicable – as a kind of witchcraft, and have pressed on me the warning: "You will never find it[s cause]! Never!"' (p. 454).

Mayer analyzed diseased and healthy plants and the soils in which they were cultivated, and patiently excluded dozens of purported causes. In reporting this research, he warned his reader against becoming so bored with the negative results as to be inattentive and thereby miss the positive conclusions that would follow (p. 455). He pointed out that, by showing the inadequacy of the many purported general causes, he had increased the likelihood that the disease was due to a specific agent – an argument like one used by Agostino Bassi nearly a century earlier. Mayer explained that, while ruling out many purported general causes, he and his colleagues had also examined diseased plants for fungi and animal parasites. At first, they found nothing. 'Then,' he wrote, 'I suddenly discovered that the sap that one could rub out of diseased plants was a reliable infectious material for healthy plants' (p. 461). According to Mayer, if one applied a small quantity of diluted sap to an incision in the stem of healthy plants, those plants usually became diseased, whereas sap from healthy plants had no effect. Mayer redoubled his efforts to discover some harmful 'body' within the sap of diseased plants but found nothing: 'I tried to culture the supposed organisms using the methods of Koch and others; in many cases I obtained bacterial vegetation, but, when used as inoculation material, none of this vegetation infected healthy tobacco plants' (p. 463). Mayer tried inoculating various bacteria and substances known to contain bacteria but all his attempts were without effect.

Mayer then tried to decide whether the success of the inoculations was due to an 'unformed or to a formed ferment' (p. 464). He admitted that a ferment of the first kind would be 'unusual as the cause of a disease' and that no 'enzyme' was known that had the capacity of 'multiplying itself' within a plant as seemed to happen in his inoculation experiments. However, 'a formed ferment could be either a fungus or a bacterium, and, elements of these groups can be distinguished mechanically [for example, by filtration] as well as by the microscope' (p. 464), and he resolved to try filtration. Mayer found that infectious agents passed through one sheet of filter paper although filtration seemed to reduce the concentration of causal agents in diluted sap. He inferred (incorrectly, as critics pointed out) that the agent could not be a fungus since all fungi would be stopped by the filter. He then found (also incorrectly, according to critics) that the infectious agent would not pass through two sheets of filter paper, and he concluded that the agent could not be an 'enzyme' since any such substance would pass through both sheets. Learning at the same time that infectious sap could be made harmless by heating it to 80 degrees, he concluded that the infectious substance was an organic ferment – a bacterium (p. 465). Mayer felt he had learned everything one could learn from filtration experiments: 'Further knowledge of the form and way of life of the guilty bacterium cannot be expected to follow from experiments of this kind, and must await future research' (p. 466).

A Russian student, Dimitri Iosifovitch Ivanovski, continued Mayer's work (Ivanovski, 1892). Ivanovski discovered that Mayer was wrong in thinking that the cause of tobacco mosaic disease could be removed from sap by two or more sheets of filter paper. Because of this realization, Ivanovski is often mentioned in connection with the discovery of filterable viruses. However, he himself believed his main contribution was recognizing that the disease Mayer studied actually included two independent disorders. In summarizing the relation of his work to Mayer's, he completely ignored the filtration experiments (Ivanovski, 1902), and he showed little interest in filtration until later researchers revealed its significance (at which time he claimed priority for its use). Like Mayer, Ivanovski believed tobacco mosaic disease was caused by a bacterium, and, while he entertained the possibility that the causal bacterium was filterable, he found it more likely that the bacterium generated a soluble poison that made sap infective (Ivanovski, 1892, p. 69, 1903, pp. 202f). He conducted no serial inoculations and never suggested that the substance that passed through the filters was itself capable of multiplying in inoculated plants. Moreover, his research 'does not appear to have had an effect on the development of the concept of the virus. His papers of 1892 had been published only in Russian journals and his work was virtually unknown in the West before 1899' (Hughes, 1977, p. 56). By then, other researchers had explicitly postulated the existence of discrete non-bacterial causal agents that replicated and were filterable.

Another scientist whose research was based on Mayer's work was Marinus Willem Beijerinck. Beijerinck was an original thinker and made significant contributions in several areas (Wilkinson, 1976, p. 117). Mayer and Beijerinck worked together at the Wageningen agricultural school, and Mayer showed Beijerinck his experiments with the sap of diseased tobacco plants. Over the next few years, Beijerinck occasionally looked for parasites in the sap of diseased plants, but he found none. For a time he suspected that the disease may be caused by anaerobic organisms, but he later saw that this idea was incorrect. Early on Beijerinck conducted diffusion experiments from which he concluded that the infective substance, which he referred to as a virus, 'must be regarded as a liquid or as dissolved, and not corpuscular' (Beijerinck, 1898, p. 6). He conducted serial inoculations from plant to plant. Given the small quantity of diluted sap that was sufficient to infect healthy plants, his serial inoculations persuaded him that 'the contagium, although liquid, replicates itself in the living plant' (Beijerinck, 1898, p. 5). Beijerinck used the term '*contagium vivum fluidum*' to refer to this unusual replicating yet liquid disease agent whose existence seemed to be implied by his experiments.

Beijerinck made the remarkable observation that injections of infective sap did not affect mature leaves, but only new growing buds and shoots in which cell division was in progress. He astutely inferred that the *contagium vivum fluidum*, being 'unable to grow independently, is drawn into the growth of the dividing cells and multiplies powerfully therein but without losing its own individuality' (Beijerinck, 1898, p. 9). Of course, contemporary scientists who were studying viral diseases in animals found no counterpart to these discoveries, and Beijerinck's observation and the inference he drew from it were inadequately appreciated. In a sequel to this paper, Beijerinck pointed out that the impossibility of culturing the contagious substance in artificial media suggested it was a liquid that could not multiply outside living protoplasm. However, he admitted that this concept was not easy to comprehend:

> The reproduction or growth of a dissolved body is not unthinkable but it is difficult to imagine. It is not easy to accept a process of division in the molecules which would lead to their multiplication, and the idea of self-sustaining molecules, which is thereby presupposed, seems unclear to me, if not contrary to nature. It is to some extent an explanation to consider that, in order to reproduce itself, the contagium must be incorporated into the living protoplasm of the cell into whose multiplication it is, so to speak, passively included. ... However, there is no denying that even if the incorporation of a virus into the living protoplasm is confirmed as factual, it cannot be regarded as a clearly comprehensible process.
>
> (Beijerinck, 1899, p. 31)

Lise Wilkinson suggested that Beijerinck's early interest in chemistry may have 'enabled him in later life to consider chemical molecules and even their possible role in biological systems in a more realistic way than could most of his fellow biologists and pathologists' (Wilkinson, 1976, p. 117).

By the time Beijerinck published his first work on tobacco mosaic disease, Friedrich Johannes Loeffler and Paul Frosch had begun publishing studies of foot-and-mouth disease (Loeffler and Frosch, 1898). Beijerinck knew of their work, and believed that Loeffler and Frosch were dealing with causal factors related to those he was studying, but he wrote that he could not support their conclusions 'in respect to the corpuscular nature of the virus' (Beijerinck, 1898, p. 7n). While Beijerinck proposed that other plant diseases may be due to other *contagium vivum fluidia*, he did not attempt to explain foot-and-mouth disease or any other animal disorders.

In respect to the etiological research programme, the most important early work on what are now called viruses was reports by Loeffler and Frosch on foot-and-mouth disease. Mayer, Ivanovski, and Beijerinck never doubted that tobacco mosaic disease had a specific cause; indeed, they all began (and Mayer and Ivanovski ended up) believing that the cause in question was a bacterium. Their work fostered the growth of an important ramification of the research programme into plant pathology – a ramification we will not pursue further. However, in respect to subsequent developments in medicine, the studies of Loeffler and Frosch were more important. In 1908, John McFadyean, an English bacteriologist, wrote that discovering the filterability of the causal agent of foot-and-mouth disease 'at once attracted general attention, and gave a great impetus to the investigation of the nature of the virus in those diseases which had hitherto baffled investigation conducted on ordinary bacteriological lines' (McFadyean, 1908, p. 66).

As early as 1840 Jakob Henle assumed, as common knowledge, that foot-and-mouth disease was contagious, and it was among the diseases for which one would have expected an explanation in terms of parasitic organisms. Both Loeffler and Frosch were bacteriologists who had been trained by Koch, and who, like Mayer, Ivanovski, and Beijerinck, began their work using standard bacteriological techniques.

Loeffler and Frosch submitted three reports to the German Ministry of Culture (17 April 1897, 14 August 1897, and 8 January 1898); the reports were published in 1898. By the time they conducted their work, technical developments had raised bacteriology to a level from which it was apparent that foot-and-mouth disease was not due to an ordinary bacterium: no such organism was found in microscopic studies of stained or unstained tissues and fluids, and none grew in culture tests using any of the standard solid or liquid media. However, Loeffler and Frosch found that apparently sterile lymph from diseased animals produced typical foot-and-mouth disease after being injected into healthy cattle (Loeffler and Frosch, 1898, p. 372). Moreover, the disease could be further conveyed from artificially infected animals, so the cause – which they referred to as a virus – was not simply a toxin produced in diseased animals.

Loeffler and Frosch emphasized the practical consequences of their work; however, near the end of their last report, they turned to certain results that seemed to have little immediate practical significance but were of interest 'not only for the further study of foot-and-mouth disease, but also for numerous other infectious diseases of humans and animals' (Loeffler and Frosch, 1898, p. 388). Independently of Mayer and Ivanovski (whose works they did not know) and of Beijerinck (whose first paper on tobacco mosaic disease had not yet appeared), they conducted filtration experiments using infectious lymph. Later, in recounting the course of their research, Loeffler attributed their use of filtration to a research tradition that began with Edwin Klebs' study of *Microsporon septicum* (Loeffler, 1911, p. 1). To insure that the filtered lymph was free from bacteria, Loeffler and Frosch added *Bacillus flourescens* to lymph before filtration. Since these bacteria were not present in the filtered lymph, they were confident it was also free from any bacterium as large or larger than *Bacillus flourescens*. Yet inoculations proved that the filtered lymph was still effective. They recognized this result as important, and they repeated their experiments several times. They could imagine only two possibilities: 'either the bacteria-free filtered lymph contains an exceptionally powerful dissolved poison, or the hitherto undiscovered causes of the disease are so small they can pass through the pores of a filter that reliably retains the smallest known bacteria' (Loeffler and Frosch, 1898, p. 389). From the quantity of filtered lymph sufficient to infect a calf, they calculated that any dissolved poison would be enormously more virulent than tetanus toxin – a possibility they dismissed as incredible (Loeffler and Frosch, 1898, p. 390). The only alternative was that the effectiveness of the filtrate was due to an agent that multiplied in living animals. Loeffler and Frosch passed foot-and-mouth disease through a series of six animals each of which died just as quickly as did the first. 'This series of trials, in each of which one fiftieth of a cubic centimeter of lymph, drawn from the previous animal, then diluted and filtered, was used to infect the succeeding animal, proves the virus of the disease is a living agent that multiplies within the body of diseased animals' (Loeffler, 1911, pp. 3f.).

The influenza bacillus was the smallest known bacterium at that time. Loeffler and Frosch calculated that if the causal agent of foot-and-mouth disease was one-tenth or even one-fifth as large, it would fall outside the theoretical limits of what could be made visible by the best microscopes. This could easily explain why the agent could not be seen in virulent lymph. They conjectured that these results could be significant for research on such other infectious diseases as smallpox, cowpox, scarlet fever, measles, typhoid, and rinderpest (Loeffler and Frosch, 1898, p. 391).

At about the same time that Loeffler and Frosch published their reports, Edmund-Isidore-Etienne Nocard and Emile Roux discovered structures in bovine pleuropneumonia that, at maximum magnification, appeared as minute points. They cultured these structures in collodion sacs inserted into the abdominal cavities of rabbits and passed the disease to healthy animals (Nocard and Roux, 1898). At a medical conference in 1898, Loeffler asked Nocard whether the minute structures were filterable. Nocard said they were not, but within a few months he advised Loeffler that, if suspended in liquids that were adequately diluted, the structures did pass through filters. In discussing these developments, Loeffler later observed that, 'a second agent was thereby recognized to be filterable' (Loeffler, 1911, p. 4). The causal agent of pleuropneumonia was at the limit of visibility with light microscopes, but everyone recognized that the existence of such a filterable organism supported the existence of other, still smaller, causal agents (Nocard and Roux, 1898, p. 248).

In an account of his discovery, Loeffler mentioned that, in the same year, Beijerinck reported conveying tobacco mosaic disease to healthy plants after filtering sap. Loeffler then noted:

> Having demonstrated the existence of infinitesimally small micro-organisms, which elude microscopic demonstration and pass through filters, one must now believe that the same methods of study should be applied to all diseases for which only unsuccessful attempts had been made to find causal agents, in the hope of discovering, in the disease products of conveyable diseases, similar minute living entities.
>
> (Loeffler, 1911, p. 5)

By 1911, he reported that filterable viruses had been discovered for 17 different diseases (Loeffler, 1911, pp. 5f).

Klebs's *Grundversuche* apply only to bacteria and, even assuming that his theory accommodates all bacterial diseases, disorders caused by other kinds of entities require different theories. One could take account of protozoal and viral diseases simply by restating the basic assumptions of the bacterial theory as disjunctions. For example, in place of the Bacterial Hypothesis one could write: every disease is caused either by bacteria or by protozoa or by viruses, and so forth. However, it is simpler to achieve the same result by formulating a disjunction of theories, each more or less parallel to the bacterial theory and designed to accommodate one kind of pathogenic organism. Each of these theories will contain an assumption, similar in form to the Bacterial Hypothesis, that specifies the domain of the theory. In seeking the cause of a new disease, one will, in effect, consider each of these theories one after another until a cause is identified. Of course, known facts about the new disease may lead one to prefer some theories over others.

Recognizing new kinds of causes also requires one to adopt new causal criteria.[3] In 1937, Thomas M. Rivers wrote:

> The idea that an infectious agent must be cultivated in a pure state on lifeless media before it can be accepted as the proved cause of a disease has ... hindered the investigations of certain maladies, inasmuch as it denies the existence of obligate parasites, the most striking phenomenon of some infections, particularly those caused by viruses
>
> (Rivers, 1937, p. 5).

In the same paper, Rivers also discussed possible causal criteria for viruses. About 20 years later, R.J. Huebner, proposed another set of causal criteria for viruses (Huebner, 1957). Both Rivers and Huebner took account of developments that came after Koch – for example, they included criteria that involved immunological reactions to pathogens. However, the only respect in which their criteria differed from those suitable for use in the study of bacteria was that neither Rivers nor Huebner had a counterpart to Koch's Rt4; they did not require that a purported causal agent be cultivated in inert media outside diseased animals. Instead, the corresponding weak sufficiency criterion stipulated only that inoculations of fluids drawn from a diseased animal (and possibly filtered) were followed by the same disease in test animals.

The discovery of filterable viruses was a greater accomplishment than one might suppose. Looking back from our point of view (which assumes a century of productive research on viruses and takes for granted tissue cultures and electron microscopes) it is easy to see a smooth path of research that required only certain empirical discoveries; but there were important conceptual obstacles to be overcome. One such obstacle concerned the distinguishability of viruses. We can approach this problem by way of the following quotation:

> Microscopy had not proved useful in positively identifying the cause of foot and month disease, although negative findings had led Löffler and Frosch to conclude that the agent was submicroscopic. They also emphasized the use of inoculation experiments on animals *whose pathological reactions were the only positive evidence then obtainable for the presence of the viruses.* ... Löffler and Frosch thus established an experimental methodology which in the early 20th century was widely adopted in research on human and animal viral diseases. It was based primarily on three techniques: microscopy and filtration to determine the absence in

infectious materials of microscopically visible organisms, and serial animal inoculation experiments to provide evidence for the presence of infectious agents in the filtrates.

(Hughes, 1977, p. 64; my emphasis)

Thus, one condition for recognizing the presence of a virus was that no causal agent could be detected by microscopy or by culturing. The only positive evidence for the existence (or of the identity or nature) of the virus was the pathological reaction that followed inoculation. Contemporary researchers were clear about this fact. In 1915, one scientist observed that varieties of non-pathogenic bacteria outnumber the pathogenic ones, and one might expect the same to be true of the 'ultra-microscopic viruses'; however, he continued, 'it is difficult to obtain proof of their existence, as pathogenicity is the only evidence we have at the present time of the presence of an ultra-microscopic virus' (Twort, 1915, p. 1241). Nocard and Roux also admitted that animal inoculations were the only way of demonstrating the presence of microscopically invisible disease agents (Nocard and Roux, 1898, p. 248). Yet the existence of the viruses was postulated precisely to explain these very pathological reactions – thus, the reasoning is circular.

Strümpell, Möbius, and Freud confronted exactly the same problem with respect to the psychological disorders: because of the nature of ideas, the only evidence for the existence or identity of a pathogenic idea seemed to be the pathological reaction that followed it. So long as Freud attributed hysteria to a sexual assault in childhood, there was a chance for independent identification and differentiation of (at least the source of some of the) supposedly pathogenic ideas. However, he later admitted that the same pathogenic ideas could stem from fantasized assaults – a concession forced on him by recalcitrant facts that would otherwise have refuted his central hypothesis. And this left him with a causal factor the only evidence for whose existence was the very pathological reaction it was intended to explain. An 1898 critic could have responded to Loeffler (or to Freud) as follows: 'You assume the existence of a virus (an idea) to explain foot-and-mouth disease (hysteria), but your only evidence for the existence of the virus (idea) is that animals (people) contract the disease.' How would this differ from the following possible response (in 1847) to Eduard Lumpe: 'You hypothesize the existence of a miasm to explain childbed fever, but your only evidence for the existence of the miasm is that women contract the disease'?[4] In all three cases, the reasoning approaches circularity. We have seen that the Distinguishability Hypothesis was necessary to avoid just this problem in dealing with bacterial diseases, but bacteria could generally be identified and distinguished other than by their pathogenicity. Since (at this point) this was no more true for viruses or for ideas than for miasms, attempts to include ideas and viruses within the research programme threatened to become what Lakatos called degenerating problem shifts (Lakatos, 1968, p. 118).

At this point, researchers could simply have abandoned these two attempts to expand the programme. By 1898, childbed fever, diphtheria, anthrax, cholera, tuberculosis, and several other bacterial diseases had been assimilated to the etiological standpoint. However, for other diseases, rather than hypothesizing the existence of viruses or ideas (each undetectable except through the very pathologicality it was intended to explain), one could have fallen back on traditional causal thinking: foot-and-mouth disease, tobacco mosaic disease, hysteria, anxiety neuroses, and the other disorders in both groups, could have been regarded as having *no* necessary causes and as being due to the traditional factors to which conventional wisdom had long ascribed them. One could simply have acknowledged that inoculations from diseased sources or sexual attacks before puberty (respectively) were among the many ways in which diseases of these two kinds could be caused. This approach would not have undercut the success of the bacterial theory and would have been compatible with all the observed facts. Moreover, in contrast to hypothesizing unknown viruses or pathogenic ideas, this would not have been question begging. However, this approach meant abandoning the quest for specific causes – the very core of the research programme. And, as Lakatos explained, in situations of this kind, the negative heuristic of the programme shields the core from refutation:

> In Newton's program the negative heuristic bids us to divert the *modus tollens* [of apparent counter-examples] from Newton's three laws of dynamics and his law of gravitation. This 'core' is 'irrefutable' by the methodological decision of its proponents: anomalies must lead to changes only in the 'protective' belt of auxiliary, 'observational' hypotheses and initial conditions.
> (Lakatos, 1968, p. 133)

At the core of our research programme was the assumption that every disease could be characterized in terms of a universal necessary cause, and this assumption simply could not be given up. Instead, researchers began looking for non-circular ways of establishing the existence and identity of the new purported causes.

Distinguishing viruses was a formidable task. At least by 1902, scientists had concluded that viruses were too small *ever* to be revealed by light microscopes, and some realized that, being obligate parasites, they could *never* be cultured in an inert medium (Joest, 1902, p. 378). This meant that, in principle, it would be impossible ever to gain knowledge about viruses through the means that had proven most enlightening in the study of bacteria. Moreover, since most viral diseases were species specific, there was no possibility of *ever* using animals in test inoculations to study most human viral diseases. Since inoculations were the only known way of learning about or even demonstrating the presence of viruses, this came close to implying that there was no possibility of any positive knowledge about the hypothesized causal agents of these diseases. However, the momentum of the research programme was sufficient that even these daunting obstacles were seen only as temporary technical inconveniences. One scientist, asked whether, facing a complete lack of positive knowledge about viruses, one should simply be resigned to ignorance? 'No!' he answered, 'for the results of previous investigation prove only that the goal cannot be achieved by way of the ordinary broad and familiar paths of bacteriological exploration. This means only that we must invent other ways and means of approaching and of learning about the unknown enemy' (Joest, 1902, p. 417). It seems never to have occurred to anyone to question the feasibility of the goal itself.

If finding ways of distinguishing viruses presented major technical difficulties, distinguishing ideas proved to be absolutely impossible. On the assumption that one's speech reflects one's ideas, Möbius, Freud, and others were driven, in one way or another, to the analysis of patients' language and to what came to be called talking cures. And, while some of these attempts have been interesting and may have contributed results of lasting value, the original goal of the project, namely, the identification of pathogenic ideas as specific causes for psychological disorders, seems to have evaporated. After a century of effort, most psychological disorders are still not associated with specific causes (ideas or otherwise), and the hypothesis of pathogenic ideas has been widely discredited as nothing more than regressive question begging. In the absence of feasible alternative hypotheses, the psychological disorders remain unassimilated anomalies and, therefore, a distraction from the credibility of the research programme as a whole.

By contrast, through the early decades of the twentieth century technical developments soon provided independent ways of identifying and differentiating viruses. By 1957, Huebner's causal criteria for viruses required one to show, by passage in laboratory animals or in cell tissues, that some new and purportedly pathogenic virus was a real entity and to fully characterize the virus and to compare it with other known disease agents (Huebner, 1957). This requirement includes a counterpart to the bacterial Distinguishability Hypothesis. Within decades, viral diseases had been fully assimilated to the etiological standpoint, and their discovery emerged as a major achievement of the programme.

Notes

1. Victoria A. Harden (1987) has given an account, compatible with the general position of this book, of elaboration of the etiology of rickettsial diseases, and Alfred S. Evans (1993) has recounted attempts to modify Koch's Postulates to encompass many different kinds of diseases.
2. Through the first three paragraphs of this section, page numbers in parentheses are references to Mayer (1886).
3. Both Gerhardt (1884, pp. 373f.) and Marchiafava and Celli (1885, pp. 805f.) made remarks that can be construed as attempts to identify such criteria for protozoa.
4. Another example of pseudoexplanation is Fracastoro's hypothesized 'seeds' (1546) which could be differentiated only by the diseases they were intended to explain and which, therefore, explained exactly nothing.

CHAPTER ELEVEN

A Nutritional
Deficiency Theory of Disease

By the beginning of the twentieth century, many diseases had been explained as infestations of microscopic parasites or of filterable viruses. However, other important diseases defied such explanations. One such disease was beriberi which, in some populations, was responsible for more deaths than all known parasitic diseases combined (Carter, 1977, p. 119[1]). Identifying the cause of beriberi required a new theory of disease: a deficiency theory.

In conventional wisdom, the bacterial theory of disease is seen only as a positive obstacle to development of a deficiency theory: Aaron J. Ihde and Stanley L. Becker claim that 'the germ concept proved a major barrier to the recognition and study of deficiency diseases' (Ihde and Becker, 1971, p. 16). C. P. Stewart writes, 'one factor which undoubtedly held up the development of the concept of deficiency diseases was the discovery of bacteria in the 19th century and the consequent preoccupation of scientists and doctors with positive infecting agents in disease' (Stewart, 1953, p. 408). Numerous writers assert that the deficiency concept was difficult to accept because the bacterial theory suggested that only a positive agent could cause something. In his history of nutrition, Emer Verner McCollum notes that 'improved microscopes and the staining and other technics applicable to the study of the problems of pathology so monopolized the attention of investigators that they had little incentive to consider any aspect of malnutrition as a cause of disease' (McCollum, 1957, pp. 225f). In *Toward the Conquest of Beriberi*, Robert R. Williams treats the bacterial theory only as the source of one false explanation for the etiology of beriberi (Williams, 1961, pp. 13–15, 18f., 35). Such claims, so frequently repeated, pass for common sense – never mind that they are usually unsupported by any evidence whatsoever. Do these authors really mean to assert that, if there had been no bacterial theory, the deficiency concept would have been more readily accepted? What evidence could there possibly be for a contrafactual claim of this kind? Who can say what *might* have been?[2]

However, all these claims are based on a serious misconstruction of the historical context. That the study of bacteria did *not* monopolize late nineteenth-century etiology is obvious from the variety of causes contemporary researchers were willing to entertain. Some diseases had been traced to minute but visible parasites such as trichinae or various fungi. Other diseases were ascribed to filterable viruses. On analogy with bacteria, some may have assumed that viruses were corpuscular, but Martinus Willem Beijerinck thought in terms of a living fluid (Beijerinck, 1899, p. 31). Even as late as 1915, one researcher speculated that viruses could be minute bacteria, tiny amoeba, or even a 'more lowly organized' form of life – a 'living protoplasm that forms no definite individuals, or an enzyme with power of growth' (Twort, 1915, p. 1242). Strümpell, Möbius, and Freud ascribed psychological disorders to pathological ideas. Even more significantly, as Thomas Schlich has discussed in a recent paper, by 1892, Theodor Kocher had proven that cretinism was due to thyroid failure, that is, to a *deficiency* (Schlich, 1994). All these possibilities were given serious attention in medical literature. In fact, rather than focusing on bacteria, medical research at the time was driven by the quest for universal necessary causes (many of which turned out to be bacteria). And, while one cannot say what *might have been* had bacteria attracted less attention, it is perfectly clear that, in the absence of the quest for universal necessary causes, no one could possibly have sought *the cause* of beriberi at all because only given the etiological standpoint could one even make sense of such a notion. Prior to assimilation by the research programme, individual cases of beriberi were ascribed to the same unlimited range of chance factors as were cases of every other disease; prior to inclusion in the programme, such causes were the sum total of the etiology of beriberi. 'The cause of beriberi' – like *the cause* of any other disease – was first given a meaning by the etiological research programme. Certainly beriberi was studied by bacteriologists who used their own techniques and found little. Given the historical context, it would have been irrational to have proceeded in any other way. However, this was an important null result, not just an obstacle. And to portray the rise of the deficiency concept only in terms of its supposed competition with the bacterial theory, rather than as part of the broader programme (of which the bacterial theory itself was a part), is exactly to blind oneself to the forest by gaping at a single (if impressive) tree.

By the beginning of the twentieth century, the etiological programme drove virtually all medical research, and this programme imposed no a priori restrictions on the nature of potential causes. While deficiency diseases obviously could not be assimilated to the *bacterial* theory, the programme itself presented no conceptual barriers to accepting deficiencies, or almost anything else, as causes. The positive heuristic of the programme provided a strategy for finding causes. Near the end of our discussion of Robert Koch (Chapter 8), we identified some of the elements of that strategy: one requires a theory defined over a domain of potential causes, the theory will include a distinguishability condition and a set of causal criteria, potential causes must explain disease phenomena, ordinarily there will be some test for weak sufficiency. None of this precludes negative causes. Ultimately, both the bacterial and the deficiency theories (like the ideational and viral theories) emerged from this common strategy. To portray the bacterial theory simply as an obstacle is to obscure a vital part of the story – in exactly the same way that traditional Freudian scholarship obscures crucial aspects of Freud's 'new' approach to hysteria by ignoring his indebtedness to the research programme.

The contrast between the histories of scurvy and of beriberi provides vivid confirmation of the dominance of the research programme in nineteenth-century medicine. We will begin with some remarks about the history of scurvy.

Scurvy as a disorder of diet

In the early nineteenth century, scurvy and rickets were generally believed to be diet-related. In 1830, *Lancet* published a series of clinical lectures by John Elliotson, Professor of Medicine in University College, London. In discussing scurvy, Elliotson noted that 'the cause ... is always, I believe, a want of fresh animal and fresh vegetable food' (Elliotson, 1830–31, p. 651). Seven years later, in a similar lecture, Marshall Hall observed

> scorbutus is generally induced by a deficiency of fresh vegetable food. It is also occasionally referred to other errors in diet, to the respiration of a crowded or otherwise impure atmosphere, to excessive fatigue, anxiety, etc. ... The prevention and cure of scorbutus consists in the administration of fresh and vegetable food, but, above all, of citric acid
>
> (Hall, 1837–38, p. 851).

Both men refer to works by Gilbert Blane (1753) and James Lind (1785) that were, by that time, recognized sources on scurvy. Neither Elliotson nor Hall suggested that his views were new or atypical; indeed, both acknowledged that lemon juice had been the standard cure for scurvy for more than 200 years.

In 1840, George Budd summarized clinical knowledge of scurvy in an article in Alexander Tweedie's *A System of Practical Medicine* (Budd, 1840). Budd discussed various fruits and vegetables generally known to cure scurvy. Knowing of François Magendie's experiments demonstrating the inadequacy of certain macronutrients, Budd speculated that 'the study of organic chemistry and the experiments of physiologists' would ultimately shed light on the essential element common to the antiscorbutic plants (Budd, 1840, p. 77). Budd's article on scurvy was frequently cited by English physicians through the turn of the century. One reason for his continued influence was that he was among the last practicing physicians to be particularly interested in the disease. By the beginning of the nineteenth century, scurvy had been virtually eliminated from the British navy (Dudley, 1953). Except for uncontrollable situations, such as famine and war, where known therapies could not be applied, scurvy gradually declined in other areas and populations (Stewart, 1953, pp. 404–12). The symptoms of scurvy were more readily controlled than were those of most other diseases. Gilbert Blane wrote that 'the efficacy of lemon juice in curing scurvy [must] be stated as singular when compared to that of any other remedy in any other disease'. Since it prevents and cures the disease so completely and with no adverse effects, 'it performs not only what no other remedy will perform in this disease, but what no known remedy will effect in any known disease whatever' (Blane, 1785, pp. 179f.). Given this, and given that the prevailing concept in medical circles was that each disease was a particular collection of symptoms, scurvy was believed to be completely understood. This attitude is reflected in an editorial written in 1858 wherein the conquest of scurvy is spoken of as a leaf in the laurel wreath on the brow of medical science (*Lancet*, 1858, p. 145).

One can gauge the attitude of nineteenth-century British physicians toward scurvy by examining references to the disease in the articles, editorials, and letters in *Lancet*. After Budd's articles there are few references to scurvy until 1848, when failure of the potato crop resulted in numerous cases of the disease in England and Ireland. Work carried out at this time by John Aldridge and (independently) by Alfred B. Garrod suggested that scurvy may have been caused by a deficiency of potash (Carter, 1977, p. 122). Through the next decade there are few references to the disease. Beginning in the late 1850s and continuing for about twenty years there are numerous letters and editorials decrying the continued appearance of scurvy in the British merchant fleet (Carter, 1977, p. 122). In these notices, scurvy is consistently treated as a disease entirely understood and completely preventable – ship owners who allow the disease to appear are regarded as criminal and, in one editorial, compared to murderers (*Lancet*, 1858, p. 146). In one of the few original opinions on scurvy to appear in this period, the disease is attributed to deficiency of protein (Oliver, 1863, p. 61). Fifteen years later, in an original article, we read that 'No fact in medicine is more clearly established than that the exclusive cause of scurvy is the prolonged and complete withdrawal of succulent plants and fruits' (Ralfe,

1877, p. 868). By the 1880s, scurvy was treated as a medical curiosity of which very few practicing physicians had had immediate experience (Eade, 1880, p. 992). In that period, however, letters and editorials begin to take account of the experiences of arctic explorers who had survived for months on fresh uncooked meat with no sign of scurvy. The chief question in these writings is whether the dietary deficiency that results in scurvy could be corrected by fresh meat as well as by fresh vegetables (Carter, 1977, p. 122).

By 1883, some bacteriologists suspected that scurvy was caused by microorganisms, but the first hint of this view in *Lancet* was in 1886. In that year, a brief editorial mentions research by a Russian pathologist, T. Stazevich, who argued that scurvy was a 'form of septic poisoning' (*Lancet*, 1886, p. 1036). Until that time *Lancet* contains no suggestion that scurvy is anything other than a nutritional deficiency disorder. In 1889, Wilhelm Koch published an ambitious study of blood diseases in which he argued that scurvy, hemophilia, and various other disorders were variant forms of an infectious blood disease, and that the obvious correlation between scurvy and the lack of fresh food (like the hereditary pattern of hemophilia) could be explained along these lines (Koch, 1889). Koch's book seems not to have had much impact, but it was reviewed seriously in *Lancet* (*Lancet*, 1890). Through the end of the century, there are scattered attempts to explain scurvy as a result of toxins or of microorganisms; these were greeted skeptically and often rebutted. In the first decade of the twentieth century, opinion was clearly shifting toward such an explanation, but, as late as December 1904, an editor of *Lancet* could still write that 'the general disposition is to regard scurvy as due to the absence of certain elements in the food which is taken, but the exact nature of those elements has not been conclusively demonstrated' (*Lancet*, 1904, p. 1660). In 1907 a letter printed in the *British Medical Journal* (*BMJ*) bemoans the fact that 'the theory that want of fresh vegetable causes scurvy dies very hard', but the author's point is only that fresh meat will also supply the necessary nourishments (*BMJ*, 1907, p. 683).

As we have seen, the preceding quotation is part of a continuous tradition that extends back beyond the time of George Budd. This quotation was published less than three years before the classic paper on scurvy by Alex Holst and Theodor Frolich that was fundamental to the development of the deficiency theory (Holst and Frolich, 1907), and less than eight years before that theory received its first full articulation by Casimir Funk (Funk, 1912). Yet in 1911, seven years after the quoted editorial, a report on vitamins published by the British Medical Research Committee stressed the difficulty of implanting 'the idea of disease as due to deficiency' (Medical Research Committee, 1919, p. 2).

Ironically, this report refers to Budd's work on scurvy and commends his treatment of the *history* of the disease (Medical Research Committee, 1919, p. 58). In 1932, a second report by the Medical Research Council retained the language about the difficulty of thinking of negative causes, dropped the reference to Budd, and added a note indicating that 'it is now difficult to understand how ... scurvy failed in practical medicine to obtain recognition as a disease due to a deficiency in food' (Medical Research Council, 1932, p. 14). It is still more difficult to understand how these false traditions could have gained credence so quickly. No doubt, part of the explanation is that there is little incentive to study scientific literature outside one's own research. For example, in reviewing early references to the deficiency concept, Holst and Frolich refer to James Lind (one of the few early British authorities who failed to identify scurvy unequivocally as a deficiency disease) and August Hirsch, and to various reports by observers of particular occurrences of the disease (Holst and Frolich, 1907, pp. 663–9). There is no recognition of the 100-year tradition in British practical medicine in which scurvy was consistently and almost unanimously regarded as a deficiency disease.

No doubt the bacterial theory fascinated medical researchers during the latter part of the nineteenth century; however, serious original work on scurvy had in fact ceased decades earlier. Through the century, practicing physicians saw fewer and fewer cases of scurvy; medical interest in the disease declined accordingly. In this period, the few chemists and physiologists who studied human nutrition showed almost no interest in the disease. By 1880 bacteriology was certainly the most promising field for medical research, but, at least in England, physicians continued to believe that scurvy was a well-understood nutritional disorder that held little practical or theoretical interest. Under these circumstances it is misleading, if not false, to speak of the bacterial theory as an obstacle to the recognition and study of scurvy as a nutritional disease.

The rise of Beriberi

Beriberi seems to have been known to Asian writers as early as the second century AD; the earliest descriptions in western literature are from the seventeenth century (Carter, 1977, p. 124). Prior to the nineteenth century, the disease was relatively unimportant even in the orient. This is evident, first, from the treatment the disease received in pre-nineteenth-century medical literature, and second, from the fact that modern steam-milling procedures, which are now recognized as having been substantially responsible for the rise of beriberi, did not become common in Asia until then. By the last quarter of the nineteenth century the disease was widespread and growing at an alarming rate.

It is difficult to gauge accurately the growth of beriberi; we must be content with a few hints. First, in the Japanese Army in 1876 there were 3,868 cases of beriberi from among 35,300 men (11 per cent), in 1877 there were 2,687 cases among 19,600 men (14 per cent), and in 1878 there were 13,629 cases among 36,100 men (38 per cent) (Scheube, 1894, p. 14). This percentage remained roughly constant through 1884 and then declined because of dietary reforms, but during the war between Japan and Russia (1904–05) there were nearly 100,000 cases of beriberi (Takaki, 1906, p. 1521). Second, in 31 district hospitals in the Malay peninsula, Chinese patients admitted for beriberi increased from 1,206 in 1881 to 3,175 in 1891, and to 6,767 in 1901. In that period, beriberi accounted for more than 100,000 deaths among Chinese laborers in the Malay States – over half the total death rate for that population (Braddon, 1907, pp. 1–4, 513–21). Third, in 1883 August Hirsch reported that within the preceding 20 years, beriberi had appeared in many areas for the first time, and that it was epidemic in coastal areas of Japan and of other Asian countries (Hirsch, 1885, pp. 573–8). Ten years later, B. Scheube reported that the disease had recently appeared for the first time in Siam and in the Philippines, that it was spreading in Africa and in South America, and that it was now endemic throughout Japan (Scheube, 1894, pp. 10–16). In 1907, Patrick Manson gave the disease an even more extensive distribution (for example, he stated that it was then common in southern China where, according to Hirsch and Scheube, it had been rare), and in most areas incidence of the disease seemed to have increased (Manson and Daniels, 1907, pp. 615–43). Finally, one can appreciate the remarkable rise of the disease by surveying the medical literature of the period. Scheube's nearly complete bibliography includes two publications on beriberi between 1800 and 1809; in subsequent decades the publications numbered 8, 10, 11, 30, 64, 80, and between 1880 and 1889, 181 (Scheube, 1894, pp. 207–18). Leonard Braddon's incomplete bibliography lists nearly 200 articles and books between 1890 and 1899 (Braddon, 1907); another incomplete bibliography lists 250 publications between 1900 and 1910 (Schaumann, 1910, pp. 699–709). A complete bibliography for this decade alone would approach 500 items. Writers in the late 1870s still regarded beriberi as an exotic and unfamiliar topic; about 30 years later, an editorial in *Lancet* observed that 'there is probably no disease concerning which so much discussion as to its etiology has taken place as beriberi' (*Lancet*, 1911, p. 842).

We can, somewhat arbitrarily, take 1880 as the beginning of serious western interest in beriberi. By that time there was a strong and broadly based opinion that the disease was diet-related. It was obvious to every-one that the disease was prominent only where rice was the staple diet. Between 1850 and 1890, several observers attributed beriberi to an 'insufficient diet or a diet not corresponding to the metabolisms and bloodmaking, or to the needs of the body' (Hirsch, 1885, p. 589). Of those who ascribed it to insufficient diet, some seem to have believed the problem was simply quantitative – those who got beriberi had too little to eat; however, others believed the problem was qualitative – sufferers had too little of certain essential foods.

Among the most important early observers to espouse a dietary ex-planation was Kamehiro Takaki. Takaki was the first to collect systematic evidence on a large scale that supported the deficiency concept. He first heard of beriberi from his father who was a guard at the Japanese Imperial Palace. Many of the guards suffered from beriberi; 'they attrib-uted the cause to food and called a provision box the "beriberi box"' (Takaki, 1906, p. 1370). Takaki became a naval doctor, spent five years studying medicine in London, and was appointed director of the Tokyo Naval Hospital. By 1882 Takaki's own observations led him to at-tribute beriberi to a poor diet. His view was that 'wide departure of nitrogen and carbon from the standard proportion (one to fifteen) essential to the maintenance of health, resulting from a great deficiency of nitrogenous substances and a great excess of carbohydrates in food, is the cause of kakke (beriberi)' (Takaki, 1885, p. 29). Takaki persuaded the skeptical Japanese admiralty to initiate massive dietary reforms – crews ate more meat (especially fresh meat), more vegetables and, at some meals, barley instead of rice. The effects were dramatic: in 1882 there were over 400 cases of beriberi for each 1,000 men, within five years the disease had been eliminated. Takaki's work was reported in major European medical periodicals, he was honored at home and abroad, and his evidence was ultimately important in understanding beriberi.

However, Takaki's ideas about the disease were inconsistent with a large, if unsystematic, body of epidemiological facts widely known before his studies even began. In 1835, John G. Malcolmson observed that 'the comparative cheapness of all kinds of grain in the Circars, and the easy circumstances of many of the native soldiers who suffered, are fatal to any supposition of the disease depending on deficient and unhealthy diet' (Hirsch, 1885, p. 592). By 1880 it was common knowl-edge that those who contracted beriberi often ate more and a better range of foods than those who did not (Hirsch, 1885, p. 592). More-over, populations that seemed especially vulnerable often lived amid a larger population that remained healthy, and the only apparent dietary difference between the groups was that the larger and immune population consumed less protein (Hirsch, 1885, p. 593). In Japan, beriberi was most prevalent in sea ports where fish was most abundant; in the East Indies, military garrisons contracted the disease while their servants (who ate less meat) did not (Rupert, 1880, pp. 509f.). Finally, specific cases were known in which beriberi appeared among persons living almost entirely on protein (Hirsch, 1885, p. 593). It was impossible to reconcile these facts with Takaki's theory. They and similar ones continued to count as evidence against dietary theories of beriberi until after the turn of the century.

Because the deficiency theory seemed incompatible with the facts, most early observers favored other explanations of beriberi. Perhaps the most popular alternative theory was that it was miasmatic or malarial. Early observers noted epidemiological similarities between beriberi and malaria. These similarities were emphasized even by persons who did not espouse the miasmatic concept. William Anderson, among the earliest western writers to investigate beriberi, noted that most Japanese doctors 'believe that the complaint is caused by some poisonous emanation from the soil'. He listed similarities between beriberi and malaria and concluded that the disease is most likely due to 'the existence of an atmospheric poison' but observed that no single cause could account for the disease (Anderson, 1876, p. 19). The *Lancet* review of Takaki's work emphasized that 'the majority of observers ... have been inclined to attribute [beriberi] ... to a specific poison which is generated in the soil under certain unsanitary conditions of local origin, and finds its way into the human body by means of the atmosphere, and perhaps of the food and drinking water also'. The reviewer observed that, Takaki's work notwithstanding, 'the weight of evidence is still in favor of the miasmatic hypothesis' (*Lancet*, 1887, p. 234).

As bacteriology became more prominent, many expected that beriberi would prove to be bacterial. Researchers sought (and often claimed to have found) the causal microorganism: Glockner identified an amoeba, Fajardo a hematozoon, Perelra a spherical microorganism, Durham a looped streptococcus, Lacerda a polymorphous ascomycete, Taylor a spirillum, Pekelharing and Winkler a micrococcus, Thomas the anchylostomum duodemale, Nepveu a strep bacillus, Rost a diplobacillus, and Dangerfield an aerobic micrococcus, and there were others (Scheube, 1894, pp. 176–91). Numerous theories linked beriberi to specific organisms. Hamilton Wright attributed the disease to an organism that entered the body by the mouth, and produced a toxin in the pyloric end of the stomach (Wright, 1902, p. 58). Herbert Durham concluded that the disease is similar to diphtheria and was communicated by fomites (Durham, 1904). Patrick Manson proposed it was a form of intoxication, not unlike alcohol intoxication, in which a toxin, manufactured outside the body (probably by microorganisms) is introduced into the body (probably through air) (Manson, 1901–02, pp. 12–16). Researchers seldom agreed which microorganism was the cause, but few seriously doubted that there was one. In 1897, M. H. Spencer wrote: 'Little doubt ... remains that [beriberi] is a germ-borne disease and that the microorganism which is the cause of it has a specially toxic influence upon the peripheral nerves' (Spencer, 1897, p. 32).

The deficiency theory of disease

In 1883, C.A. Pekelharing and A. Winkler were sent to Java by the Dutch government to study beriberi. Christiaan Eijkman, who had studied with Koch in Berlin, was a staff bacteriologist with the expedition. He was specifically instructed to find the organism that caused beriberi (Williams, 1961, p. 19). When Pekelharing and Winkler returned to Europe, they reported that the disease was definitely parasitic but that they had not yet conclusively identified the agent (Van der Berg, 1889, pp, 941f.).

Eijkman remained in Java as director of a bacteriological laboratory connected with a military hospital. While there he made two important discoveries, the first of which was that under certain conditions, chickens spontaneously contracted a disease whose symptoms and histological features resembled those traditionally connected with beriberi. For years, dogs, rabbits, guinea pigs, and monkeys had been used by bacteriologists in beriberi research and, although Eijkman is not explicit on this point, it seems likely that the chickens used in his laboratory were intended for that purpose. He reported making this discovery, by accident, when his chickens began to show signs of polyneuritis (Eijkman, 1897a, p. 525). The chickens were examined carefully and no pathological organisms were found; nor was he able to infect healthy chickens by exposure to those with polyneuritis. Eijkman then discovered that, whereas the chickens in his laboratory were generally fed a low-grade uncooked rice, it had happened that for some weeks they had been fed surplus cooked rice from the hospital kitchen.

His second important discovery was that, while ordinary chicken feed was unpolished rice, rice from the kitchen was polished. Here is one account of the sequence of events leading to these:

> Eijkman's original research in connection with beriberi began in a curiously accidental way. He wished to carry out certain investigations on fowls, and in order to economize on their food he fed them on scraps from the wards of the military hospital to which he was attached. On these scraps, which consisted chiefly of cooked,

polished rice, the fowls developed paralyses, whose nature was at first obscure. A clue thereto was unintentionally given by a newly appointed director of the hospital, who refused to let Eijkman feed his fowls any longer on scraps from the wards. Henceforward they were fed on gaba (rice still in the husks) and on this diet they recovered.

(Lancet, 1930, pp. 1097f.)

Eijkman soon became convinced that the consumption of polished rice was associated with the inception of polyneuritis gallinarum, as he called the chicken disease. Without assuming that polyneuritis gallinarum was the same as beriberi, Eijkman wondered whether beriberi was also correlated with the consumption of polished rice.

Rice was commonly prepared for human consumption in three ways:

1. Rice could be milled immediately after being harvested. If so, both outer and inner husks were generally removed, leaving only the white grain. This rice was called uncured, polished, or decorticated rice.
2. In some areas, newly harvested rice was soaked, steamed, and dried before milling. In this event, milling usually left some of the inner layers of husk, called pericarp, and certain light brown inner coverings of the grain. This rice was called cured or unpolished rice (Grist, 1965, p. 404).
3. In some primitive areas, rice was not machine milled at all but was stored unhusked and then pounded and winnowed just prior to eating. Local custom, and the ethnic origin and the economic status of consumers were among the factors determining which kind of rice was eaten (Braddon, 1907, p. 137–50).

In Java, prison inmates were usually fed whichever form of rice was commonly consumed by the local population. As it happened, in 27 prisons inmates ate unpolished rice, while in 74 others the rice was decorticated to some extent. This provided an ideal opportunity for determining whether beriberi was correlated with the consumption of decorticated rice. Eijkman's colleague, A. G. Voderman, who was then a Civil Medical Inspector, conducted surveys of the prisons in Java. The preliminary results were astonishing: of nearly 300,000 prisoners, only one in 10,000 of those who ate unpolished rice had beriberi while one in 39 of those who ate polished rice had the disease (Eijkman, 1897b). These results exhibited a striking correlation between the incidence of beriberi and the consumption of particular kinds of rice.

Within a few years, studies of other populations confirmed these results. Braddon noted that in the Malay States, Chinese, who ate polished rice, were seriously afflicted whereas Tamils, who ate unpolished rice, and native Malays, who ate rice that was not mechanically milled, were almost free from the disease (Braddon, 1907, pp. 150–198). Both Voderman's and Braddon's evidence was demographic and not subject to controls. Eijkman's studies on fowl could yield only analogical arguments that many found unconvincing. 'The favorite view of most physicians who knew of [Eijkman's] work at all, was to dismiss the matter with the assertion that polyneuritis in fowls had no relation to human beriberi' (Williams, 1961, p. 14). However, toward the end of the decade, William Fletcher (Fletcher, 1907), and Henry Fraser and Thomas Stanton (Fraser and Stanton, 1909) published important studies on small but carefully controlled populations. These studies probably did more than anything else to persuade physicians that consumption of decorticated rice was connected with beriberi.

By 1910, the evidence was clear enough for a meeting of the Far Eastern Association of Tropical Medicine to adopt a motion stating that 'in the opinion of this association sufficient evidence has now been produced in support of the view that beriberi is associated with the continuous consumption of white (polished) rice as the staple article of diet' (*BMJ*, 1910, p. 1000). In a 1911 meeting of the Society of Tropical Medicine and Hygiene, the consensus of opinion favored a dietary theory for beriberi, and Patrick Manson, admitting that his ideas about beriberi 'belong to a past age', was almost alone in expressing reservations about such a theory (Manson, 1911–12, p. 85).

Numerous theories were proposed to explain the relation between beriberi and polished rice and, not surprisingly, most of these were modelled in one way or another on the bacterial theory. Braddon proposed that polished rice was the locus within which a toxin was created by microorganisms and by which it was transferred to potential victims (Braddon, 1907, pp. 39–48). Eijkman's original hypothesis was also a version of the toxin theory:

> under the assumption that all polyneuritis ultimately seems to be intoxication, we must assume that the starch in these cases carries a poison or that from it – either in the alimentary canal (under the influence of a microorganism?) or in the nerves – a poison is produced by the chemical process of metabolism. In the pericarp of the grain, then, the material(s) would be present, through which the poison is, in some way, made harmless or, perhaps, its creation is prevented.
>
> (Eijkman, 1897a, pp. 529f.)

There were other theories as well (Williams, 1961, pp. 14f).

In 1901, Gerrit Grijns, a bacteriologist who succeeded Eijkman as director of the pathology laboratory in Batavia, first proposed that there may be some unknown ingredient in the pericarp whose absence resulted in beriberi (Grijns, 1901). Grijns asserted that recent developments were leading away from the idea that beriberi was infectious. Moreover, in his own experiments he had induced polyneuritis in chickens by feeding them concentrated protein (cooked horse meat) and this, he felt, counted heavily against Eijkman's hypothesis. The most likely conclusion seemed to be 'that there are various natural foodstuffs that cannot be missed without particular damage in the peripheral nerves' (Grijns, 1901, p. 45). Grijns's hypothesis, which appeared in a relatively minor journal, seems to have received little attention.

For the next few years, most researchers continued to favor a toxic or infectious explanation for beriberi, and this obviously reflects the prominence of the bacterial theory. However, it does not imply that facts about beriberi were blindly or irrationally forced into the bacterial mold. First, as we have seen, there were persuasive arguments against a strictly dietary explanation of beriberi. Second, through the first decade of the twentieth century, explanations of beriberi based on the bacterial theory continued to yield significant new results. Fletcher and Braddon both conducted their demographic studies in connection with infectious theories of the disease. In testing Eijkman's toxin hypothesis, Grijns obtained important results from animal experiments. Because he believed that the pericarp contained a natural antitoxin that neutralized the harmful influence of the starchy rice grain, Eijkman himself began an active chemical investigation in the effort to isolate the antitoxin. He was able to show that an aqueous extract from rice polishings cured polyneuritis gallinarum; he also showed that, when foods were heated above 120°C, they lost their effectiveness in preventing and curing the disease (Eijkman, 1906, pp. 164–70). All these results were consequences of the assumption that bacteria were somehow involved in the etiology of beriberi, so it was reasonable to continue thinking that bacteria may somehow be involved.

The success achieved by Eijkman and Grijns suggested profitable avenues of investigation for researchers working on a different disease. Beginning in 1894, crews on Norwegian ships were recognized as suffering from a disease some of whose symptoms resembled beriberi. This disease was therefore called ship-beriberi. In 1902, a Norwegian research commission concluded that ship-beriberi was a non-infectious intoxication from tainted foods (*Lancet*, 1903). In the same year, Alex Holst visited Grijns in Batavia, and Grijns showed him the experiments he was performing on fowls (Holst, 1907). Holst was impressed with the work of Eijkman and Grijns, and he adopted a similar approach in his own study of ship-beriberi. He tried to induce the disease in pigeons and chickens, and later, having been joined by Theodor Frolich, in guinea pigs (Holst and Frolich, 1907). The results of controlled feeding experiments were curious: while Holst and Frolich were trying to study ship-beriberi, the guinea pigs regularly contracted a disease that bore every similarity to scurvy. Holst and Frolich did not verify that similar diets would induce scurvy in humans, but they did mention that earlier evidence connected scurvy with deficient diet, and that scurvy and beriberi often appeared together. They also cited B. Nocht, a German observer, who had argued that ship-beriberi was a form of scurvy. Because of these publications, beriberi, scurvy, and ship-beriberi were all seen as *causally* linked to deficient diets and, therefore, as *theoretically* linked to one another.

In 1910 Fraser and Stanton showed that the substance that prevented beriberi was soluble in strong alcohol, and that the effectiveness of a given grain in combating beriberi seemed to depend on the amount of phosphorus it contained (Fraser and Stanton, 1910). By obtaining a purer specimen of the ingredient in rice husks that protected test animals from beriberi, Casimir Funk was soon able to show that the disease was not due to phosphorus deficiency, but the idea that beriberi and scurvy were due to a deficiency of some essential nutrient or nutrients was becoming more plausible.

By this time, several lines of work were converging: epidemiological studies (Takaki, Voderman, Braddon, Fletcher, Stanton and Fraser) and animal experiments (Eijkman, Grijns, Holst and Frolich) had exhibited a connection between the consumption of milled grain and various distinctive disorders; chemical studies (Eijkman, Fraser and Stanton, Funk) had isolated and characterized with fair precision the particular ingredient in rice polishings that would prevent and cure some of these disorders; an important negative result was that, after 30 years of searching, bacteriologists could not agree in identifying a particular microorganism that was causally responsible for any of the diseases in question. Given the importance of the bacterial theory, it would have been difficult for any deficiency hypothesis to have been accepted without this negative result. The strands were finally assembled in Casimir Funk's 'The Etiology of the Deficiency Diseases' (Funk, 1912). Funk announced – somewhat prematurely as it turned out – the isolation of a concentrated form of the protective substance for beriberi; he proposed that it be called vitamine (Funk, 1912, p. 347). Funk classified beriberi, polyneuritis in birds, epidemic dropsy, scurvy, infantile scurvy, experimental scurvy in animals, ship-beriberi, pellagra, and rickets as deficiency diseases. He stated that these diseases are due to different deficiencies. Funk noted that about twenty years of experimental work had been required to establish that these various diseases were caused by a deficiency of essential nutrients. He admitted that this view was still not generally accepted, but claimed that there was enough evidence 'to convince everybody of its truth, if the trouble be taken to follow step by step the development of our knowledge on this subject' (Funk, 1912, p. 341).

The deficiency theory in relation to the etiological research programme

As we have seen, in 1910 the Far Eastern Association of Tropical Medicine concluded that 'sufficient evidence has now been produced in support of the view that beriberi is associated with the continuous consumption of white (polished) rice as the staple article of diet' (*BMJ*, 1910, p. 1000). There are unmistakable parallels between this conclusion and beliefs about scurvy that prevailed 80 years earlier in the 1830s. In both cases physicians discovered an empirical correlation between a symptomatically defined disorder and a particular dietary pattern. In both cases, also, the disorder could be effectively controlled by changing what people ate. The remarkable difference is that, whereas in the 1830s this empirical understanding of scurvy effectively satisfied scientific interest in the disease, in 1910 recognition of the empirical correlation between beriberi and the consumption of polished rice only intensified research on the etiology of the disease. How can one explain this difference? The obvious answer is the research programme to which, by 1910, virtually all medical scientists subscribed. In the 1830s, the understanding of scurvy enabled physicians to control symptoms (and, as then conceived, that was all there was to the disease), but, by the turn of the century, in comparison to the explanations emerging from the identification of universal necessary causes, even effective control was seen as inconclusive. As Adolf Strümpell observed:

> The empty generalities of the past only appeared, superficially, to satisfy the need for causes; this need can only be met through the discovery of causes that operate in every single case, only through a knowledge of their nature, of the manner of their operation, of the site of their influence, and of the necessity of their consequence.
> (Strümpell, 1893, p. 22f.)

The etiological standpoint carried a new standard for comprehension – a standard that was obligatory for the acceptance of any etiological account.

By 1910 the most impressive achievements in the quest for specific causes involved bacteria. Largely because these successes were so striking, medical science in general had become converted to the etiological standpoint. Having accepted this way of thinking, researchers looked for universal necessary causes for all diseases. Many diseases proved to be non-bacterial. However, since all this research was informed by the etiological standpoint, and since the etiological standpoint itself was accepted largely because of the striking successes of the bacterial theory, it is clearly a mistake to regard the bacterial theory only as an obstacle to research on non-bacterial diseases. The truth is almost exactly the opposite. Conventional wisdom is that 'improved microscopes and the staining and other [bacteriological] technics ... monopolized the attention of investigators' and left them with 'little incentive to consider ... malnutrition as a cause of disease' (McCollum, 1957, pp. 225f.). Even if this were true (which it is not), without the successes of bacteriology, there would have been neither a reason to look for universal necessary causes nor even a theoretical framework within which such causes could have been conceived. The quest for a universal necessary cause for beriberi makes sense only within the context of the etiological standpoint.

In a recent book, Kenneth J. Carpenter concludes that:

> [It was] the repeated failure of lime juice after 1860 that was most important in leading investigators to doubt the whole structure of experience and conclusions about scurvy that had been built up in the previous two hundred years ... . In this situation the investigator was induced to look at the whole subject anew, rejecting earlier knowledge which now seemed unreliable, and accepting only the first-hand experiences and ways of thought of his own generation.
> (Carpenter, 1986, pp. 250f.)

It may well have been that the failure of lime juice after 1860 motivated scientists to look again at the etiology of scurvy. But, quite obviously, the 'ways of thought of his own generation' that the early twentieth-century investigator found most compelling were those dictated by the quest for universal necessary causes. Without this 'way of thought' there was no universal cause of scurvy (or of beriberi) and, therefore, while there may have been piecemeal changes in what people thought about the disease and how to control it, there was no possibility for doubting 'the whole structure of [earlier] experience and conclusions' about the disease. Unfortunately, except for this one vague allusion, Carpenter totally misses the broader story.

Thus, as with every other etiological investigation in the period, research on the deficiency diseases was informed by the heuristic of the research programme of which it was a part. And, more than anything else, the stunning success of the bacterial theory insured universal acceptance of that programme. Thus, far from merely presenting an obstacle to researchers studying the deficiency (and other non-bacterial) diseases, the success of the bacterial theory was the most vivid source both of motivation for their work and of the standards for comprehension that their etiological investigations were required to satisfy.

Notes

1. In this earlier paper ('The Germ Theory, Beriberi, and the Deficiency Theory of Disease'), which forms the basis for this chapter, I took a position that I now regard as incorrect. It was not 'the germ theory [*per se*] that revived interest in scurvy and ... motivated researchers to seek a theoretical understanding of scurvy' (Carter, 1977, p. 136), but rather what I am here calling the etiological research programme of which the germ theory [more precisely the bacterial theory] of disease was a part. So while I still think that my earlier argument is essentially correct, the conclusion as stated in the earlier paper requires modification.
2. Kenneth J. Carpenter has recently written books on scurvy and beriberi (1986, 2000). Carpenter is much more reserved in his judgments about the relation of bacteriology and the deficiency concept than those quoted above so they constitute the foil for my argument. Carpenter provides more details about research on both scurvy and beriberi, but, from the point of view of this book, what he says neither adds to nor (with one minor exception to be discussed below) challenges the position I advocated in my 1977 paper or that I now present. Therefore, his interesting and engaging work has not occasioned any substantial change in my argument.

Some Final Thoughts

In these case studies, my goals have been twofold: to present modern medicine as a Lakatosian research programme focusing on the quest for universal necessary causes, and to identify some of the heuristic principles required in that undertaking. The cases we have examined are by no means exhaustive. Alfred S. Evans has shown that Koch's Postulates can be expanded to encompass diseases of several different kinds – for example, those caused by 'slow viruses' and occupational and immunological diseases (Evans, 1993). Given the broad interpretation of the Postulates proposed in Chapter 8, Evans's account is obviously compatible with my objectives. In the last two decades, other writers have discussed still other diseases in ways that also fit well with the point of view here presented (Ghesquier, 1999; Harden, 1987 and 1992; Kunitz, 1988; Schlich, 1994). The process by which causes were finally identified for chromosomal disorders provides a further example (Carter, 2002).

This way of thinking reveals mistakes in current beliefs about the rise of modern medicine. Thinking that nineteenth-century medicine means the germ theory, historians have almost totally ignored the broader movement of which it was a part. As a result, most writers entirely overlook the role of the research programme in the origins of Freudian psychology. A related flaw is evident in accounts of the deficiency theory: historians see only competition with the germ theory and are oblivious of the movement that nurtured them both and endowed each with its own objectives and research orientation. By failing to grasp the nature of the programme, historians also misconstrue the work of those who contributed to it. For example, Semmelweis is seen only as having introduced chlorine washings – in spite of his own clear and repeated claims that his *opinions* mattered most and distinguished him from other early advocates of disinfection and in spite of subsequent obstetricians who praised his *theory* of childbed fever because of its explanatory power. Finally, as another example, there has been almost universal neglect of early nineteenth-century studies of parasitic diseases, yet these were arguably more important in the rise of medicine than was pathological anatomy (which, partly through the unfortunate influence of Foucault, has attracted far more attention than its significance warrants). In my view, Rennucci, Bassi, and Gruby, Semmelweis, Davaine, Klebs, Pasteur and Koch, the early Freud, Loeffler and Frosch, Eijkman and Funk (each of whose work was, demonstrably, focused almost exclusively on the quest for universal necessary causes) and virtually every other medical researcher since the demise of *chimbuki*-medicine have all contributed to the same research programme. 'The final hope and aim of medical science is the establishment of monogenic disease entities' (Taylor, 1979, p. 21); it can't be made clearer than that.

By identifying heuristic principles essential to this programme – for example, the Distinguishability Hypothesis – our investigation has also underscored the importance of theory in the quest for causes. One might expect that historians of medicine, like many who write on the history of the physical sciences, would give careful attention to medical theories. No such luck. Theory, and every other manifestation of reason, gets short shrift these days. In William F. Bynum's recent book, *Science and the Practice of Medicine in the Nineteenth Century*, the phrase 'etiological theories' appears only once; it appears in the following subordinate index entry: 'see also germ theory, miasmata, etiological theories' (Bynum, 1994, p. 262). But there is nothing else to see; the phrase 'etiological theories' appears nowhere else in the index and, so far as I can determine, Bynum never once used the phrase in the entire body of his book (Carter, 1995, p. 496). To be sure, in a five-page section entitled 'bacteriology', Bynum devotes just over one page (!) to Koch's Postulates (Bynum, 1994, pp. 129f.). Otherwise there is no discussion whatsoever of what Adolf Strümpell called 'the most characteristic thrust of modern pathology (Strümpell, 1884a, p. 2) – namely, the quest for universal necessary causes. Bynum's neglect is typical and symptomatic. Influenced by one brand of postmodernism – the French Disease – historians have become suspicious of anything that smacks of rationality, so scientific theories are marginalized. Today's historians look, instead, at the power structures of medicine (professional organizations, medical schools) and at medicine among the unempowered (irregular practitioners, treatment of the insane, the Poor Laws). As a result, we know less about the nature and origin of the medical theories that affect our lives than about, say, eighteenth-century quackery or the average income of general practitioners in Victorian England. And that, I think, is an abrogation of responsibility.

'But,' one early reviewer, asked: 'what would Carter say about Latour?'. Bruno Latour has shown (in a lively manner replete with the quaint metaphors one has come to expect in Gallic 'philosophy') how Pasteur and members of the early French Hygienic movement managed to *Pasteurize* France – that is, managed *bilaterally* to leverage themselves into nearly absolute hegemony (Latour, 1984). But we are not talking here about hula-hoops or polyester leisure suits. At the end of the day, Pasteur advanced rational scientific theories in support of which he gave evidence and made arguments. As an exercise in 'let's pretend', suppose none of Pasteur's evidence was relevant to the process by which his theories won out (which, by the way, reduces Pasteur himself to little more than a fool). Suppose, as Latour seems to fancy, power relations alone explain why any one theory surpasses its rivals (p. 153). So what? Even if this were true, at some point scientific theories deserve attention as examples of the best *thinking* the species has yet achieved ('There's no point in listening to Bach's music any more; now we understand the system of patronage that gave him influence at court.'). So what can be the point (other than to sustain a fad nearly on a par with leisure suits) of writing books arguing that one can dispense with arguments? Moreover, Latour, like everyone else, sees only bacteriology – not the quest for universal necessary causes. French bacteriology, a local phenomenon after all, is less in need of explanation than is the research programme of which it was one part. Perhaps Latour should be arguing that the origin and growth of the entire international programme can be reduced to social forces. That would be a more interesting thesis and it has a certain plausibility – the broader an intellectual change, the less likely it can be explained in strictly rational terms. Moreover, that thesis might at least force one to transcend Gallic chauvinism.

As Koch's Postulates are usually explained in introductory textbooks, the goal seems to be proving causation by routine procedures (isolation, cultivation, and inoculation) that generate empirical evidence of sufficiency; these accounts invariably ignore the theoretical assumptions that, alone, can breathe life and meaning into such procedures. However, ever since Kant refuted Hume we have known that causation is not an empirical relation. Apparently without realizing that they are re-enacting history, some writers suggest that causes can be conjured from the dusty boneyard that is empiricism through the judicious use of induction (Parascandola, 1998, p. 320). But since we can't observe causes in individual cases, we can't induce universal causes from particular cases either. Rather, causation is inherently theoretical and, in the absence of an accepted theory, no amount of empirical evidence can demonstrate causal relations – as we saw illustrated in Davaine's dispute with his critics.

While it is often overlooked, Koch was clear that empirical correlations alone can never prove causality. In 'Investigations of the Etiology of Wound Infections', he repeatedly insisted that proving causation required showing that 'the number and distribution of bacteria [is] appropriate to explain completely the disease symptoms' (Koch, 1878a, pp. 27, 29, 48), and his papers on tuberculosis and cholera contain similar language. More recent scientists have made analogous observations. For example, in concluding an essay on the application of Koch's Postulates to viruses, Thomas M. Rivers urged that research be 'tempered by the priceless attributes of common sense, proper training and sound reasoning' (Rivers, 1937, p. 11). But the need for such attributes varies directly with the degree to which one's work involves theoretical considerations: counting requires little training or common sense. In a reflective paper on proving the etiological significance of non-living toxins, J. Yerushalmy and Carroll E. Palmer advised researchers to examine the relation between similar and related possible causal factors and the disease in question (Yerushalmy and Palmer, 1959, p. 38). But such examinations can yield only analogical arguments that are inherently theoretical and not subject to direct empirical confirmation – how, after all, does one decide which factors are *similar* and *related* except by an appeal to theory? At the end of his own list of mostly empirical causal criteria, Alfred S. Evans notes that 'the whole thing should make biologic and epidemiologic sense' (Evans, 1976, p. 192). He later wrote that he added this requirement 'with tongue in cheek' (Evans, 1989, p. 108). The problem with his last criterion – perhaps the reason he regarded it as less than fully serious and why it is so seldom addressed explicitly – may be that, while everyone recognizes intuitively that 'making sense' of the world is the whole point in looking for causes and an essential standard against which purported causes must always be judged, it is absolutely impossible to specify, in advance, what it will take to make sense of the world or how one goes about doing it. It is nearly impossible, sometimes until long after the fact, to be sure that the causes we hypothesize really do make sense of anything at all. Thus, the maximally and irremediably *vague* notion of 'making sense' lies at the heart of the concept of causation. This shows how totally pointless, hopeless, and downright silly it is to think one can ever state *precisely* what it is for one thing to cause another.[1]

So, popular versions of Koch's Postulate suggest that causation is ultimately an empirical relation and that establishing causation resembles counting. But all the while we know in our hearts – and our bright students quickly figure out – that our hypotheses must *also* satisfy a different standard, one on a completely different conceptual level, because ultimately, making sense (biological relevance, theoretical adequacy, explanatory power) matters at least as much as any empirical correlation.[2]

We have traced some aspects of the rise of the etiological research programme and we have seen the enormous increase in explanatory power that this programme achieved. What, if anything, can we expect of future causal thinking in medicine? Will the quest for universal necessary causes continue to dominate medical research? We begin with a minor philosophical dispute in contemporary epidemiology.

Nowadays epidemiologists get criticized for how they talk (Stehbens, 1992), and sometimes this seems to foster a sense of insecurity – some epidemiologists apparently worry about whether theirs is only 'second-rate science' (Parascandola, 1998). But do the criticisms make sense?

'At the crux of the issue', William E. Stehbens insists, 'is the use and meaning of *cause* in medicine' (Stehbens, 1992, p. 97). He finds current epidemiological usage teetering on the brink of imprecision, and the fate of scientific medicine seems to hang in the balance: 'If epidemiology continues to disregard the misusage of terminology ... it threatens the very survival of logic and science in medicine' (Stehbens, 1992, p. 116). How can we save our way of life? our civilization? the self-respect of our embattled epidemiologists? Stehbens recommends paying strict heed to what Aristotle, Spinoza, Hume, Mill, and Bertand Russell had to say about causes.

However, one must be cautious about using philosophy to regulate scientific discourse, because most of philosophy is inherently retrospective. Hegel put it this way: 'When philosophy paints its gray in gray, then has a shape of life grown old. By philosophy's grey in grey it cannot be rejuvenated but only understood. The owl of Minerva spreads its wings only with the falling of the dusk' (Hegel, 1821, p. 7). As Hegel saw, while philosophy describes the way words have been used, it says little about how words will be (or should be) used in the future. Anthony Flew (borrowing an image from Rudolf Carnap) explained that to think otherwise would be like an explorer saying: 'This country has its rivers in the wrong place! Look, my map shows where they are supposed to be' (Flew, 1966, p. 150). Philosophy occasionally contributes new ways of thinking or helps us refine our use of specific terms, but past philosophers seldom provide much help when it comes to deciding how words should be used in the future.

In contrast to philosophy, most important scientific advances depend on changes in how we talk. 'As ideas are preserved and communicated by means of words, it necessarily follows that we cannot improve the language of any science without at the same time improving the science itself; neither can we, on the other hand, improve a science without improving the language or nomenclature which belongs to it' (Lavoisier, 1789, p. 1). Between about 1830 and 1880, medicine reorganized itself around the concept of universal necessary causes. Robert Koch referred to the new way of thinking as the etiological standpoint (Koch, 1901, p. 905). As we have seen, before that time, no one spoke about *the cause of anthrax* or *the cause of tuberculosis* – such phrases literally had no meaning. This is because, as diseases were then defined, virtually none of them could have had that sort of cause. Recharacterizing diseases in terms of necessary causes was a major advance that made possible coherent explanations of disease phenomena as well as systematic treatment and prophylaxis. Currently, medical science seeks such characterizations. But this tells us nothing about whether we will continue, in the future, to characterize diseases in this way. The reason is that one can never know in advance what kinds of explanations will be required to make sense of future observations. Judging from current developments in cosmology, our observations are likely to get weirder and weirder, and our explanations will probably follow suit.

One reason science is no longer done in Latin is that dead languages cannot accommodate the linguistic adjustments on which all good science depends. And any contemporary who favors quaint anachronisms like *causa vera* sine qua non (Stehbens, 1992, p. 115) is either confused or making a naked attempt to obfuscate the reader – probably both.

We make up words and give them meanings, and they can be used however we like. But this does not imply that meanings should be changed capriciously. Current scientific usage embodies what is arguably the best thinking that our species has achieved through several thousand years of intellectual groping, and it should be adjusted cautiously only when there are compelling reasons for doing so. On the other hand, as we have seen, language must be open to change if science is to progress at all.

It isn't a fact about the world that some cases of illness come packaged together with universal necessary causes; rather, it's a fact about how we have learned to characterize diseases. When possible, we define diseases so they have necessary causes because there is great utility in doing so. But there may be diseases for which this is impossible either in principle or simply in fact.

On the one hand, it is impossible, in principle, to explain why one unstable atom decays at a certain time while identical atoms around it do not. As currently understood, there are *no* sufficient causes for such events; they simply happen. This is a metaphysical issue not an epistemological one; it stems from the way the world is, not from the weakness of our intellects. By a loose analogy, there could conceivably be individual cases of illness (perhaps those that start on the chromosomal level) whose beginnings have no sufficient causes; they may simply happen. It would obviously be impossible to group such cases in such a way that a new disease could be so characterized that all its instances would share a necessary cause. If this is how the world turns out to be, the very most one could hope for would be risk factors (and even these may ultimately prove impossible). Of course, even if there were such illnesses, we would probably never come to know it and, in the absence of such knowledge, we could continue seeking non-existent causes for as long as the species shall live.

Alternatively, there could be cases of illness that *do* share sufficient causes but causes whose identification requires more intellectual, financial and/or temporal assets than the human species will ever have at its disposal. In short, there could be causes that we simply are not smart enough to identify.

As a species, we have spent more time and money on cancer research than on any other single problem in our history. Yet, while we have learned a lot, we may be no closer to identifying sufficient causes in terms of which classes of cancers can be characterized than we were 100 years ago.[3] And this could be because there simply are no such causes or it could be because, so far (and maybe forever), we are not smart enough to find them. Perhaps at this point (and maybe forever), the best we can do is find risk factors. So how should we respond? By wringing our hands and insisting that no one speaks until we find *causae verae* sine qua non? Of course not. We do our best to understand and to control the world in whatever ways we can, and this may require changes in how we talk.

We all know that risk factors are different from the causes Koch identified. So what? At some point we may confront diseases for which causes of *his* kind can never be found. But language evolves to accommodate and to foster new ways of thinking. What form of speech should we adopt? We cannot prescribe for the future, but here are two obvious candidates: either we could exploit the similarity (family resemblance) between traditional causes and theory-poor statistical correlations and simply broaden our concept of causation to include some risk factors; or we could continue to talk about risk factors as different from traditional causes. At this point, the choice seems arbitrary. Scientific medicine is unlikely to collapse, whichever course we adopt. But, however we end up speaking, this much is absolutely certain: just as dead languages have no names for whatever new concept of causation may emerge, dead philosophers (Aristotle, Hume, Mill, Popper, and so on) are in no position to advise epidemiologists about how to talk.

Half a century from now, historians may document when and how we resolved these issues (assuming they finally get around to looking at theories again), and philosophers, with their gray in gray, may clarify why the resolution took the form it did. But how *we* talk about causes will certainly be no more binding on scientists in 2060 than James L.

Bardsley's way of talking about the causes of diabetes is binding on us today.

Notes

1. Which, of course, doesn't deter the bold from trying. First try: '*Cause* is here used as the essential antecedent [i.e. the cause] or sole prerequisite determinant [i.e. the cause] by which the disease is brought about [i.e. caused]' (Stehbens, 1992, pp. 99f.). In short: a cause is the cause by which the disease is caused. Second try: '*Cause* is something that occasions [i.e. causes], produces [i.e. causes], or effects [i.e. causes] a disease' (Stehbens, 1992, p. 102). In short: a cause is something that causes, causes, or causes a disease.
2. And that, by the way, seems to me to have been – at least at the beginning – the real point of contention between Peter Duesberg and his opponents in the AIDS establishment. While the arguments were generally stated in terms of the necessity and sufficiency conditions of Koch's Postulates, the real issue was usually whether a retrovirus like HIV could possibly explain AIDS.
3. To be sure, we *may* be a whole lot closer, but, until such causes are found, there is no telling – not knowing where the goal lies, we can't be sure whether we are getting closer to it or not.

Bibliography

l'Académie Impériale de Médecine (1858), *De la fièvre puerpérale*, Paris: Baillière et fils.

Ackerknecht, Erwin H. (1946), 'Natural Diseases and Rational Treatment in Primitive Medicine', *Bulletin of the History of Medicine*, 19:467–497.

Adelon, Nicholas Philibert (ed.) (1832–46), *Dictionnaire de médecine*, 2nd edn, 30 vols, Paris: Bechet.

Anderson, William (1876), 'On Kakke, or the Beri-beri of Japan', *Saint Thomas Hospital Reports*, 7:5–30.

Andersson, Ola (1962), *Studies in the Prehistory of Psychoanalysis*, Stockholm: Svenska Bokförlaget.

Andral, Gabriel (1832–33), 'Hydrophobia', *Lancet*, 1:806–808.

Audouin, Jean Victor (1836a), 'Recherches anatomiques et physiologiques sur la maladie contagieuse qui attaque les vers à soie, et qu'on désigne sous le nom de muscardine', *Annales des Sciences Naturelle: Zoologie*, 2nd series, 8:229–245.

——— (1836b), 'Nouvelles expériences sur la nature de la maladie contagieuse qui attaque les vers à soie, et qu'on désigne sous le nom de muscardine', *Annales des Sciences Naturelle: Zoologie*, 2nd series, 8:257–269.

Balsamo-Crivelli, Joseph (1839), 'Ueber den Ursprung und die Entwicklung der *Botrytis bassiana* und eine andere schmorotzende Art von Schimmel', *Linnaea*, 16:118–123.

Bamberger, Heinrich von (1883), 'Hysterie', *Allgemeine wiener medizinische Zeitung*, 28:529f.

Bar, Paul (1883), *Des méthodes antiseptiques en obstétrique*, Paris: Alexandre Coccoz.

Bardsley, James L. (1845), 'Diabetes', in Dunglison (1845), vol. 1, pp. 606–625.

Barlow, Edward (1845a), 'Education (Physical)', in Dunglison (1845), vol. 1, pp. 750–765.

——— (1845b), 'Plethora', in Dunglison (1845), vol. 3, pp. 553–574.

Barnes, David S. (2000), 'Historical Perspectives on the Etiology of Tuberculosis', *Microbes and Infection*, 2:431–440.

Bassi, Agostino (1835), *Del mal del segno, calcinaccio o moscardino*, trans. P.J. Yarrow, ed. G.C. Ainsworth, (1958), Ithaca, NY: Phytopathological Classics, Number 10.

Beaude, Jean Pierre (1849), 'Anthrax', in J.-P. Beaude (ed.), *Dictionnaire de médecine usuelle à l'usage des gens du mode*, 2 vols, Paris: Didier, vol. 1, pp. 129f.

Beijerinck, Martinus Willem (1898), 'Ueber ein Contagium vivum fluidum als Ursache der Flackenkrankheit der Tabaksblätter', *Verhandelingen koniinklijke Akademie van Wetenscharppen te Amsterdam*, **65**:3–21.

—— (1899), 'Ueber ein Contagium vivum fluidum als Ursache der Fleckenkrankheit der Tabaksblätter', Abteilung II, *Centralblatt für Bakteriologie, Parasitenkunde und Infektionskrankheiten*, **5**:27–33.

Berliner klinische Wochenschrift (1877), [Review of Klebs' 'Ueber die Umgestaltungen der medicinischen Anschauungen in den letzten drei Jahrzehnten'], *Berliner klinische Wochenscrift* **14**: 594.

Bert, Paul (1876), 'Nouvelles recherches sur le sang de rate', *Comptes rendus de Séances et Mémoires de la Société de Biologie*, **28**:380–381.

—— (1877), 'Sur la nature du charbon', *Comptes rendus de Séances et Mémoires de la Société de Biologie*, **29**:317–321.

Biett, L. (1836), 'Gale', in Adelon (1932–46), vol. 13, pp. 545–549.

Billet, Léon (1872), *De la fièvre puerpérale et de la réforme des maternités*, Paris: H.-B. Baillière et fils.

Birch-Hirschfeld, Felix Victor (1872), 'Die neuern pathologischanatomischen Untersuchungen über krankmachende Schmarotzerpilze', *Schmidts Jahrbücher der in- und ausländischen Medizin*, **155**:97–109.

—— (1875), 'Die neuern pathologischanatomischen Untersuchungen über Vorkommen und Bedeutung niederer Pilzformen (Bakterien) bei Infektionskrankheiten', *Schmidts Jahrbücher der in- und ausländischen Medizin*, **166**:169–223.

—— (1877), *Lehrbuch der pathologischen Anatomie*, Leipzig: F.C.W. Vogel.

Blane, Gilbert (1785), *Observations on the Diseases Incident to Seamen*, in Christopher C. Lloyd (ed.) (1965), *The Health of Seamen*, London: Naval Records Society, pp. 1–211.

Bloomfield, Arthur L. (1958), *A Bibliography of Internal Medicine: Communicable Diseases*, Chicago: The University of Chicago Press.

Boehr, Max (1868), 'Ueber die Infectionstheorie des Puerperalfiebers und ihre Consequenzen für die Sanitäts-Polizei', *Monatsschrift für Geburtskunde und Frauenkrankheiten*, **32**:401–433.

Bollinger, Otto (1875), 'Infectionen durch thierische Gifte (Milzbrand)', in Hugo Wilhelm von Ziemssen (ed.), *Handbuch der speciellen Pathologie und Therapie*, 4 vols, Leipzig: F.C.W. Vogel, vol. 3, pp. 447–490.

Böttger, Herbert (1955), 'Förderer der Semmelweisschen Lehre', *Sudhoffs Archiv*, **39**:341–362.

Braddon, W. Leonard (1907), *The Cause and Prevention of Beriberi*, London: Rebman.

Brauell, Friedrich August (1857), 'Versuche und Untersuchungen betreffend den Milzbrand des Menschen und der Thiere', *Archiv für pathologische Anatomie, Physiologie, und klinische Medizine (Virchows Archiv)*, 11:132–144.

—— (1858), 'Weitere Mittheilungen über Milzbrand und Milzbrandblut', *Archiv für pathologische Anatomie, Physiologie, und klinische Medizine (Virchows Archiv)*, 14:432–466.

—— (1866), 'Zur Milzbrand-Frage', *Archiv für pathologische Anatomie, Physiologie, und klinische Medizine (Virchows Archiv)*, 36:292–297.

Braun, Carl (1855), 'Kindbettfieber', in J.B. Chiari, C. Braun and J. Späth (eds), *Klinik der Geburtshilfe und Gynakologie*, Erlangen: Ferdinand Enke.

—— (1857), *Lehrbuch der Geburtshülfe*, Wien: Wilhelm Braumüller.

Breisky, August (1861), 'Semmelweis: Die Aetiologie, der Begriff und die Prophylaxis des Kindbettfiebers', *Vierteljahrschrift für praktsche Heilkunde*, 18, Literärischer Anzeiger, pp. 1–13.

Breuer, Josef and Sigmund Freud (1893), 'On the Psychical Mechanism of Hysterical Phenomena: Preliminary Communication', in Strachey (1955–74), vol. 2, pp. 3–17.

British Medical Journal (1898), 'An Eccentric Physician', *British Medical Journal*, 2:1705.

—— (1907), 'Scurvy', *British Medical Journal*, 1:683.

—— (1910), 'The Far Eastern Association of Tropical Medicine', *British Medical Journal*, 1:999f.

Brock, Thomas D. (1988), *Robert Koch: A Life in Medicine and Bacteriology*, Madison, WI: Science Tech Publishers.

Brown, Joseph (1845), 'Contagion', in Dunglison (1845), vol. 1, pp. 500–505.

Bruce-Chwatt, Leonard J. (1988), 'History of Malaria from Prehistory to Eradiction', in Walter H. Wernsdorfer and Ian McGregor (eds), *Malaria: Principles and Practice of Malariology*, 2 vols, Edinburgh: Churchill Livingstone, vol. 1, pp. 1–59.

Budd, George (1840), 'Scurvy', in Alexander Tweedie (ed.), *A System of Practical Medicine*, 5 vols, London: Whittaker, vol. 5, pp. 58–95.

Bynum, William F. (1994), *Science and the Practice of Medicine in the Nineteenth Century*, Cambridge: Cambridge University Press.

Campbell, William C. (1979), 'History of Trichinosis: Paget, Owen and the Discovery of *Trichinella Spiralis*', *Bulletin of the History of Medicine*, 53:520–552.

Carpenter, Kenneth J. (1986), *The History of Scurvy and Vitamin C*, Cambridge: Cambridge University Press.

—— (2000), *Rice, Beriberi and Vitamin B*, Berkeley: University of California Press.

Carter, K. Codell (1977), 'The Germ Theory, Beriberi, and the Deficiency Theory of Disease', *Medical History*, 21:119–136.

—— (1980), 'Germ Theory, Hysteria, and Freud's Early Work in Psychopathology', *Medical History*, 24:259–274.

—— (1982a), 'On the Decline of Bloodletting in 19th Century Medicine', *The Journal of Psychoanalytic Anthropology*, 5:219–234.

—— (1982b), 'Nineteenth-Century Treatments for Rabies as Reported in the *Lancet*', *Medical History*, 26:67–78.

—— (1985a), 'Ignaz Semmelweis, Carl Mayrhofer, and the Rise of Germ Theory', *Medical History*, 29:33–53.

—— (1985b), 'Koch's Postulates in Relation to the Work of Jacob Henle and Edwin Klebs', *Medical History*, 29:353–374.

—— (trans.) (1987a), *Essays of Robert Koch*, New York: Greenwood Press.

—— (1987b), 'Edwin Klebs' Criteria for Disease Causality', *Medizinhistorisches Journal*, 22:80–89.

—— (1991), 'Causes of Disease and Death in the Babylonian Talmud', *Medizinhistorisches Journal*, 26:94–104.

—— (1993), 'The Concept of Quackery in Early Nineteenth Century British Medical Periodicals', *The Journal of Medical Humanities*, 14:89–97.

—— (1995), 'Essay Review: Toward a Rational History of Medical Science', *Studies in the History and Philosophy of Medical Science*, 26:493–502.

—— (1997), 'Causes of Disease and Causes of Death', *Continuity and Change*, 12:189–198.

—— (2002), 'Early Conjectures that Down Syndrome is Caused by Chromosomal Nondisjunction', *Bulletin of the History of Medicine*, 76:528–563.

—— and George S. Tate (1991), 'The Earliest-Known Account of Semmelweis's Initiation of Disinfection at Vienna's Allgemeines Krankenhaus', *Bulletin of the History of Medicine*, 65:252–257.

——, Scott Abbott, and James L. Siebach (1995), 'Five Documents Relating to the Final Illness and Death of Ignaz Semmelweis', *Bulletin of the History of Medicine*, 69:255–270.

Castiglioni, Arturo (1947), *A History of Medicine*, 2nd edn, trans. E.B. Krumbhaar, New York: Alfred A. Knopf.

Charcot, Jean Martin (1883), 'Deux cas de contracture hystérique d'origine traumatique', *Progrès médical*, 11:37–39.

—— (1888–94), *Oeuvres complètes*, M. Babinski et al. (eds), 9 vols, Paris: Bureaux du Progrès Médical.

—— (1889), *Clinical Lectures on Diseases of the Nervous System*, trans. Thomas Savill, London: New Sydenham Society.

—— (1892–95), *Poliklinische Vorträge*, trans. Sigmund Freud, 2 vols, Leipzig: Franz Deuticke.

Chomel, M. (1835), 'Etiologie', in Adelon (1832–46), vol. 12, pp. 415–425.

—— (1842), 'Pneumonie', in Adelon (1832–46), vol. 25, pp. 144–232.

Cohn, Ferdinand (1872), 'Untersuchungen über Bakterien', *Beiträge zur Biologie der Pflanzen*, **2**:128–222.

—— (1875), 'Untersuchungen über Bakterien', *Beiträge zur Biologie der Pflanzen*, **3**:141–204.

Cohn, Martin (1883), 'Ueber die Psychosen im kindlichen Alter', *Archiv für Kinderheilkunde*, **4**:28–64, 102–107.

Cohnheim, Julius Friedrich (1877), *Vorlesungen über allgemenine Pathologie*, 2 vols, Berlin: August Hirschwald.

—— and Carl Julius Salomonsen (1877) [Report of discussion] *Jahresbericht der schlesische Gesellschaft für vaterländische Kultur*, **55**:222f.

Colin, Léon (1880a), 'Présentation d'ouvrages manuscrits et imprimés', *Bulletin de l'Académie de médecine*, 2nd series, **9**:1235f.

—— (1880b), 'Présentation d'ouvrages manuscrits et imprimés', *Bulletin de l'Académie de médecine*, 2nd series, **9**:1346f.

Collard, Patrick (1976), *The Development of Microbiology*, Cambridge: Cambridge University Press.

Conolly, John (1845), 'Disease', in Dunglison (1845), vol. 1, pp. 674–689.

Conrad, Peter and Joseph W. Schneider (1980), *Deviance and Medicalization: From Badness to Sickness*, St Louis: C.V. Mosby.

Copi, Irving R. (1979), *Symbolic Logic*, 5th edn, New York: Macmillan Publishing Co.

Coze, Leon and Victor-Timothee Feltz (1866), 'Recherches expérimentales sur la présence des infusoires et l'état du sang dans les maladies infectieuses', *Gazette médical de Strasbourg*, 2nd series, **6**:61–64, 115–125, 208f., 225–229.

—— and —— (1872), *Recherches cliniques et expérimentales sur les maladies infectieuses*, Paris: J.B. Baillière et fils.

Crede, Carl S.F. (1861), 'Die Aetiologie, der Begriff und die Prophylaxis des Kindbettfiebers von Ignaz Philipp Semmelweis', *Monatsschrift für Geburtskunde*, **18**:406f.

Cuboni, Giuseppe and Ettore Marchiafava (1881), 'Neue Studien über die Natur der Malaria', *Archiv für experimentelle Pathologie und Pharmakologie*, **13**:265–280.

Cumin, William (1845), 'Scrofula', in Dunglison (1845), vol. 4, pp. 125–145.

D'Espine, H.-A. (1873), *Contribution a l'étude de la septicémie puerpérale*, Paris: J.-B. Baillière et fils.

Darwin, Charles (1876), *The Origin of Species*, Vol 49, Great Books of the Western World, ed. Robert M. Hutchins (1952), Chicago: Encyclopaedia Britannica.

Davaine, Casimir (1863a), 'Recherches sur les infusoires du sang dans la maladie connue sous le nom de *sang de rate*', *Comptes rendus de l'Académie des sciences*, 57:220–223.

────── (1863b), 'Nouvelles recherches sur les infusoires du sang dans la maladie connue sous le nom de *sang de rate*', *Comptes rendus de l'Académie des sciences*, 57:351–353, 386–387.

────── (1864a), 'Nouvelles recherches sur la nature de la maladie charbonneuse connue sous le nom de *sang de rate*', *Comptes rendus de l'Académie des sciences*, 59:393–396.

────── (1864b), 'Recherches sur les Vibrioniens', *Comptes rendus de l'Académie des sciences*, 59:629–633.

────── (1868a), 'Sur la nature des maladies charbonneuses', *Archives générales de Médicine*, Series 4, 11:i:144–148.

────── (1868b), 'Expériences relative à la durée de l'incubation des maladies charbonneuses et à la quantité de virus nécessaire à la transmission de la maladie', *Bulletin de l'Académie de médecine*, 33:816–821.

────── (1870a), 'Études sur la contagion du charbon chez les animaux domestiques', *Bulletin de l'Académie de médecine*, 35:215–235.

────── (1870b), 'Études sur la genèse et la propagation du charbon', *Bulletin de l'Académie de médecine*, 35:471–498.

────── and Raimbert (1864), 'Sur la présence des Bactéridies dans la pustule maligne chez l'homme', *Comptes rendus de l'Académie des sciences*, 59:429–431.

Decker, Hannah S. (1977), *Freud in Germany*, Psychological Issues, Vol. 11, Monograph 41, New York: International Universities Press.

Dolman, Claude E. (1974), 'Robert Koch' in Charles Coulston Gillispie (ed.), *Dictionary of Scientific Biography*, 15 vols, New York: Charles Scribner's Sons, vol. 7, pp. 420–435.

Douglas, Mary (1975), 'Environments at Risk' in *Implicit Meanings*, London: Routledge & Kegan Paul, pp. 230–248.

Dracobly, Alex (2000), 'Therapeutic Innovation and Philippe Ricord's "New Doctrine" of the Venereal Diseases', paper presented at the American Association for the History of Medicine conference, Bethesda, 20 May 2000.

Dubois, Paul (1842), 'Puerpérale (Fièvre)' in Nicholas Philibert Adelon et al. (eds), *Dictionnaire de médecine*, 2nd edn, Paris: Bechet, vol. 26, pp. 336–359.

Dudley, Sheldon F. (1953), 'The Lind Tradition in the Royal Naval Medical Service', in C.P. Stewart and Douglas Guthrie (eds), *Lind's Treatise on Scurvy*, Edinburgh: Edinburgh University Press, pp. 369–385.

Duméril et al. (1838), 'Rapport sur divers travaux entrepris au sujet de la maladie des vers à soie, connue volgairement sous le nom de muscardine', *Comptes rendus de l'Académie des sciences*, 6:66–102.

Dunglison, Robley (ed.) (1845), *Cyclopaedia of Practical Medicine*, American Edition, 4 vols, Philadelphia: Lea and Blanchard.

Durham, Herbert E. (1904), 'Notes on Beriberi in the Malay Peninsula and on Christmas Island (Indian Ocean)', *Journal of Hygiene, Cambridge*, 4:112–155.

Eade, Peter (1880), 'Civil Practice', *Lancet*, 1:992f.

Eijkman, Christiaan (1897a), 'Eine beriberi-ähnliche Krankheit der Huhner', *Archiv für pathologische Anatomie, Physiologie, und klinische Medizine (Virchows Archiv)*, 148:523–532.

——— (1897b), 'Ein Versuch zur Bekampfung der Beriberi', *Archiv für pathologische Anatomie, Physiologie, und klinische Medizine (Virchows Archiv)*, 149:187–194.

——— (1906), 'Ueber Ernährungspolyneuritis', *Archiv für Hygiene*, 58:150–177.

Ellenberger, Henri F. (1970), *The Discovery of the Unconscious*, New York: Basic Books.

Elliotson, John (1830–31), 'Clinical Lectures: Scurvy', *Lancet*, 1:650–655.

——— (1844), *Principles and Practice of Medicine*, 2nd edn, Philadelpia: Carey and Hart.

Evans, Alfred S. (1976), 'Causation and Disease: The Henle-Koch Postulates Revisited', *Yale Journal of Biology and Medicine*, 49:175–195.

——— (1989), 'Does HIV Cause AIDS? an Historical Perspective', *Journal of Acquired Immune Deficiency Syndromes*, 2:107–113.

——— (1993), *Causation and Disease: A Chronological Journey*, New York: Plenum Medical Book Company.

Evans-Pritchard, E.E. (1976), *Witchcraft, Oracles, and Magic Among the Azende*, abridged edn, Oxford: Oxford University Press.

Farr, William (1839), 'Letter to the Registrar-General', in *First Annual Report of the Registrar-General of Births, Deaths, and Marriages in England*, London: W. Clowes and Sons.

——— (1840), 'Letter to the Registrar-General', in *Second Annual Report of the Registrar-General of Births, Deaths, and Marriages in England*, London: W. Clowes and Sons.

Ferber, Rudolf H. (1868), 'Die Aetiologie, Prophylaxis und Therapie des Puerperalfiebers', *Schmidts Jahrbucher der in- und ausländische Medizin*, **139**:318–346.

Fischel, Wilhelm (1882), 'Zur Therapie der puerperalen Sepsis', *Archiv für Gynaekologie*, **20**:1–70.

Fitzgerald, Thomas J. (1991), 'Treponema', in Samuel Baron (ed.), *Medical Microbiology*, 3rd edn, New York: Churchill Livingstone, pp. 491–504.

Fletcher, William (1907), 'Rice and Beriberi', *Lancet*, **1**:1776–1779.

Flew, Anthony (1966), *God and Philosophy*, New York: Dell.

Forbes, John (1845), 'Angina Pectoris', in Dunglison (1845), vol. 1, pp. 103–117.

Foster, George M. (1976), 'Disease Etiologies in Non-Western Medical Systems', *American Anthropologist*, **78**:773–782.

Foster, W.D. (1965), *A History of Parasitology*, Edinburgh: E. & S. Livingstone.

Foucault, Michel (1973), *The Birth of the Clinic*, New York: Pantheon Books.

Frankfort, H.A., John A. Wilson and Thorkild Jacobsen (1949), *Before Philosophy*, Baltimore, MD: Penguin Books.

Fraser, Henry and A. Thomas Stanton (1909), 'An Inquiry Concerning the Etiology of Beriberi', *Lancet*, **1**:451–455.

—— and —— (1910), 'The Etiology of Beriberi', *Lancet*, **2**:1755–1757.

Freud, Sigmund (1886), 'Report on my Studies in Paris and Berlin' in James Strachey (ed.) (1955–74), *The Standard Edition of the Complete Psychological Works of Sigmund Freud*, London: Hogarth Press, vol. 1, pp. 5–15.

—— (1888), 'Hysteria,' in Strachey (1955–74), vol. 1, pp. 41–59.

—— (1893), 'On the Theory of Hysterical Attacks', in Strachey (1955–74), vol. 1, pp. 151–154.

—— (1894), 'The Neuro-Psychoses of Defense', in Strachey (1955–74), vol. 1, pp. 45–61.

—— (1895), 'On the Grounds for Detaching a Particular Syndrome from Neurasthenia under the Description "Anxiety Neurosis"', in Strachey (1955–74), vol. 3, pp. 90–117.

—— (1896a), 'Heredity and the Aetiology of the Neuroses', in Strachey (1955–74), vol. 3, pp. 143–156.

—— (1896b), 'Further Remarks on the Neuro-Psychoses of Defence', in Strachey (1955–74), vol. 3, pp. 162–185.

—— (1896c), 'The Aetiology of Hysteria', in Strachey (1955–74), vol. 3, pp. 191–221.

—— (1909), 'Five Lectures on Psycho-Analysis', in James Strachey (1955–74), vol. 11, pp. 9–55.

—— (1925), *An Autobiographical Study*, in James Strachey (1955–74), vol. 20, pp. 7–74.

—— (1954), *The Origins of Psycho-Analysis: Letters to Wilhelm Fliess, Drafts and Notes: 1887–1902*, ed. Marie Bonaparte, Anna Freud and Ernst Kris, New York: Basic Books.

Funk, Casimir (1912), 'The Etiology of the Deficiency Diseases', *Journal of State Medicine*, 20:341–368.

Garrison, Fielding H. (1929), *Introduction to the History of Medicine*, 4th edn, Philadelphia: W.B. Saunders.

Geison, Gerald L. (1974), 'Pasteur', in Charles Coulston Gillispie (ed.), *Dictionary of Scientific Biography*, 15 vols, New York: Charles Scribner's Sons, vol. 10, pp. 350–416.

—— (1995), *The Private Science of Louis Pasteur*, Princeton, NJ: Princeton University Press.

Gelfand, Toby (1989), 'Charcot's Response to Freud's Rebellion', *Journal of the History of Ideas*, 50:293–307.

Gerhardt, C. (1884), 'Ueber Intermittens-Impfungen', *Zeitschrift für klinische Medizin*, 7:372–377.

Ghesquier, Danièle (1999), 'A Gallic Affair: The Case of the missing Itch-Mite in French Medicine in the early 19th Century', *Medical History*, 43:26–54.

Gras, Albin (1836), 'Du rôle que joue l'acarus de l'homme dans la production de la gale', *Bulletin de l'Académie de Médecine* 1:77–82.

Grijns, Gerrit (1901), 'Over polyneuritis gallinarum', *Geneeskundig Tijdschrift voor Nederlandsch-Indië*, 41:3–110.

Grist, D.H. (1965), *Rice*, 4th edn, London: Longmans.

Györy, Tiberius von (1905), *Semmelweis' gesammelte Werke*, Jena: Gustav Fischer.

Hall, Marshall (1837–38), 'Lectures on the Theory and Practice of Medicine: Scorbutus', *Lancet* 2:851f.

Hamlin, Christopher (1992), 'Predisposing Causes and Public Health in Early 19th-Century Medical Thought', *Social History of Medicine*, 5:43–70.

Hanson, Norwood Russell (1963), *The Concept of the Positron*, Cambridge: Cambridge University Press.

—— (1969), *Patterns of Discovery*, Cambridge: Cambridge University Press.

Harden, Victoria A. (1987), 'Koch's Postulates and the Etiology of Rickettsial Diseases', *Journal of the History of Medicine and Allied Sciences*, 42:277–295.

—— (1992), 'Koch's Postulates and the Etiology of AIDS', *History and Philosophy of the Life Sciences*, 14:249–269.

Haussmann, David (1870), *Die Parasiten der weiblichen Geschlechtsorgane*, Berlin: August Hirschwald.

—— (1874), 'Untersuchungen und Versuche über die Entstehung der übertragbaren Krankheiten des Wochenbettes', *Beiträge zur Geburtshülfe und Gynäkologie* 3:311–421.

Hegel, G.W.F. (1821), Preface to *Philosophy of Right*, Vol. 46, Great Books of the Western World, ed. Robert M. Hutchins (1952), Chicago: Encyclopaedia Britannica.

Henle, Jacob (1840), *Pathologische Untersuchungen*, Part 2 'Miasmata and Contagia', trans. George Rosen, *Bulletin of the History of Medicine*, 1938, 6:911–983.

—— (1844a) 'Medicinische Wissenschaft und Empirie', *Zeitschrift für rationelle Medizin*, 1:1–35.

—— (1844b) 'Miasmatisch-Contagiöse Krankheiten', *Zeitschrift für rationelle Medizin*, 2:287–412.

Henoch, Eduard Heinrich (1881), *Vorlesungen über Kinderkrankheiten*, Berlin: August Hirschwald.

Herbst, G. (1851–52), 'Beobachtungen über *Trichina spirallis* in Betreff der Uebertragung der Eideweidewürmer', *Nachrichten Georg-August Universität. Königlich Gesellschaft für Wissenschaft Göttingen*, 2:260–264, 183–204.

Herz, Maximilian (1885), 'Uber Hysterie bei Kindern', *Wiener medizinische Wochenschrift*, 34:cols 1305–1308, 1338–1342, 1368–1371, 1401–1405.

Heymann, Bruno (1932), *Robert Koch*, Leipzig: Akademische Verlag.

Hirsch, August (1885), 'Beriberi', in *Handbook of Geographical and Historical Pathologie*, 2nd edn, trans. Charles Creighton, London: New Sydenham Society.

—— (1935), 'Klebs', *Biographisches Lexikon hervorragenden Aerzte*, 2nd edn, Berlin: Urban and Schwarzenberg.

Hoag, Junius C. (1887), 'Puerperal fever and its treatment', *American Journal of Obstetrics and Diseases of Women and Children*, 20:828–844, 941–957.

Holmes, Oliver Wendell (1843), 'The Contagiousness of Puerperal Fever', reprinted in *Medical Essays* (1883), New York: Houghton Mifflin.

Holst, Alex (1907), 'Experimental Studies Relating to Ship-Beriberi and Scurvy', *Journal of Hygiene, London*, 7:619–633.

—— and Theodor Frolich (1907), 'Experimental Studies Relating to Ship-Beriberi and Scurvy', *Journal of Hygiene, London*, 7:634–671.

Huebner, Robert J. (1957), 'The Virologist's Dilemma', *Annals of the New York Academy of Science*, 67:430–438.

Hughes, Sally Smith (1977), *The Virus: a History of the Concept*, New York: Science History Publications.

Huppert (1865), [Review of Anthrax Literature], *Schmidts Jahrbucher der in- und ausländische Medizin*, **132**:37–43.

Ihde, Aaron J. and Stanley L. Becker (1971), 'Conflict of Concepts in Early Vitamin Studies', *Journal of the History of Biology*, **4**:1–33.

Iwanovski, Dimitri Iosifovitch (1892), 'Ueber die Mosiakkrankheit der Tabakspflanze', *Bulletin Académie Impériale de Science St. Petersburg*, **3**:67–70.

——— (1902), 'Die Mosiak- und die Pockenkrankheit der Tabakspflanze', *Zeitschrift für Pflanzenkrankheiten*, **7**:202f.

——— (1903), 'Ueber die Mosaikkrankheit der Tabakspflanze', *Zeitschrift für Pflanzenkrankheiten*, **13**:1–41.

J.F.S. (1836), 'Discovery of an Insect in Itch', *Lancet* **1**:59–62.

Jaggard, W.W. (1884), 'The Pathology, Etiology, Prophylaxis, and Treatment of Puerperal Fever, from the Vienna Standpoint', *Medical News*, **44**:442–445.

Jeannel, Maurice (1880), *L'infection purulente ou pyohémie*, Paris: J.-B. Baillière et fils.

Joest, Ernst (1902), 'Unbekannte Infektionsstoffe', *Centralblatt für Bakteriologie Parasitenkunde und Infektionskrankheiten*, Abt. I, **31**:361–384, 410–422.

Jones, Ernest (1953), *The Life and Works of Sigmund Freud*, 3 vols, New York: Basic Books.

Kamminga, Harmke (1993), 'Taking Antecedent Conditions Seriously: A Lesson in Heuristics from Biology', in Steven French and Harmke Kamminga (eds), *Correspondence, Invariance and Heuristics: Essays in Honor of Heinz Post*, Dordrecht: Kluwer.

Kaufmann (1866), 'Ueber die Ursachen des epidemischen Puerperalfiebers in Gebäranstalten', *Monatsschrift für Geburtskunde und Frauenkrankheiten*, **26**:422–424.

King, Lester S. (1982), *Medical Thinking: A Historical Preface*, Princeton, NJ: Princeton University Press.

Klebs, Edwin (1865), 'Zur Pathologie der epidemischen Meningitis', *Archiv für pathologische Anatomie, Physiologie, und klinische Medizine (Virchows Archiv)*, **34**:327–379.

——— (1871), 'Die Ursache der infectiösen Wundkrankheiten', *Correspondenz-blatt für Schweizer Aerzte*, **1**:241–246.

——— (1872), *Beiträge zur pathologischen Anatomie der Schusswunden*, Leipzig: V.C.W. Vogel.

——— (1873), 'Beiträge Zur Kenntniss der Micrococcen', *Archiv für experimentelle Pathologie und Pharmakologie*, **1**:31–64.

—— (1874a), 'Beiträge Zur Kenntniss der Micrococcen', *Archiv für experimentelle Pathologie und Pharmakologie*, 2:206–210.

—— (1874b), 'Micrococcen als Krankheitsursache', *Verhandlungen der physicalische-medizinische Gesellschaft in Würzburg* 6:vi–viii.

—— (1875–76), 'Beiträge zur Kenntniss der pathogenen Schistomyceten', *Archiv für experimentelle Pathologie und Pharmakologie*, 3:305–324, 4:107–136, 207–247, 409–488.

—— (1877), 'Pathologisch-anatomische Demonstrationen', *Prager medizinische Wochenschrift*, 2:529–535.

—— (1878a), 'Ueber die Umgestaltung der medizinische Anschauungen in den letzten drei Jahrzehnten', *Gesellschaft der Deutsche Naturforscher und Aerzte in München*, Leipzig: Vogel.

—— (1878b), 'Ueber Cellularpathologie und Infectionskrankheiten', *Gesellschaft der deutsche Naturforscher und Aerzte in Cassel*, Cassel: Baier und Lewalter.

—— (1878c), 'Notiz über die Ursache des Milzbrandes', *Archiv für experimentelle Pathologie und Pharmakologie*, 8:269f.

—— (1880), 'Der Ileotyphus, eine Schistomycose', *Archiv für experimentelle Pathologie und Pharmakologie*, 12:230–236.

—— (1881), 'Der Bacillus des Abdominaltyphus und der typhöse Process, *Archiv für experimentelle Pathologie und Pharmakologie*, 13:381–460.

—— and C. Tommasi-Crudeli (1879a), 'Studien über die Ursache des Wechselfiebers und über die Natur der Malaria', *Archiv für experimentelle Pathologie und Pharmakologie*, 11:311–398.

—— and —— (1879b), 'Einige Sätze über die Ursachen der Wechselfieber und die Natur der Malaria', *Archiv für experimentelle Pathologie und Pharmakologie*, 11:122–126.

Koch, Robert (1876), 'The Etiology of Anthrax, Founded on the Course of development of the *Bacillus Anthracis*', in K. Codell Carter (trans.) (1987), *Essays of Robert Koch*, New York: Greenwood Press, pp. 1–17.

—— (1878a), 'Investigations of the Etiology of Wound Infections', in Carter (1987), pp. 19–56.

—— (1878b), 'Neue Untersuchungen über die Mikroorganismen bei infektiösen Wundkrankheiten', in J. Schwalbe (ed.) (1912), *Gesammelte Werke von Robert Koch*, Leipzig: Georg Thieme, vol. 1, pp. 57–60.

—— (1881a), 'Zur Untersuchung von pathogenen Organismen,' in Schwalbe (1912), vol. 1, pp. 112–163.

—— (1881b), 'On the Etiology of Anthrax', in Carter (1987), pp. 57–81.

—— (1882a), 'The Etiology of Tuberculosis', in Carter (1987), pp. 83–96.

—— (1882b), 'On the Anthrax Inoculation', in Carter (1987), pp. 97–115.

—— (1882c), 'Ueber die Aetiologie der Tuberkulose', in Schwalbe (1912), vol. 1, pp. 446–453.

—— (1884a), 'Experimentelle Studien über die künstliche Abschwächung der Milzbrandbazillen und Milzbrandinfektion durch Fütterung', in Schwalbe (1912), vol. 1, pp. 232–270.

—— (1884b), 'The Etiology of Tuberculosis', in Carter (1987), pp. 129–150.

—— (1884c), 'On Cholera Bacteria', in Carter (1987), pp. 171–177.

—— (1884d), 'Lecture at the First Conference for Discussion of the Cholera Question', in Carter (1987), pp. 151–170.

—— (1887), 'Ueber die Pasteurschen Milzbrandimpfungen', in Schwalbe (1912), vol. 1, pp. 271–273.

—— (1890), 'On Bacteriological Research', in Carter (1987), pp. 179–186.

—— (1901), 'Massnahmen gegen die Pest', in Schwalbe (1912), pp. 905–907.

—— (1909), 'Antrittsrede in der Akademie der Wissenschaften am 1. Juli 1909', in Schwalbe (1912), vol. 1, pp. 1–4.

Koch, Wilhelm (1889), *Die Bluterkrankheit in ihren Varianten*, Stuttgart: Ferdinand Enke.

Kunitz, Stephen J. (1987), 'Explanations and Ideologies of Mortality Patterns', *Population and Development Review*, **13**:379–408.

—— (1988), 'Hookworm and Pellagra: Exemplary Diseases in the New South', *Journal of Health and Social Behavior*, **29**:139–148.

Lagasquie, A. (1849), 'Causes', in Jean Pierre Beaude (ed.), *Dictionnaire de médecine usuelle à l'usage des gens du mode*, 2 vols, Paris: Didier, vol. 1, p. 313.

Lakatos, Imre (1968), 'Falsification and the Methodology of Scientific Research Programmes', in Imre Lakatos and Alan Musgrave (eds) (1974), *Criticism and the Growth of Knowledge*, Cambridge: Cambridge University Press, pp. 91–196.

—— (1971), 'History of Science and its Rational Reconstructions', in John Worrall and Gregory Currie (eds) (1974), *The Methodology of Scientific Research Programmes*, Cambridge: Cambridge University Press, pp. 102–138.

Lancet (1842–43), 'London Medical Society', *Lancet*, 1:879.

Lancet (1858), 'Scurvy in the Merchant Fleet', *Lancet*, 1:145f.

Lancet (1886), 'Pathology of Scurvy', *Lancet*, 1:1036.

Lancet (1887), 'Kakké, or Japanese Beriberi', *Lancet*, 2:233f.

Lancet (1890), [Review of William Koch, *Die Bluterkrankheit in ihren Varianten*], *Lancet*, 1:1186f.

Lancet (1903), 'Report of the Norwegian Beriberi Committee', *Lancet*, 1:378.

Lancet (1904), 'The Etiology of Scurvy', *Lancet*, 2:1659f.

Lancet (1911), 'The Etiology of Beriberi', *Lancet*, 2:842.

Lancet (1930), 'Christiaan Eijkman', *Lancet*, 2:1097f.

Landau, Leopold (1874), 'Zur Aetiologie der Wundkrankheiten', *Archiv für klinische Chirurgie*, 17:527–554.

Latour, Bruno (1984), *The Pasteurization of France*, trans. Alan Sheridan and John Law (1988), Cambridge, MA: Harvard University Press.

Laveran, Charles Louis Alphonse (1881), 'De la nature parasitaire des accidents de l'impaludisme', *Comptes rendus de l'Académie des sciences*, 93:627–630.

Lavoisier, Antoine (1789), *Elements of Chemistry*, Vol. 45, Great Books of the Western World, ed. Robert M. Hutchins (1952), Chicago: Encyclopaedia Britannica.

Lechevalier, Hubert A. and Morris Solotorovsky (1974), *Three Centuries of Microbiology*, New York: Dover Publications.

Leplat, Emile-Claude and Pierre-François Jaillard (1864), 'De l'action des bactéries sur l'économie animale', *Comptes rendus de l'Académie des sciences*, 59:250–252.

Leuckart, Rudolf (1860), 'Der Geschlechtsreife Zustand der Trichina spiralis', *Zeitschrift für rationelle Medizin*, 8:259–262, 334f.

Loeffler, Friedrich (1887), *Vorlesungen über die geschichtliche Entwickelung der Lehre von den Bacterien*, Leipzig: F.C.W. Vogel.

—— (1911), 'Ueber filtrierbares Virus', *Centralblatt für Bakteriologie, Parasitenkunde und Infektionskrankheiten*, 50: Beiheft:1–12.

—— and P. Frosch (1898), 'Berichte der Kommission zur Erforschung der Maul- und Klauenseuche bei dem Institut für Infektionskrankheiten in Berlin', *Centralblatt für Bakteriologie Parasitenkunde und Infektionskrankheiten*, 23:371–391.

Lomer, M. (1884) 'Ueber den heutigen Stand der Lehre von den Infectionsträgern bei Puerperalfieber', *Zeitschrift für Geburtshülfe und Gynäkologie*, 10:366–397.

Loudon, Irvine (2000), *The Tragedy of Childbed Fever*, Oxford: Oxford University Press.

Lumpe, Eduard (1845), 'Die Leistungen der neuesten Zeit in der Gynäkologie', *Zeitschrift der k. k. Gesellschaft der Aerzte zu Wien*, 1:341–371.

—— (1850), 'Zur Theorie der Puerperalfieber', *Zeitschrift der k. k. Gesellschaft der Aerzte zu Wien*, 6:392–398.

Major, Ralph H. (1944), 'Agostino Bassi and the Parasitic Theory of Disease', *Bulletin of the History of Medicine*, 16:97–107.

Malkin, Harold (1986), 'Louis Pasteur and "le rage" – 100 Years Ago', *Perspectives in Biology and Medicine*, **30**:40–46.

Manninger, Vilmos (1904), *Der Entwickelungsgang der Antiseptik und Aseptik*, Breslau: J.U. Kerns.

Manson, Patrick (1901–02), 'The Etiology of Beriberi', *Transactions of the Epidemological Society*, **21**:1–17.

—— (1911–12), '[Discussion following] The Etiology of Beriberi [by Alex Holst]', *Transactions of the Society for Tropical Medicine and Hygiene*, **5**:81–90.

—— and C.W. Daniels (1907), 'Beriberi', in T.C. Allbutt and H.D. Rolleston, *A System of Medicine*, 9 vols, London: Macmillan, vol. 2, part 2, pp. 615–643.

Marchiafava, Ettore and Angelo Celli (1883), 'Die Veränderung der rothen Blutscheiben bei Malaria-Kranken', *Fortschritte der Medizin*, **1**:573–575.

—— and —— (1885a), 'Untersuchungen über die Malariainfection', *Fortschritte der Medizin*, **3**:339–354.

—— and —— (1885b), 'Weitere Untersuchungen über die Malariainfection', *Fortschritte der Medizin*, **3**:787–806.

Marjolin (1833), 'Anthrax', in Adelon (1832–46), vol. 3, pp. 193–200.

Mayer, Adolf (1886), 'Ueber die Mosaikkrankheit des Tabaks', *Landwirtschaftlichen Versuchs-Stationen*, **32**:451–467.

McCollum, Elmer Verner (1957), *A History of Nutrition*, Boston: Houghton Mifflin.

McFadyean, John (1908), 'The Ultravisible Viruses', *Journal of Comparative Pathology and Therapeutics*, **21**:58–68, 168–175, 232–242.

Medical Research Committee (1919), *Report on the Present State of Knowledge Concerning Accessory Food Factors (Vitamines)*, Special Report No. 38, London: HMSO.

Medical Research Council (1932), *Vitamins: a Survey of Present Knowledge*, London: HMSO.

Mendel, Emanuel (1884), 'Ueber Hysterie beim mannlichen Geschlecht', *Deutsche Medizinische Wochenschrift*, **10**: 241–244.

Misner, Charles W., Kip S. Thorne and John Archibald Wheeler (1973), *Gravitation*, San Francisco: W.H. Freeman and Company.

Möbius, P.J. (1888), 'Ueber den Begriff der Hysterie', *Centralblatt für Nervenheilkunde und gerichtliche Psychiatrie*, **11**:66–71.

—— (1892), 'Ueber die Eintheilung der Krankheiten', *Centralblatt für Nervenheilkunde und Psychiatrie*, **15**:289–301.

Mollaret, H.H. (1983), 'Contribution à la connaissance des relations entre Koch et Pasteur', *NTM-Schriftenreihe für Geschichte der Naturwissenschaften, Technik, und Medizin*, **20**:57–65.

Monatsschrift für Geburtskunde und Frauenkrankheiten, (1861),

'Deutsche Naturforscher und Aerzte in Speier: Dritte Sitzung', *Monatsschrift für Geburtskunde und Frauenkrankheiten*, 18:376–382.

Mujeeb-ur-Rahman, M. (ed.) (1977), *The Freudian Paradigm: Psychoanalysis and Scientific Thought*, Chicago: Nelson-Hall.

Murphy, Frank P. (1946), 'Ignaz Philipp Semmelweis: an Annotated Bibliography', *Bulletin of the History of Medicine*, 20:653–707.

Nepveu, Gustave (1872), 'Note sur la présence des bactéries dans le sang des érysipélateux', *Comptes rendus Société de biologie*, 5th series, 2:164–168.

Nocard, Edmund-Isidore-Etienne and Emile Roux (1898), 'Le Microbe de la Péripneumonie', *Annales de l'Institut Pasteur*, 12:240–249.

Obermeier, Otto (1873), 'Vorkommen feinster, eine Eigenbewegung zeigender Fäden im Blute von Recurrenskranken', in Heinz Zeiss (ed.) (1926), *Otto Obermeier: Die Entdeckung von fadenförmigen Gebilden im Blut von Rückfallfieberkranken*, Leipzig: Johann Ambrosius.

Oliver, W.S. (1863), 'Scurvy: Its Cause', *Lancet*, 1:61.

Oppenhelm, Herman (1890), 'Thatsächliches und Hypothetisches über das Wesen der Hysterie', *Berliner klinische Wochenschrift*, 27:553–556.

Orth, Johannes (1873), 'Untersuchungen über Puerperalfieber', *Archiv für pathologische Anatomie, Physiologie, und klinische Medizine (Virchows Archiv)*, 58:437–460.

Oxtoby, David W. and Norman H. Nachtrieb (1990), *Principles of Modern Chemistry*, Chicago: Saunders College Publishing.

Paget, James (1866), 'On the Discovery of Trichina', *Lancet*, 1:269.

Parascandola, M. (1998), 'Epidemiology: Second-Rate Science?', *Public Health Reports*, 113:312–320.

Pasteur, Louis (1857a), 'Mémoire sur la fermentation appelée lactique', in Vallery-Radot Pasteur (ed.) (1922–39), *Oeuvres de Pasteur*, 7 vols, Paris: Masson, vol. 2, pp. 3–13.

—— (1857b), 'Mémoire sur la fermentation alcoolique', in V.R. Pasteur (1922–39), vol. 2, pp. 18–22.

—— (1859a), 'Lettre manuscrite de Pasteur à Pouchet', in V.R. Pasteur (1922–39), vol. 2, pp. 628–630.

—— (1859b), 'Note remise par Pasteur au Ministre de l'instruction publique et des cultes', in V.R. Pasteur (1922–39), vol. 3, pp. 481f.

—— (1860), 'Suite à une précédente communication relative aux générations dites spontanées', in V.R. Pasteur (1922–39), vol. 2, pp. 202–205.

—— (1861a), 'Animalcules infusoires vivant sans gaz oxygène libre et déterminant des fermentations', in V.R. Pasteur (1922–39), vol. 2, pp. 136–138.

—————— (1861b), 'Expériences et vues nouvelles sur la nature des fermentations', in V.R. Pasteur (1922–39), vol. 2, pp. 142–147.

—————— (1861c), 'Mémoire sur les corpuscules organisés qui existent dans l'atmosphère. Examen de la doctrine des générations spontanées', in V.R. Pasteur (1922–39), vol. 2, pp. 210–294.

—————— (1862), 'Quelques faits nouveaux au sujet des levures alcooliques', in V.R. Pasteur (1922–39), vol. 2, pp. 150–158.

—————— (1863a), 'Lettre au Colonel Favé', in V.R. Pasteur (1922–39), vol. 7, pp. 8f.

—————— (1863b), 'Examen du rôle attribué au gaz oxygène atmosphérique dans la destruction des matières animales et végétales après la mort', in V.R. Pasteur (1922–39), vol. 2, pp. 165–171.

—————— (1864), 'Études sur les vins. Deuxième partie: des altérations spontanées ou maladies des vins, particulièrement dans la Jura', in V.R. Pasteur (1922–39), vol. 3, pp. 396–406.

—————— (1865a), 'Procédé pratique de conservation et d'amélioration des vins', in V.R. Pasteur (1922–39), vol. 3, pp. 409–412.

—————— (1865b), 'Observations sur la maladie des vers à soie', in V.R. Pasteur (1922–39), vol. 4, pp. 427–431.

—————— (1865c), 'Note au sujet de la communication de MM. Leplat et Jaillard', in V.R. Pasteur (1922–39), vol. 6, pp. 161–163.

—————— (1866a), *Études sur le Vin*, in V.R. Pasteur (1922–39), vol. 3, pp. 111–386.

—————— (1866b), 'Observations verbales présentées après la lecture de la note de M. Donné', in V.R. Pasteur (1922–39), vol. 2, pp. 352–355.

—————— (1866c), 'Nouvelles études sur la maladie des vers a soie', in V.R. Pasteur (1922–39), vol. 4, pp. 436–448.

—————— (1866d), 'Observations au sujet d'une note de M. Balbiani relative à la maladie des vers à soie', in V.R. Pasteur (1922–39), vol. 4, pp. 471–472.

—————— (1867a), 'Nouvelle note sur la maladie des vers à soie, présentée à la commission impériale de sériciculture, dans sa séance du 12 janvier 1867', in V.R. Pasteur (1922–39), vol. 4, pp. 454–468.

—————— (1867b), [report of discussion held 24 June 1867], in V.R. Pasteur (1922–39), vol. 4, pp. 505–510.

—————— (1867c), 'Sur la nature des corpuscles des vers à soie. Lettre à M. Dumas', in V.R. Pasteur (1922–39), vol. 4, pp. 498–499.

—————— (1868a), 'Éducations précoces de graines des races indigènes provenant de chambrées choisies. Lettre à M. Dumas', in V.R. Pasteur (1922–39), vol. 4, pp. 524–528.

—————— (1868b), 'Rapport à S. Exc. M. le Ministre de l'Agriculture sur la mission confiée à M. Pasteur, en 1868, relativement à la maladie des vers a soie', in V.R. Pasteur (1922–39), vol. 4, pp. 547–576.

———— (1868c), 'Remarques à propos de la note de M. Chauveau sur la nature du virus-vaccin', in V.R. Pasteur (1922–39), vol. 6, p. 469.

———— (1869a), 'Note adressée à l'empereur sur la sériciculture', in V.R. Pasteur (1922–39), vol. 7, pp. 18–20.

———— (1869b), 'Résultats des observations faites sur la maladie des morts-flats, soit héréditaire, soit accidentelle', in V.R. Pasteur (1922–39), vol. 4, pp. 590–594.

———— (1870), *Études sur la maladie des vers à soie*, in V.R. Pasteur (1922–39), vol. 4, pp. 1–284.

———— (1873a), 'Réponse à une note de M. Trécul', in V.R. Pasteur (1922–39), vol. 2, pp. 411–415.

———— (1873b), 'Observations sur la putréfaction et la fermentation', in V.R. Pasteur (1922–39), vol. 6, pp. 3–5.

———— (1874a), 'Discussion sur la fermentation putride', in V.R. Pasteur (1922–39), vol. 6, pp. 13–16.

———— (1874b), 'Discussions sur la putréfaction', in V.R. Pasteur (1922–39), vol. 6, pp. 6–12.

———— (1875a), 'Discussion sur la fermentation', in V.R. Pasteur (1922–39), vol. 6, pp. 37–58.

———— (1875b), 'Sur les urines ammoniacales', in V.R. Pasteur (1922–39), vol. 6, pp. 77–80.

———— (1876a), *Études sur la bière*, in V.R. Pasteur (1922–39), vol. 5.

———— (1876b), 'Sur la fermentation de l'urine', in V.R. Pasteur (1922–39), vol. 6, pp. 80–84.

———— (1877a), 'Étude sur la maladie charbonneuse', in V.R. Pasteur (1922–39), vol. 6, pp. 164–171.

———— (1877b), 'Charbon et septicémie', in V.R. Pasteur (1922–39), vol. 6, pp. 172–188.

———— (1878a), 'Sur les découvertes relatives à la maladie charbonneuse', in V.R. Pasteur (1922–39), vol. 6, pp. 197–200.

———— (1878b), 'Congrès international séricicole tenu à Paris du 5 au 10 Septembre 1878', in V.R. Pasteur (1922–39), vol. 4, pp. 691–696.

———— (1878c), 'Discussion sur l'étiologie du charbon; poules rendues charbonneuses', in V.R. Pasteur (1922–39), vol. 6, pp. 210–214.

———— (1878d), 'La théorie des germes et ses applications à la médecine et à la chirurgie', in V.R. Pasteur (1922–39), vol. 6, pp. 112–130.

———— (1878e), 'Discussion sur la flacherie', in V.R. Pasteur (1922–39), vol. 4, pp. 698–725.

———— (1879a), 'Septicémie puerpérale', in V.R. Pasteur (1922–39), vol. 6, pp. 131–135.

———— (1879b), 'Étiologie du charbon', in V.R. Pasteur (1922–39), vol. 6, pp. 232–238.

—————— (1879c), 'Discussion sur la peste en orient', in V.R. Pasteur (1922–39), vol. 6, pp. 493–497.

—————— (1879d), 'Commission dite de la peste', in V.R. Pasteur (1922–39), vol. 6, pp. 497–502.

—————— (1880a), 'De l'extension de la théorie des germes a l'étiologie de quelques maladies communes', in V.R. Pasteur (1922–39), vol. 6, pp. 147–158.

—————— (1880b), 'Sur l'étiologie du charbon', in V.R. Pasteur (1922–39), vol. 6, pp. 254–263.

—————— (1880c), 'Sur la non-récidive de l'affection charbonneuse', in V.R. Pasteur (1922–39), vol. 6, pp. 316–322.

—————— (1881a), 'De la possibilité de rendre les moutons réfractaires au charbon par la methode des inoculations préventives', in V.R. Pasteur (1922–39), vol. 6, pp. 339–343.

—————— (1881b), 'De l'atténuation des virus et de leur retour à la virulence', in V.R. Pasteur (1922–39), vol. 6, pp. 332–338.

—————— (1881c), 'Vaccination in relation to chicken-cholera and splenic fever', in V.R. Pasteur (1922–39), vol. 6, pp. 370–378.

—————— (1881d), 'Sur la rage', in V.R. Pasteur (1922–39), vol. 6, pp. 573f.

—————— (1881e), 'Expériences faites avec la saline d'un enfant mort de la rage', in V.R. Pasteur (1922–39), vol. 6, pp. 553–555.

—————— (1882), 'De l'atténuation des virus' in V.R. Pasteur (1922–39), vol. 6, pp. 391–411.

—————— (1883), 'La vaccination charbonneuse: réponse à un mémoire de M. Koch', in V.R. Pasteur (1922–39), vol. 6, pp. 418–440.

—————— (1884), 'Microbes pathogènes et vaccins', in V.R. Pasteur (1922–39), vol. 6, pp. 590–602.

—————— (1885), 'Méthode pour prévenir la rage après morsure', in V.R. Pasteur (1922–39), vol. 6, pp. 603–612.

—————— (1887), 'A propos de la vaccination charbonneuse', in V.R. Pasteur (1922–39), vol. 6, pp. 460f.

Pasteur, Vallery-Radot (ed.) (1922–39) Oeuvres de Pasteur, 7 vols, Paris: Masson et cie.

Pollender, Franz Aloys Antoine (1855), 'Mikroskopische und mikrochemische Untersuchungen des Milzbrandblutes sowie über Wesen und Kur des Milzbrandes', Vierteljahrschrift für gerichtliche Medizin und Oeffentliches Sanitätswesen, 8:103–114.

Prichard, J.C. (1845a), 'Hypochondriasis', in Dunglison (1845), vol. 2, pp. 554–562.

—————— (1845b), 'Insanity', in Dunglison (1845), vol. 3, pp. 26–76.

r (1882), [Obituary of Karl Mayrhofer], Wiener medizinische Blätter, 5:col. 725.

Ralfe, Charles Henry (1877), 'General Pathology of Scurvy', *Lancet*, 1:868–71.

Ravitsch, J. (1872), *Zur Lehre von der putriden Infection und deren Beziehung zum sogenannten Milzbrande*, Berlin: August Hirschwald.

Rayer, Pierre-François-Olive (1850), 'Inoculation du sang de rate', *Comptes rendus des séances et mémoires de la Société de biologie*, 2:141–144.

Recklinghausen, Friedrich Daniel von (1872), 'Ueber Pilzmetastasen', *Verhandlungen der Würzburger physikalischemedicinische Gesellschaft*, 2:xiif.

Richard, M. (1882), 'Sur le parasite de la malaria', *Comptes rendus de l'Académie des sciences*, 94:496–499.

Richmond, Phyllis A. (1978), 'The Germ Theory of Disease' in Abraham M. Lilienfeld (ed.), *Times, Places and Persons*, Baltimore, MD: Johns Hopkins University Press.

Richter, Hermann Eberhard (1867), 'Die neuern Kenntnisse von den krankmachenden Schmarotzerpilzen', *Schmidts Jahrbucher der in- und ausländische Medizin*, 135:81–98.

Ricord, B. [*sic*] (1835), 'Correspondance médicale: Lettre de M. Ricord sur la syphilis, adressée au président de la Société royale académique de Nantes', *Gazette médicale de Paris*, 2nd series 3:540–541.

Ricord, Philippe (1838), *Traité pratique des maladies vénériennes*, Paris: Just Rouvier et E. Le Bouvier.

Rindfleisch, Eduard (1867–69), *Lehrbuch der pathologischen Gewebelehre zur Einführung in das Studium der pathologischen Anatomie*, Leipzig: Engelmann.

Rivers, Thomas M. (1937), 'Viruses and Koch's Postulates', *Journal of Bacteriology*, 33:1–11.

Rokitansky, Carl Jun. (1874), 'Untersuchungen der mikroskopischen Zusammensetzung der Lochien', *Medizinische Jahrbücher*, 30:161–178.

Rosenberg, Charles E. (1979), 'The Therapeutic Revolution: Essays in the Social History of America', in Morris J. Vogel and Charles E. Rosenberg (eds), *The Therapeutic Revolution: Medicine, Meaning, and Social Change in 19th-Century America*, Philadelphia: University of Pennsylvania Press.

———— (1989), 'Body and Mind in 19th-Century Medicine: Some Clinical Origins of the Neurosis Construct', *Bulletin of the History of Medicine*, 63:185–197.

Rosenthal, Moritz (1879), 'Untersuchungen und Beobachtungen über Hysterie', *Wiener medizinische Presse*, 20:569–805 (*passim*).

Roser, W. (1860), 'Die specifische Natur der Pyämie', *Archiv der Heilkunde*, 1:39–50.

———— (1867), 'Zur Verständigung über den Pyämiebegriff', *Archiv für Heilkunde*, 8:15–24.

Röthlin, Otto Mario (1962), *Edwin Klebs*, Zürich: Juris.

Rupert, J. (1880), 'Uber Beriberi', *Deutsches Archiv für klinische Medizin*, 27:95–110, 499–519.

Scanzoni, Wilhelm Friedrich (1850), '[Review of Josef] Skoda['s], Ueber die von Dr. Semmelweis entdeckte wahre Ursache der in der Wiener Gebäranstalt ungewöhnlich häufig vorkommenden Erkrankungen der Wöchnerinen', *Vierteljahrschirft für das praktische Heilkunde*, Literarische Anzeiger, 26:25–33.

———— (1855), *Lehrbuch der Geburtshilfe*, 3rd edn, 2 vols, Vienna: L.W. Seidel.

Schäfer (1884), 'Ueber Hysterie bei Kindern', *Archiv für Kinderheilkunde*, 5:401–428.

Schaumann, H. (1910), 'Die Aetiology der Beriberi', *Archive für Schiffs- und Tropenhygiene*, 14: Beiheft 8: 325–329.

Scheube, B. (1894), *Die Beriberikrankheit*, Jena: Gustav Fischer.

Schlich, Thomas (1994), 'Changing Disease Identities: Cretinism, Politics and Surgery (1844–1892)', *Medical History*, 38:421–443.

———— (1996), 'Die Konstruktion der notwendigen Krankheitsursache: Wie die Medizin Krankheit beherrschen will', in Cornelius Borck (ed.), *Anatomien medizinischen Wissens*, Frankfurt am Main: Fischer Taschenbuch.

Schönlein, Johann Lucas (1832), *Allgemeine und specielle Pathologie und Therapie*, 2nd edn, Würzburg: C. Etlinger.

———— (1839), 'Zur Pathologie der Impetigines', *Archiv für Anatomie, Physiologie und wissenschaftliche Medicin*, 6:82.

Schrödinger, Erwin (1969), *What is Life?*, Cambridge: Cambridge University Press.

Schüller, Max (1876), 'Experimentelle Beiträge zum Studium der septischen Infection', *Deutsche Zeitschrift für Chirurgie*, 6:113–190.

Schwalbe, J. (ed.) (1912), *Gesammelte Werke von Robert Koch*, 2 vols, Leipzig: Georg Thieme.

Schweninger, Franz (1866), 'Ueber die Wirkung faulender organischer Substanzen auf den lebenden thierischen Organismus', *Aertzliches Intelligenz-blatt* 13:590–672 (*passim*).

Seeligmuller, Ludwig (1881), 'Ueber Chorea magna und ihre Behandlung', *Deutsche Medizinische Wochenschrift*, 7:584.

Semmelweis, Iganz (1861a), *Die Aetiologie, der Begriff, und die Prophylaxis des Kindbettfiebers*, Pest: C.A. Hartleben.

———— (1861b), *The Etiology, Concept, and Prophylaxis of Childbed Fever*, trans. K. Codell Carter (1983), Madison, WI: University of Wisconsin Press.

Signol (1863), 'Présence des bactéries dans le sang', *Comptes rendus de l'Académie des sciences*, 57:348–351.

Sontag, Susan (1979), *Illness as Metaphor*, New York: Vintage Books.

Späth, Josef (1864), 'Statistische und historische Rückblicke auf die Vorkommnisse des Wiener Gebärhauses während der letzten dreissig Jahre mit besonderer Berücksichtigung der Puerperal-Erkrankungen', *Medizinische Jahrbücher*, 20:145–164.

Spencer, M.H. (1897), 'Notes on beriberi as observed at the Seamen's Hospital, Greenwich', *Lancet*, 1:30–32.

Stamm, August Theodor (1865), 'Grösse und Einrichtung von Gebäranstalten', *Gesellschaft der Deutsche Naturforscher und Aerzte in Giessen*, Biessen: Keller.

Stehbens, William E. (1992), 'Causality in Medical Science with Particular Reference to Heart Disease and Atherosclerosis', *Perspectives in Biology and Medicine*, 36:97–119.

Steudener, Friedrich (1872), 'Ueber pflanzliche Organismen als Krankheitserreger', *Volkmann's klinische Vorträge, Innere Medizin*, 1:283–308.

Stewart, C.P. (1953), 'Scurvy in the 19th Century and after', in C.P. Stewart and Douglas Guthrie (eds), *Lind's Treatise on Scurvy*, Edinburgh: Edinburgh University Press.

Strachey, James (ed.) (1955–74), *The Standard Edition of the Complete Psychological Works of Sigmund Freud*, 24 vols, London: Hogarth Press.

Strümpel, Adolf von (1884a), 'Ueber die Ursachen der Erkrankungen des Nervensystems', *Deutsche Archiv für klinische Medizin*, 35:1–17.

—— (1884b), *Krankheiten des Nervensystems*, Leipzig: F.C.W. Vogel.

—— (1885), *Krankheiten des Nervensystems*, 2nd edn, 2 vols, Leipzig: F.C.W. Vogel.

—— (1893), 'Ueber die Entstehung und die Heilung von Krankheiten durch Vorstellungen', *Berliner klinische Wochenschrift*, 30:22–25.

Susser, Mervyn (1973), *Causal Thinking in the Health Sciences*, Oxford: Oxford University Press.

Symonds, J.A. (1845), 'Tetanus', in Dunglison (1845), vol. 4, pp. 364–376.

Takaki, Kamehiro (1885), 'On the Cause and Prevention of Kakke', *Trans. Sei-i-kwai*, 4:29–37.

—— (1906), 'The Preservation of Health Amongst the Personnel of the Japanese Navy and Army', *Lancet*, 1:1369–1374, 1451–1455, 1520–1523.

Taylor, F. Kräupl (1979), *The Concepts of Illness, Disease and Morbus*, Cambridge: Cambridge University Press.

Théodoridès, Jean (1966), 'Casimir Davaine (1812–1882): a Precursor of Pasteur', *Medical History*, **10**:155–165.

Tiegel, E. (1871), 'Die Ursache des Milzbrandes', *Correspondenzblatt für Schweizer Aerzte*, **1**:275–280.

Tigri (1863), 'Sur la présence d'infusoires du genre *Bacterium* dans la sang humain', *Comptes rendus de l'Académie des sciences*, **57**:633.

Trousseau, A. (1835), 'Croup', in Nicholas Philibert Adelon (ed.), *Dictionnaire de médecine*, 2nd edn, Paris: Bechet, vol. 9, pp. 334–401.

Tuczek, F. (1886), 'Zur Lehre von der Hysterie der Kinder', *Berliner klinische Wochenschrift*, **31**:511–515, 534–537.

Turner, Victor (1967), *The Forest of Symbols*, Ithaca, NY: Cornell University Press.

Tweedy, Alexander (1845), 'Fever (Continued)', in Dunglison (1845), vol. 2, pp. 153–201.

Twort, F.W. (1915), 'An Investigation on the Nature of Ultra-Microscopic Viruses', *Lancet*, **2**:1241–1243.

Van der Berg, C.L. (1889), 'Reviews and Notices of Books: C.A. Pekelharing and A. Winkler, *Onderzoek naar den aard en de Orzaak der Beriberi*', *Lancet*, **1**:892f, 941f.

Van der Steen, Wim J. and Harmke Kamminga (1991), 'Laws and Natural History in Biology', *British Journal of the Philosophy of Science*, **42**:445–467.

Veit, A.C. Gustav (1865), 'Ueber die in der geburtshilflichen Klinik in Bonn im Sommer 1864 und 1864–65 aufgetretenen puerperalen Erkrankungen', *Monatsschrift für Geburtskunde und Frauenkrankheiten*, **26**:127–155, 161–208.

——— (1867), *Krankheiten der weiblichen Geschlechtsorgane*, 2nd edn, Erlangen: Ferdinand Enke.

Villemin, Jean Antoine (1868), *Études sur la tuberculose*, Paris: J.B. Baillière.

Virchow, Rudolf (1880), 'Krankheitswesen und Krankheitsursachen', *Archiv für pathologische Anatomie, Physiologie, und klinische Medizine (Virchows Archiv)*, **79**:1–19, 185–228.

Waldeyer, Wilhelm (1871), 'Ueber die pathologische Bedeutung der Bacterien, Vibrionen, etc.', *Jahresbericht der schlesische Gesellschaft für vaterländische Kultur*, **49**:205–208.

——— (1872), 'Ueber das Vorkommen von Bacterien bei der diphtheritischen Form des Puerperalfiebers', *Archiv für Gynaekologie*, **3**:293–296.

Warner, John Harley (1986), *The Therapeutic Perspective*, Cambridge, MA: Harvard University Press.

Watson, Thomas (1858), *Lectures on the Principles and Practice of Physic*, Philadelphia: Blanchard and Lea.

Weiss, J. (1884), 'Die infantile Hysterie', *Archiv für Kinderheilkunde*, 5:451–461.

Wertheimer, M. (1888), *Von dem Verhalten der Lochialsecretion zur Pathogenese des Kindbettfiebers*, Freiburg: H.M. Poppen & Sohn.

Wilkinson, Lise (1976), 'The Development of the Virus Concept as Reflected in Corpora of Studies on Individual Pathogens; 3. Lessons of the Plant Viruses – Tobacco Mosaic Virus', *Medical History*, 20:111–134.

Williams, Robert R. (1961), *Toward the Conquest of Beriberi*, Cambridge, MA: Harvard University Press.

Wilson, Adrian (2000), 'On the History of Disease-Concepts: The Case of Pleurisy', *History of Science*, 38:271–319.

Winckel, Franz Karl Ludwig Wilhelm (1866), *Die Pathologie und Therapie des Wochenbettes*, Berlin: Hirschwald.

Worboys, Michael (2000), *Spreading Germs: Disease Theories and Medical Practice in Britain, 1865–1900*, Cambridge: Cambridge University Press.

Wright, Hamilton (1902), *An Inquiry into the Etiology and Pathology of Beriberi*, Singapore: Kelly and Walsh.

Wulff, Henrik R. (1984), 'The Causal Basis of the Current Disease Classification', in Lennart Nordenfelt and Ingemar B. Lindahl, *Health, Disease, and Causal Explanations in Medicine*, Dordrecht: D. Reidel, pp. 169–177.

Yerushalmy, J. and Carroll E. Palmer (1959), 'On the Methodology of Investigations of Etiologic Factors in Chronic Diseases', *Journal of Chronic Diseases*, 10:27–40.

Zakon, S.J. and T. Benedek (1944), 'David Gruby and the Centenary of Medical Mycology 1841–1941', *Bulletin of the History of Medicine*, 16:155–168.

Zenker, F.A. (1860), 'Ueber die Trichinen-Krankheit des Menschen', *Archiv für pathologische Anatomie, Physiologie, und klinische Medizine (Virchows Archiv)*, 18:561–572.

—— (1865), 'Beiträge zur Lehre von der Trichinenkrankheit', *Deutsches Archiv für klinische Medizin*, 1:90–124.

Zuber (1882) [Review of Koch's 1881 anthrax paper], *Revue d'hygiène*, 2:104f.

Index